An African Perspective on the Thought of Benedict XVI

Other Books of Interest from St. Augustine's Press

Maurice Ashley Agbaw-Ebai, *Light of Reason, Light of Faith: Joseph Ratzinger and the German Enlightenment*

Maurice Ashley Agbaw-Ebai, *The Essential Supernatural: A Dialogical Study in Kierkegaard and Blondel*

Maurice Ashley Agbaw-Ebai and Matthew Levering, Editors, *Africae Munus: Ten Years Later*

Peter Kreeft, *Ha!: A Christian Philosopher of Humor*

Peter Kreeft, *If Einstein Had Been a Surfer*

Peter Kreeft, *A Socratic Introduction to Plato's Republic*

Kenneth Weisbrode, *Real Influencers: Fourteen Disappearing Acts that Left Fingerprints on History*

Peter Kreeft, *The Philosophy of Jesus*

Peter Kreeft, *Socratic Logic (3rd Edition)*

Marvin R. O'Connell, *Telling Stories that Matter: Memoirs and Essays*

Jean-Luc Marion, *Descartes's Grey Ontology: Cartesian Science and Aristotelian Thought in the Regulae*

Josef Pieper, *A Journey to Point Omega: Autobiography from 1964 Winston Churchill on Politics as Friendship*

Joseph Bottum, *Spending the Winter*

Richard Ferrier, *The Declaration of America: Our Principles in Thought and Action*

Roger Scruton, *An Intelligent Person's Guide to Modern Culture*

Roger Scruton, *The Meaning of Conservatism: Revised 3rd Edition*

Roger Scruton, *The Politics of Culture and Other Essays*

Roger Scruton, *On Hunting*

Anne Drury Hall, *Where the Muses Still Haunt: The Second Reading*

Chilton Williamson, *The End of Liberalism*

Marion Montgomery, *With Walker Percy at the Tupperware Party*

An African Perspective on the Thought of Benedict XVI

EDITED BY

MAURICE ASHLEY AGBAW-EBAI
AND KIZITO FORBI S.J.

ST. AUGUSTINE'S PRESS
South Bend, Indiana

Manufactured in the United States of America.

1 2 3 4 5 6 28 27 26 25 24 23

Library of Congress Control Number: 2022948199

Paperback ISBN: 978-1-58731-044-7
Hardback ISBN: 978-1-58731-048-5
Ebook ISBN: 978-1-58731-046-1

∞ The paper used in this publication meets the minimum requirements of the American National Standard for Information Sciences – Permanence of Paper for Printed Materials, ANSI Z39.48-1984.

St. Augustine's Press
www.staugustine.net

Table of Contents

Preface
Francis Cardinal Arinze

Pope Benedict XVI is a blessing for Church and society in our times. Working with the rich talents with which Divine Providence gifted him, he has enriched the Church with theological, scriptural, pastoral, philosophical and cultural teachings and explorations which have a wide-spanning vision. Having participated in the Second Vatican Council as a "peritus" (theological expert), taught in universities in a time of transition, and served as a pastor in the Church, he has transmitted to posterity, a hermeneutic of continuity for the Church after that General Council. As a Bishop and Vicar of Christ on earth, he has encouraged Africa as a continent of hope.

Deep gratitude is due to the Benedict XVI Institute for Africa, together with the Catholic University of Central Africa, for organizing the International Colloquium: "The African Perspective of Benedict XVI's Thought" in Yaoundé, Cameroon, from 27-29 November 2019.

In this book are put together the erudite papers read in that symposium by eminent African thinkers who have allowed the powerful light of the studies and teaching of Cardinal Joseph Ratzinger/Pope Benedict XVI to pour its liberating and encouraging light over Africa in four principal fields: Philosophy, Theology, Sociology and Canon Law.

Pope Benedict's love of truth, search for truth, exposition and defense of sound doctrine and demasking of the error of the dictatorship of relativism, come out clearly in these pages. So does his love for Africa and his encouragement of that continent of hope.

I join the public in thanking the Benedict XVI Institute for Africa and the Catholic University of Central Africa for having put together this symposium and for sharing its riches with the public through this publication.

Africae Munus, the Post-Synodal Apostolic Exhortation of Pope Benedict to Africa after the Second African Synod held in October 2009, can be regarded as the summit of the encouragement of Pope Benedict to Africa. In this document, the Pope is, as it were, saying to Africa: "Stand up; take up your mat and walk" (Jn 5:8). In paragraph 149 of that comprehensive exhortation, Pope Benedict says: "What Africa needs most is neither gold nor silver; she wants to stand up, like the man at the pool of Bethzatha; she wants to have confidence in herself and in her dignity as a people loved by her God. It is this encounter with Jesus which the Church must offer to bruised and wounded hearts yearning for reconciliation and peace, and thirsting for justice. We must provide and proclaim the word of Christ which heals, sets free and reconciles."

The 2019 Yaoundé symposium is a help in this direction. Every reader of this book will feel enriched.

+ Francis Card. Arinze
Vatican City
30 September 2022

Introduction

Summary of the International Colloquium: An African Perspective on the Thought of Benedict XVI
Catholic University of Central Africa, Yaoundé, 27th–29th November 2019

From Wednesday 2th to Friday 29th November 2019, the Catholic University of Central Africa played host to an international colloquium entitled "**African Perspective of Benedict XVI's Thought.**" This international colloquium was organized to mark the 10th anniversary of the visit of Pope Benedict to Cameroon, an event which took place from 18th to 20th of March 2009. This conference was organized jointly by the Catholic University of Central Africa, and the Benedict XVI Institute for Africa, which had just organized a similar conference for African Scholars from North America and Europe in the month of October 2019 at the University of St. Mary of the Lake/ Mundelein Seminary, USA. In the three days of deep exchange, scholars, researchers, and pastors from Cameroon and abroad engaged in an interdisciplinary reflection on the visit, writings, and pastoral solicitude of Pope Emeritus Benedict XVI, and the reception of these by the African Church and society.

Day One: Opening Ceremony, Wednesday 27th, November, 2019

Three main events characterized the opening ceremony. First, there was an Opening Prayer, in which the light of the Holy Spirit was invoked for the smooth flow of the Conference. This was followed by a series of brief speeches, starting with a word of welcome presented on behalf of the Rector of UCAC (who was unavoidably absent) by Mr. Ettiene Manga, Administrative Secretary General of the same university. He recalled the memorable stay of Pope Benedict XVI in Cameroon, and appreciated the interdisciplinary study of the pastoral solicitude of Pope Benedict XVI towards Africa, which the Pope had often described as "the beloved land of Christ" and his "new homeland." While thanking all the stakeholders involved in the organization of the conference, he wished all the participants a pleasant stay and fruitful exchange. After this came a word from the representative of the Benedict XVI Institute for Africa, Fr. Maurice Agbaw-Ebai, from Boston College, USA who situated the Conference within the framework of the international initiatives targeting the furtherance of the legacy of Pope Benedict XVI, a discussion in which the Church in Africa had been somewhat absent.

The next key point was the presentation of the Structure of the Colloquium, by Fr. Stephen Kizito Forbi, S.J., on behalf of the Scientific Committee that prepared the event. Beginning with a brief spotlight on the person and work of Joseph Ratzinger/Benedict XVI, Fr. Forbi showed the Pope to be a Theologian within his own right, with over 30 publications to his credit before his assumption of the Petrine office. As a key participant in the Second Vatican Ecumenical Council, Joseph Ratzinger ensured its right interpretation by co-founding the Theological Journal *Communio* alongside Hans Urs Von Balthazar and Henri De Lubac. Ratzinger's constant return to the Fathers of the Church revealed the ecclesial vocation of the Theologian, who must expound the timeless truths about God, man, and the world in fidelity to Scripture, in communion with the Magisterium, and in continuity with Tradition. Benedict XVI was not just a teacher of the faith; he was first of all a believer, who embodied a personal holiness that showed his belief that true theology must be done "on one's knees." After this presentation, Fr. Forbi outlined the four main themes that would constitute the African reading of the thought of Pope Benedict XVI. These were the Theological, the Canonical, the Philosophical, and the Social Science/Social panels. He ended his presentation with a message of support and blessing from the office of the Apostolic Nuncio to Cameroon and Equatorial Guinea, Archbishop Julio Murat. On this note he declared the Conference officially opened, and invited everyone to join in a family photo to mark the opening ceremony.

The third event for the opening session was the keynote address, presented by Fr. Charles Moukala, entitled "**Benedict XVI and Africa: Hope as a utopic model.**" The speaker situated the message of Pope Benedict XVI to the Church in Africa as rooted in hope, a theological virtue alongside Faith and Love, which the Pope had made the object of his encyclicals. Using the Biblical models of Abraham and also St. Joseph, who had "hoped against all hope," Benedict XVI was convinced that Africa was a "spiritual lung" and a blessing for the Church. Hope is not just some rhetoric or appeal to resignation, but an invitation to plunge oneself into the Gospel which changes life. Fr. Moukala went on to dissect a threefold hermeneutic of hope that could be discerned from the writings of Pope Benedict XVI. The spiritual-theological dimension of hope consists in the fact that the Gospel does not directly target the transformation of political structures, but rather the change of human hearts, for Jesus Christ is not a social revolutionary like Spartacus or Barabbas, but the chief shepherd of our souls. The ecclesial-communal dimension of hope consists in the fact that hope is not individualistic, nor can it be equated to the Enlightenment's notion of Progress by Kant or Marx. Mere scientific progress cannot redeem man, for man is not a mere product of economic factors. The third dimension of hope is eschatological, for Christian hope does not have its ultimate goal in an earthly reality, but in making men and women "citizens of heaven." However, this theology of hope is radically different from the utopia of contemporary thinkers like Ernst Bloch and Jorgen Moltmann. Christian hope, in preparing us for eternity, does not ignore the need for Christian involvement in creating a more just social order and uprooting the structures of sin that thwart the harmony of that order.

The keynote address whetted the appetite and provoked a lively exchange of remarks and questions, some of which were answered, and others deferred for the next day's conferences.

Day Two: Thursday, 28th November 2019

This day featured two panels, the Theology panel in the morning and the Philosophy panel in the afternoon. The morning session started at 9:10 a.m. with three theological conferences moderated by Prof. Paul Bitchick. The first conference, presented by Dr. Antoine Essomba, was entitled: **"Benedict XVI's vision of liturgical reform vis-à-vis the Challenge of Inculturation in the Church in Africa."** The author notes that Benedict XVI championed the right interpretation of Vatican II, and thus insisted on a hermeneutic of continuity in liturgical reform. The liturgy is at the heart of the Church's life, because the Church in its foundation is an "ekklesia," that is, a community gathered in worship. For Benedict XVI then, the "ars celebrandi" or art of celebrating should foster the sense of mystery and reverence towards what Christ, the principal actor in the Liturgy, is doing and in which we are called to participate. Benedict's vision of liturgical reform thus lays accent on the equal reverence to the Table of the Word and the Table of the Sacraments, reinstating the place of silence, rediscovering the inner meaning of acts of piety, and a proper implementation of liturgical norms laid out in *Sacrosanctum Concilium*. The author noted that although Inculturation is a priority in our local Church, it should not lead to a disintegration of the Church's liturgy. He cautioned against the introduction of profanity in liturgical celebrations, especially during weddings, funerals, and the choice of songs during Mass. For liturgy to transform, it must touch the lives of Christians, giving them reasons to hope, to love, and to believe.

The Second conference was entitled: **"The Place of Africa in the Social Teaching of Benedict XVI"** and was given by Dr. Thomas Bienvenu Tchoungui. The author noted that the approach of Pope Benedict XVI with Africa was shaped by previous decisive encounters with the African Church. First as a *peritus* at the Second Vatican Council, he interacted with the African prelates present. Secondly, during his supervision of Barthelemy Adoukounou's doctoral thesis, "An Essay on Christian Hermeneutics of Dahomian Vodun," he was introduced to the future debates on inculturation, a theme he would later discuss as Prefect of the Congregation for the Doctrine of the Faith on the 21st of June 1987 Meeting with African prelates in Kinshasa, DR Congo. Benedict XVI's social doctrine makes his thought further relevant to Africa because of his handling of themes like charity as a primordial commandment for Christian living, the preferential option for the poor, the duty to justice, ecological challenges, the rightful use of public goods, human rights, and other themes as treated in the encyclical *Caritas in Veritate*. The author ended by employing the figure of Simon of Cyrene to argue for hospitality and a Theology of the Cross, as the model for interpersonal relations in African society and the Church.

The Third Conference was entitled "**Joseph Ratzinger and the Universality of Logos in Cultures: The Preference for Inter-Culturality over Inculturation**" and was given by Dr. Maurice Agbaw-Ebai. The author's point of departure was Pope Benedict XVI's September 12, 2006, lecture at the University of Regensburg, Germany. The leitmotiv of that lecture could be captured from the assertion: "Not to act in accordance with reason is contrary to the nature of God." For the Greeks, logos was an impersonal force that animated the cosmos, just as the soul animated the body. But for the Fathers, the Logos is a person, the Word of God through whom the world was made, and who became flesh. Using three pre-pontifical texts of Benedict XVI, the author showed Ratzinger's preference of "inter-culturality" over "inculturation." By becoming flesh and dwelling among us, the Son of God dignified human cultures. Jesus Christ as the Logos makes it possible to speak of inter-culturality, because Christ sustains all cultures, and makes them open to the transformative power of the truth. Inculturation on the other hand, presumes an already designed line of action between an antecedent culture and a receiving one.

Ratzinger, therefore, opens up new roads of thinking and so, African Theology needs not attempt to have a de-hellenized theological orientation for the 21st century. This is captured in Benedict's call for the reopening of Origen's Catechetical School of Alexandria, albeit in a different model. After this talk, there was a question-and-answer session that lasted until 12:30 pm. Before the lunch break, there was a moment of silence for the repose of the soul of Fr. Christian Mofor, former Rector of the Catholic University of Central Africa. The afternoon session brought together three philosophy speakers, and the panel was directed by Prof. Kondjo Brossala Diddy.

The first Paper was delivered by Fr. Fabrice Nsemi, entitled **"Love and Truth in the Thought of Ratzinger/Benedict XVI."** In tackling the twin concepts of love, the author made recourse to Ratzinger's dependence upon Augustine, who was the first patristic thinker to develop a Christian theory of love. At the same time, he noted that Pope Benedict avoided the constant opposition between agape and eros, by showing in the encyclical *Deus Caritas Est* that even God loves with eros. Eros thus needs to be disciplined and purified, so that it can rise above mere carnality to its divine potential. A key starting point for the purification of love is at the level of language, for love is one of the most used, misused, and misunderstood concept. For the author, truth is practically a leitmotiv for Benedict XVI, who since his Episcopal ordination chose for his motto: "Co-worker the truth." His papacy was a long defense of truth against the dictatorship of relativism. Fusing the two concepts, then, the author concluded by saying Pope Benedict XVI calls us to love one another in the truth of each other's being, for deprived of truth, love becomes mere sentiment.

The Second paper, entitled "**The Defense of Reason in Benedict XVI,**" was delivered by Prof. Gabriel Ndinga. In it, the author showed that Benedict XVI's defense of reason avoids two dangers—first, the absolute and self-sufficient reason of thinkers of German Idealism, such as Kant and Hegel. It also avoids the skepticism of postmodern thought, which has lost faith in thepower of reason to discern truth. Reason, for Benedict, is ordered to and capable of finding truth. The university milieu is thus a laboratory in the service (diakonia) of truth. As a result, it must be characterized by objective research and the transmission of knowledge. Using examples of Ratzinger's exchanges with Jurgen Habermas, the author concluded that there is need for a dialogue of intellectuals, of cultures, and sciences in the search of the truth. The true man of science, shaped by a right philosophical mind, should be able to rise to the realm of faith, which opens human reason more fully to the Truth found in God.

The Third paper, delivered by Prof. Stephen Kizito Forbi, S.J., was captioned "**Benedict XVI and the Philosophy of Hope: From Africa the Forgotten to Africa of Authentic Hope.**" The author evoked the contemporary debate also tackled in Benedict XVI's *Africae Munus*, on whether Africa is a cursed continent or a continent of hope. From one standpoint, the socio-political landscape of Africa is marked by multiple coups d'etat, inter-tribal conflicts, and fragile political institutions. To this could be added a certain anthropological crisis, marked by a spirit of mediocrity, the memory of historical wounds, extreme poverty, sickness, and new forms of slavery. But Africa is not only bad news. For *Africae Munus* sees in Africa a continent of hope, and challenges the faithful more than seven times to "rise up" and "march toward" the future. This hope is not mere utopia, but has its basis in the rich intellectual and cultural heritage of Africa. This is what, for the Pope, makes Africa a spiritual lung for humanity. The new African man, therefore, is a man rooted in the justice of love, reconciliation, and peace.

The afternoon session ended with a question-and-answer exchange that lasted until 4:30 p.m. before the participants retired for the day.

Day Three: Friday, 29th November 2019

Two panels comprised this day: Canon Law and Social Teaching of the Church. The Canon Law panel, moderated by Prof. Claude Kiamba, sought to examine the canonical reforms made during the Pontificate of Pope Benedict XVI.

In the first presentation, **"Benedict XVI and the Question of Sexual Abuse of Minors Committed by Clergy,"** Prof. Jean-Marie Signe noted that the papacy of Pope Benedict XVI was marked by the unveiling of scandals of sexual abuse of minors by clerics, even if some of these offences were perpetrated long before. As prefect of the Congregation of the Doctrine of the Faith, the then Cardinal Joseph Ratzinger was already charged with the implementation of the measures put in place by *Sacramentorum Sanctitatis* promulgated by Pope John Paul II in the wake of the 2001 sex abuse scandals. This experience would further bear fruit in the reforms the Cardinal would later make as Pope. Faced with the lack of necessary structures and qualified personnel in many African dioceses to handle technical canonical procedures of inquiries and proceedings, the Pope gave a concession to the Congregation for the Evangelization of peoples to handle directly cases coming from these local churches.

Other reforms include Pope Benedict XVI's revision of *Sacrementorum Sanctitatis* (2010). In this, for example, he assimilated to the definition of "minor" even vulnerable majors or those who lacked habitual use of reason, while also adding to the definition of "abuse" the actions of possession of and dissemination of child pornography. He also increased the span of inquiry to twenty years, and made provision for the forwarding of extreme cases to the Pope for dismissal from the clerical state. For Prof. Signe, the message in Pope Benedict XVI's letter of solidarity to the Church in Ireland speaks clearly to Africa, because the enhancing factors of sexual abuse of minors by clergy are also prevalent here: namely, inadequate scrutiny of candidates for clerical and religious formation, insufficient human and spiritual formation that aims at affective maturity, and the tendency of defending clergy and religious under the guise of soiling the Church's image. In sum, the message for Africa from Benedict XVI's magisterium is that: sexual abuse is not only a canonical offense, but a crime punishable by civil law; it is an anti-witness to the Gospel, and weakens the faith of the people of God. Therefore the Church, in solidarity to victims, should ensure not just their healing but work to prevent future abuse cases.

The Second intervention presented by Prof. Jean-Paul Betengne, was entitled **"The Preparation for Priesthood in the Legislative Reform of Pope Benedict XVI."** In continuity with the first presentation, this paper situated Pope Benedict's measures to curb sexual abuse by clerics, by paying attention to norms regarding priestly formation. The first point of note was the transfer of the supervision of seminaries from the Congregation for Catholic Education to the Congregation for Clergy. This move highlighted the distinction (but not opposition) of Catholic Education, which is destined for all persons without distinction of status or category; and priestly formation, which prepares pastors of souls. The next reform was the revision of the philosophical studies, which was aimed at making future priests capable of proposing a reasonable ministerial accompaniment that is pertinent both intellectually and pastorally adapted to today's world. Pope Benedict XVI saw the priest as an agent of the New Evangelization, which he was convinced was the most pertinent response to our age of secularism, characterized by an "eclipse" of God. Key pontifical acts show Benedict XVI's commitment to this ideal, in continuity with his predecessor: First, the creation of a *Pontifical Council for the Promotion of the New Evangelization* in 2010. The next was the convocation in October 2012, of an Ordinary Assembly of the Synod of Bishops on *The New Evangelization for the Transmission of the Christian Faith*. These, put together with the *Year of the Priesthood* celebrated in 2009 under the patronage of St. John Mary Vianney showed clearly the Pope's conviction that an interior renewal of the priesthood was required to guarantee a decisive evangelical witness in today's world.

To put these reflections into context, Prof. Betengne drew inspiration from the writings of Eloi Messi Metogo to assert that religious indifference, secularism, and atheism are not problems far off from Africa. He warned that if candidates for seminary formation choose to question the pertinence or practical use of some aspects of formation to their future ministry, rather than configure themselves to Christ in prayer, studies, and celebration of the sacraments, they would have lost the goal. The disposition to learn, the openness to culture and humility, as highlighted by the *Ratio Fundamentalis*, is needed not only for initial but for ongoing formation.

In the third intervention of the day, **"Benedict XVI and Marriage,"** Prof. Angéle Makiang showed clearly the essential continuity between Holy Orders and Matrimony as Sacraments at the service of the Church and humanity. Restricting herself to Benedict XVI's Motu Proprio *Omnium in Mentem* (2010), Prof. Makiang examined the reforms regarding the obligation to canonical form in the contraction of marriage for Catholics who leave the Church. Given the difficulties in some cases to ascertain "formal departure" from the Church, the pastoral solicitude to facilitate the return of former Catholics, and the pastoral need to avoid clandestine marriages, Benedict XVI, without contradicting Church discipline, ruled out from Canons 1117, 1086 par 1 and 1124, the clause about "formal departure from the Church" as one of the conditions that render invalid the marriage between a baptized and a non-baptized person. In doing this he sought to remain attentive to the needs of the flock, and keep a gate open for lost sheep to return. Given that the Sacrament of Marriage and the Family Apostolate constitute recurrent areas for pastoral challenges in Africa, Prof. Makiang invited all speakers to endeavour to inform and form themselves and also disseminate documents of the Holy See on such matters.

In the last paper of the day, Dr. Engelbert Meyongo treated the audience to **"An African Reading of Benedict XVI's Resignation."** Beginning with a historical survey of examples from antiquity, like the Roman Emperor Diocletian, the French Emperor Charlemagne, and Cameroon's first president Ahmadou Ahidjo, he demonstrated that resignation from power always comes as a surprise to the public, because it runs contrary to the great temptation to eternalize oneself in power. After exploring terminological nuances of renunciation, understood as "resignation," a "surrender/abandonment" of power, he showed that the canonical requirement for the validity of an act of resignation is that it be done consciously, freely, and wilfully. The act of Benedict XVI was premeditated, as was shown by the deposition of the Pallium, symbol of Episcopal authority on the relics of Pope Celestine V, in Italy. The act, however, took its meaning from his desire to ensure the common good, and to follow the will of Christ which, according to his discernment, was no longer served by his fragile health, age, and physical strength. Far away from running from care of the sheep in the face of wolves, Pope Benedict pledged to remain associated by his obedience to his successor, and a withdrawal to a life of prayer in the example of the monk St. Benedict, his patron. This resignation has pastoral and canonical implications. First, it invites leaders in every walk of life to think of the common good first before their private interests. Secondly, it invites retired leaders (even bishops, in line with the instruction *Apostolorum successores,*) to avoid raising any competition or parallel administration with the successor. Third, with the inspiration of St. Francis of Assisi, resignation shows that no one is more important than the office he occupies.

This presentation was followed by brief question-and-answer session, which ended the third panel of discussion.

4th Panel:
Social Sciences and Social Teaching of the Church

The fourth panel of discussion, moderated by Fr. Giles Ngwa Forteh, was another interdisciplinary appreciation of the thought of Benedict XVI from the perspective of social sciences and the social teaching of the Church.

The first speaker, Dr. Augusta Anata Mawata, presented on **"The Thought of Benedict XVI to open a breach in the blockade of the ideology of development of Africa."** Starting from the assertion that the term "development," which is an ideal sought by all, targets the transformation of the human being in all its dimensions. However, without a good foundation, efforts at development could be detrimental to some societies, as in the case where, in the name of "development," local languages have been abandoned for foreign ones, rural homes destroyed for road construction, or imported products have supplanted local ones. The move towards development often follows one of the following three pathways: first, that of total adhesion to technology; second, the attempt to combine African culture with Western technology; and third, the option to approach development from the daily life of people. Benedict XVI criticizes the model of development marked merely in scientific progress, as put forward by Francis Bacon, Karl Marx, and Auguste Comte. These models sacrifice transcendence at the altar of an auto- sufficient reason. In his encyclical *Caritas in Veritate*, Benedict XVI holds that the world of finance, politics, and science should be evangelized, so that individuals should recognize that personal conscience is more vital than the multiplication of structures. For this to take place, education of conscience in virtue and responsibility is irreplaceable.

The second speaker, Dr. Aime Martial Wakeu, made an expose on **"The Impact of Justice and Peace Commissions in the Civic Engagement of Catholic Christians in Cameroon."** The paper was inspired by Pope Benedict XVI's call in *Africae Munus* for Africa to be a witness to Reconciliation, Justice, and Peace, and also by the vocation of the laity to penetrate the world. Linking the above, the speaker affirmed that Reconciliation restores peace, while to work for peace is to establish harmony and concord between people. Justice is not only giving to others their due, but also maintaining a preferential option for the poor. To build a society of reconciliation, justice, and peace needs active not passive citizens. Christians especially need to foster this through their involvement in Commissions of Justice and Peace at the parish, diocesan, and national levels. Using the example of the Yaoundé Archdiocese, the speaker showed how the Justice and Peace Commission with the aid of media and personal contact enlightened Christians on active citizenship and civic engagement. Despite the successes encountered, areas of challenge included: a general political (voter) apathy among Christians, resistance of politicians to allow Christians to "meddle" in their affairs, inadequacy of personnel, formation, structures, and resources needed to effectively carry out the tasks related to these Commissions. For Dr. Wakeu, eight years after the publication of *Africae Munus* was the right time to muster more commitment to working for Reconciliation, Justice, and Peace.

In the last paper of the day, termed **"The African Reception of the Social Teaching of Benedict XVI: Between Engagement and Non-engagement in Politics,"** Mr. Marcel Enama Saint-Daniel formulated what he termed the "social credo" for Benedict XVI, namely that the task of the Church is to form right consciences capable of responding to the demands of justice and the training of men and women to live responsibly. The social gospel of the Church goes beyond its involvement in health, education, and communication, not with the aim of creating a parallel social order, but rather of penetrating the ordinary world with its spirit. In the African milieu, like elsewhere, the Church often meets a double challenge in centralized political systems: if she is silent, she would have renounced her prophetic role; at the same time, she has to denounce injustice and stand in favour of suffering humanity, while recognizing the separation of the Church from the state. The challenge consists in taking a proper position that does not sacrifice its mission to the truth. The speaker ended by saying the challenges of implementing the social magisterium of Benedict XVI in the dense socio-political reality of Africa should not lead to discouragement, but hope. With the continuous evangelization and formation of consciences, more progress will be made.

The exchange that followed between the participants and panelists showed the appropriation of the talks by the assembly, especially in the perspective of applying the question of justice, development, and civic engagement in the Cameroonian context.

In three days therefore, the Franz-Kamphaus amphitheatre of the Catholic University of Central Africa played host to an intense reflection on the import of Benedict XVI's thought to Africa from the perspective of Theology, Exegesis, Ethics, Phenomenology, Philosophy,

Canon Law, Politics, and Social Sciences. The themes explored in this international colloquium gave fresh impetus once more to the visit of the Pontiff to Cameroon from 17–20 March 2009. The cooperation between the Benedict XVI Institute for Africa and the Scientific Preparatory Council thus bore fruit in this second conference, a sequel to the first already held in Mundelein Seminary, Chicago in October 2019. The eight years of papacy and the three papal visits to Africa were rich in content and inspiration to this continent of hope. African theologians had indeed taken to heart Pope Benedict XVI's recommendation for a rebirth of theological activity in Africa akin to that of the golden era of the Alexandrian Schools. But the task is not over, for as a Church, the task still lies before us, to be salt of the earth, and light to the world, a bastion of hope despite the surrounding bad news, a church at the service of reconciliation, justice, and peace.

Fr. Herbert Niba
Secretary of the Colloquium

Presentation of the Colloquium

Benedict XVI's commitment to Africa is not only summarised through his writings such as *Africae Munus* addressed to all Africans and which urges them to be at the service of reconciliation, justice, and peace on the continent. It was also seen through his numerous visits to the continent: Cameroon (March 2009), Angola (March 2009) and Benin (2011).

Before undertaking his first visit to Africa, Benedict XVI gave the purpose of his visit: *"I am leaving for Africa aware that I have nothing else to propose and to give to those I meet besides Christ and the Good News of His Cross."* On the second day of his arrival in Yaoundé, Cameroon, he reiterated that: "In the face of suffering or violence, in the face of poverty or hunger, in the face of corruption or abuse of power, a Christian can never remain silent. The saving message of the Gospel must be proclaimed loudly and clearly, so that the light of Christ may shine in the darkness into which people are plunged." (Yaoundé Nsimalen International

Airport. *Tuesday 17 March 2009*). This speech is the Pope's reminder of the Church's responsibility in Africa. After the first Synod on Africa in 1995, John Paul II's exhortation, *Ecclesia in Africa,* focused on the Church as the human family of the black continent, and more attention was given to inculturation of Catholicism. More than 15 years later, as Benedict XVI said in Cameroon in 2009, "local and regional conflicts, massacres and genocides that have developed on the continent must appeal to us in a very special way." The text published by the Pope on Saturday 19 November 2009 draws the conclusions of the second Synod on Africa, and poses more directly the question of the Church's action in this situation.

The *Africae Munus* exhortation calls for an internal reordering of the African Church. It questions the contribution of the Catholic Church in Africa to the shaping of reconciled, more just, and peaceful societies. Benedict XVI embodies the reconciliation of reason and divine light. It was in this light that he gave a lecture in Regensburg on 12 September 2006 to "representatives of the scientific community" in the main amphitheatre of the university where he taught during his youth (as part of a five-day apostolic trip to Germany). He stressed that God could not be excluded from reason (and more generally from science), and vice versa. The Regensburg discourse was undoubtedly one of the most striking of his papacy because it was publicized following a controversy. Some Muslims had thought unfortunately and wrongly so that they could trace in the Pope's words insults against Islam. But to Benedict XVI the focus was to argue for the legitimate space for faith in an increasingly secularized Western work that was suffering not only from a crisis of faith, but even more, from a crisis of reason as well.

Benedict XVI's main guidelines of intellectual activity are found in this speech: Faith and philosophical reason,[1] faith and scientific reason, and faith and political reason.[2] Concerning the relationship between faith and reason, Benedict XVI said this on the tenth anniversary of John Paul II's *Fides et Ratio*: "The love for Truth impels us to go within ourselves to discover the inner man and the profound meaning of our life. An authentic philosophy must accompany everyone in knowing the Truth of Revelation."[3] On the issue of the dialogue between science and faith, he regrets the "shift" of modern science towards technicality. Benedict XVI defines the role of the Church in politics as follows: "The Church, on her part, is committed to promoting a culture enshrined in the rule of law within the church and in the society... To yield to the temptation to transform yourselves into political or social guides would mean compromising your priestly mission and serving the society, which expects prophetic words and deeds from you."[4] As such, the convergence of the Christian faith on the one hand and philosophy, science, and politics on the other is an issue Benedict XVI cherishes.

Although one might be tempted to make systemic and spiritual theology in Pope Benedict XVI's teaching more prominent, the significance of his contribution in the sphere of ethics should be noted as well. This is the objective of our research, which intends to focus on Benedict XVI's social teaching by examining some major texts addressed to the churches and peoples of Africa.

In the course of his visit to France in September 2008, Benedict XVI addressed issues that go beyond the confines of believers and are of interest to all men of good will: man, the creator. In the image of God, man is a creator and must transform the planet for the good of all. Economic activity is no longer an issue for slaves, as in ancient times; it has become an essential dimension of the human being. It has made man a creator of services for others and therefore a servant of others. As far as secularism is concerned, he used Nicolas Sarkozy's "beautiful expression" on "positive secularism" as he put it; freedom of worship is essential in our societies. And he recalled the "Christian roots of France." He also recalled the words of Jesus on God and Caesar ("Give to God what is God's and to Caesar what is Caesar's," affirming that "the Church does not seek the place of the State. She does not want to replace her." So, there is no issue of fundamentalism. Religion wants its rightful place, nothing more; it reiterates ethical constraints, it does not bear a political project.

Joseph Ratzinger was born in the diocese of Passau (Germany) on 16 April 1927 (Holy Saturday) and was baptized on the same day. From 1946 to 1951 he studied philosophy and theology at the Freising Higher Institute and at the University of Munich. In 1953 he defended his doctorate in theology having as thesis: "The People and the house of God in Augustine's Doctrine of the Church." In 1972, alongside Hans Urs von Balthasar, Henri de Lubac, and other leading theologians, he launched the theological journal *Communio*.

Describing him as a theologian is also stating an essential trait of his personality. He is a man of practice and books, deeply involved in research, which does not prevent him from being attuned to the situation of the Church and the world. Pope Francis, in the preface to a collection of homilies, characterizes Benedict XVI's theology as a "theology on the knees": "Every time I read the works of Joseph Ratzinger / Benedict XVI, I realize more and more clearly that he has done and is still doing theology on his knees, because, even before being a very great theologian and master of the faith, we see that he is a man who really believes, who really prays; we see that he is a man who personifies holiness, a man of peace, a man of God." The search for truth is the basis and the challenge of Benedict XVI's theology. His interest in African theological research is in the same line as the *intellectus fidei* in the African context.

Benedict XVI is also a jurist. During his eight-year papacy (2005–2013), he brought about important norms in the canonical legislation, some of which constitute real mild reforms. These legislative acts can be seen in the context of the essential concerns expressed by Benedict XVI when he occupied Peter's throne. Indeed, we know this Pope's concern for unity among Christians, for the improvement of the quality of ecclesiastical studies, for the accountability of ordinary persons in punishing the perpetrators of sexual abuse of minors within the Church, etc. His legislation has thus focused on various areas that can be the object of a historical and prospective review in order to better understand and appreciate them in the current African religious context.

Benedict XVI is also a philosopher. In his Regensburg address, we find the main guidelines of his intellectual activity: Faith and philosophical reason, faith and scientific reason, and faith and political reason. Concerning the relationship between faith and reason, Benedict XVI said this on the tenth anniversary of John Paul II's *Fides et Ratio*,"The love for Truth impels us to go within ourselves to discover the inner man and the profound meaning of our life. An authentic philosophy must accompany everyone in knowing the Truth of Revelation."[5] On the issue of the dialogue between science and faith, he regrets the "shift" of modern science towards technicality. As such, the convergence of the Christian faith on the one hand and philosophy, science, and politics on the other, is an issue Benedict XVI cherishes. The Philosophy Panel will bring this up to date.

Benedict XVI is committed to the Social Teachings of the Church. Although one might be tempted to make systemic and spiritual theology in Pope Benedict XVI's teaching more prominent, the significance of his contribution in the sphere of ethics should be noted as well. This is the objective of the Fourth Panel, which intends to focus on Benedict XVI's social teaching by examining some major texts addressed to the churches and peoples of Africa. Why must we not ask about the contribution of his social doctrine in the face of socio-political challenges such as the management of the common good in our "democracies in the making," the mastery of violence-producing mechanisms and the implementation of peace in an Africa torn by wars of interest and fratricidal conflicts? Why don't we take seriously the emergence of an African identity in this increasingly global culture? Can we remain indifferent to the ecological threats in an Africa devastated by the exploitation of multinational companies and subjected to the dictatorship of a liberal and essentially capitalist economy? These are all areas of interest that deserve our attention in dialogue with the social doctrine of Benedict XVI.

The interest of a symposium on *the African perspective of Benedict XVI* is to gather the multidisciplinary heritage of this intellectual and writer, especially with regard to his interest and

commitment to the Church and the people of Africa. This symposium will examine his writings, homilies, and speeches during
his visits to Africa.

We thank all those that took part in the Colloquium, especially
the authorities of the Catholic University of Central Africa, Yaoundé,
Cameroon, and the speakers that so generously shared their thoughts in
the thought-provoking lectures delivered. Our gratitude likewise extends
to Virginia M. Greeley, Clauvis K. Komalo, and Fr. James Ajombu for
their proofreading work on the manuscript. Immense gratitude goes as
well to the Benedict XVI Institute for Africa for providing the
needed funding, and to St. Augustine's Press, South Bend, IN, for
accepting to publish this volume, which will hopefully help the Church
in Africa to increasingly become producers and not simply consumers
of the science of theology. In the spirit of Ratzinger, may this volume contribute to fostering love for Christ and Christ's Church
in the hearts of all.

Maurice Agbaw-Ebai and Kizito Forbi, S.J.

Keynote Address:
Benedict XVI and Africa:
Hope as a Utopian Model
Charles Moukala

"On March 17, 2009, Benedict XVI got on the plane to reach Africa. This is the first time that Benedict will visit the African continent as Pope, and he is visibly delighted. He travels to Cameroon and Angola, (...), in order to deliver to the bishops gathered in Yaoundé the *Instrumentum laboris*, the initial text which will then be discussed at the Second Synod of Bishops celebrated in the Vatican in the Fall. This trip to Africa, the "land of hope" as he calls it (...)."[1] This is how Elio Guerriero introduces the paragraph concerning the trips to Africa in his "ample biography" on Pope Benedict XVI, published in 2017 under the title: *Servant of God and Humanity*. In fact, if Pope Benedict XVI wanted to refocus the life of the Church on the theological virtues, as evidenced by his three encyclicals devoted to two of them, hope and charity, it is the first of the two which he always particularly wanted to put at the heart of his message for the Church of God which is in Africa. It is, therefore, quite natural as the bearer of a message of hope that he presents himself to Africa during these two trips to this continent.

During his first trip mentioned above, in his homily of March 19, 2009, at the Amadou Ahidjo stadium in Yaoundé, he commended hope according to the model of St. Joseph (whose memory is celebrated on this day according to the liturgical calendar of the Church) despite difficult situations, especially in family life, likely to lead to discouragement:

> Is there a fatality here, an inevitable evolution? Certainly not! More than ever, we must 'hope against all

hope' (Rm 4, 18) (…) Sons and daughters of Africa, do not be afraid to believe, to hope and to love (…) 'Hoping against all hope': isn't that a magnificent definition of a Christian? Africa is called to hope through you and in you! With Christ Jesus, who walked on African soil, Africa can become the continent of hope (…) If discouragement overwhelms you, think of the faith of Joseph; If you are worried, think of the hope of Joseph, a descendant of Abraham who hoped against all hope.

In his homily of March 21, 2009, in the Sao Paolo church in Luanda, Pope Benedict XVI calls for announcing the message of hope to those who, for lack of Christ, light, and new life, risk remaining in darkness. And this, following the example of the Apostle Paul as well as the missionaries in his suite, in particular those who succeeded by their announcement in giving birth to the first sub-Saharan Christian kingdom from the 16th to the 17th century:

With gratitude and full of hope, I greet you all—men and women given to the cause of Jesus—who are here and who represent so many others (…) At this moment, it pleases me to recall that, five hundred years earlier, that is to say, around the years 1506 and following, when on this land, while the Portuguese were present, the first sub-Saharan Christian kingdom was formed, thanks to faith and to the political determination of King Dom Afonso Mbemba I Mbemba-a-Nzinga (…) The Lord makes us his friends, He entrusts himself to us, He entrusts his body to us in the Eucharist, He entrusts his Church to us (…) May this be our common commitment: to do, together, his holy will: 'Go into the whole world. Proclaim the Good News to all creation.'(Mk 16:15)[3]

And in his homily of October 4, 2009, during the opening Mass of the Second Special Assembly for Africa of the Synod of Bishops, Pope Benedict XVI did not change his tune either. He hoped that the synod will be an opportunity for Africa to turn, in the light of the Word of God, to its spiritual and cultural heritage, namely and in particular the primacy of God, creator and Lord, and its deep sense of God, whom humanity needs more than raw materials, so that it (Africa) is precisely an immense spiritual lung for a humanity in crisis of faith and hope. This, while taking heed of two major pathologies: practical materialism, associated with relativist thought, and religious fundamentalism: *"Thus open to the grace of Christ, Africa will be ever more enlightened by his light and, by allowing itself to be guided through the Holy Spirit, she will become a blessing for the universal Church, bringing her qualified contribution to the building of a more just and fraternal world."*[4]

The same applies to his second trip to Africa, from November 18 to 20, 2011, in Benin, for the delivery of the post-synodal apostolic exhortation, *Africae Munus*, to the bishops of Africa. Already in his speech of November 19, 2011, at the presidential palace in Cotonou, during the meeting with the members of the government, the representatives of the institutions of the Republic, the diplomatic corps, and the representatives of the main religions, Pope Benedict XVI reiterated his message of hope, which hope consists, in this case, in expanding one's heart not only by hope in God but also by openness to the concerns of bodily and temporal realities for the glory of God. In the process, he calls on political representatives not to deprive their people of hope, not to amputate their future by mutilating their present. It also indicates that interreligious dialogue, in an African context marked by the pluralism of religions—dialogue not to be equated with confusion or syncretism—constitutes a field where hope can flourish.[5] Finally in the homily, pronounced during the mass at the *Stade de l'Amitié* in Cotonou on Sunday, November 20, 2011, the Pope returns to his call to be witnesses of the hope received from the announcement of the missionaries, namely that the ultimate goal of man is not the pursuit of selfish happiness, easy gain or power. This hope also passes through conversion, solidarity, and compassion, following the example of the crucified King, for those who suffer, especially the sick:

> The Church in Benin has received a lot from the missionaries: she owes to her in turn bring this message of hope to the peoples who do not know or who no longer know the Lord Jesus. Dear brothers and sisters, I invite you to have this concern for evangelization, in your

country and among the peoples of your continent and of the whole world: The recent Synod of Bishops for Africa reminds us insistently: man of hope, the Christian cannot be uninterested in his brothers and sisters.[6]

It can also be noted from this quotation that for Pope Benedict XVI, the post-synodal apostolic exhortation itself, *Africae Munus*, falls within the same line of the message of hope, by calling on us to assume the tasks of reconciliation, justice, and peace.

It thus appears that if there is a constancy that runs through the various teachings and messages of Pope Benedict XVI vis-à-vis Africa, it could not be better substantiated than by the virtue of hope, proposed to Africa as a utopia mobilizing all its values, its strengths, and above all its faith with a view to its full development, and with it all of humanity, according to God's plan of salvation. The pope himself affirms it even more explicitly, as in a precise summary, in the already quoted speech of November 19, 2011: "Often, in my previous interventions, I have combined the word Africa with that of hope. I did it in Luanda two years ago and already in a synodal context. The word hope also appears several times in the Post-Synodal Apostolic Exhortation Africae Munus that I am going to sign shortly. When I say that Africa is the continent of hope, I am not making easy rhetoric, but quite simply expressing a personal conviction, which is also that of the Church."[7]

This, so to speak, is the factual positivity of the discursive given of Benedict XVI's message for and in Africa. And since it is a question of doing a work of theology, it is, therefore, appropriate to proceed to the systematic and theological analysis of the said conviction in order to extract the theological grammar. And it is again Pope Benedict XVI himself who furnishes us with one of the hermeneutic keys, when he entrusts, still in the same speech of November 19, 2011—which moreover has the particularity of being certainly more systematically reflexive than kerygmatic, in that the latter partakes much more of the style of those given respectively by the Pope in Regensburg in 2006, at the Collège des Bernardins in Paris in 2008, and at the Bundestag in Berlin also in 2011: "I am aware that the words do not have the same meaning everywhere. But that of hope varies little according to culture. A few years ago, I dedicated an encyclical letter to Christian hope."[8] Thus the pope unveils in a way the doctrinal foundation of his conviction which he presents as also being that of the Church: it is a question of the doctrinal development on Christian hope as deployed in the encyclical letter *Spe Salvi* of November 30, 2007.[9] Examined in the light of the said encyclical, the hope at the heart of the essential message of Pope Benedict XVI vis-à-vis Africa can, among other things, be apprehended theologically according to three dimensions: Christologico- soteriological, ecclesiastical-community, and eschatological.

Hope from a Christologico-Soteriological Perspective

The Christologico-soteriological perspective of the doctrinal development of Pope Benedict XVI on hope is already stated from the beginning of *Spe salvi*. The pope actually opens his encyclical with a quotation from the Letter of Saint Paul to the Romans. A quote that hides a confession of faith in the saving redemption offered in Christ, which opens to whoever adheres to it a reliable hope allowing him to face the present, even the difficult one, with an indestructible optimism and an unshakable confidence in the future: *"In hope, we have been saved"* (Rom 8:24). The pope thus establishes a link that could not be more inchoate between hope and faith, as adherence to the saving mystery of Christ. From this perspective, the pope's doctrinal development on hope can then be read as a theological declension which presents itself as a sort of philosophy of history in the light of the soteriological perspective of the mystery of Christ, having allowed the eruption of the infinite in the finite, thus giving back to history and to human life as a whole a direction, a goal, and therefore, a meaning. This, in the sense of what Roger Garaudy was already saying: "The Judeo-Christian faith has defatalized history."[10] If, therefore, Christ has devitalized history by drawing the future into the present, then those who believe in him can hope for a more than certain future. As the encyclical tirelessly emphasizes, which makes it its central line: Christians have a future, their lives do not end in a vacuum.[11] This, according to Pope Benedict XVI, is the theological foundation from which the great Christian hope draws its source. Hope which, therefore, cannot be reduced to the caricatural image of a reward in the future or a call to resignation, but which is rather to be perceived as a mobilizing utopia which sets man in motion:

> It is only when the future is secured as a positive reality that the present becomes so livable. So, we can now say: Christianity was not just "good news"—the communication of content hitherto ignored. In our language, we would say: the Christian message was not only "informative," but "performative." This means that the gospel is not just knowable communication, but fact-producing, life-changing communication. The dark door of time, of the future, has been opened wide. He who has hope lives differently; a new life has already been given to him.[12]

This resounds precisely as an echo of the vibrant appeal of Pope Benedict XVI to African Christians, particularly at the conclusion of his homily on Sunday, March 22, 2009, at the Cimangola esplanade in Luanda: "Get up! Hit the road (cf. 2 Ch 36, 239). Look to the future with hope, trust in God's promises and live in his truth. In this way, you will build something that is destined to endure and you will leave to future generations a lasting legacy of reconciliation, justice and peace."[13] This follows, in the same vain, his exhortation to "hope against all hope," in his homily, already mentioned above, of March 19, 2009, at the Amadou Ahidjo stadium in Yaoundé.[14]

This theological foundation of Christian hope also induces, according to Pope Benedict XVI, its first and foremost deeply spiritual-theological dimension. Indeed, believes the pope, contrary to a certain theology of liberation, if Christian hope transforms the world, it does so from within, by changing hearts through conversion: "Christianity did not bring a message of social revolution like that of the illfated Spartacus, whose struggle led to so much bloodshed. Jesus was not Spartacus, he was not engaged in a fight for political liberation like Barabbas or Bar-Kokhba. Jesus, who himself died on the Cross, brought something totally different: an encounter with the Lord of all lords, an encounter with the living God and thus an encounter with a hope stronger than the sufferings of slavery, a hope which therefore transformed life and the world from within."[15] It is, therefore, deduced that it is not a question, for the pope, of structural transformation, but rather of the conversion of hearts (!).

Was the pope already thinking of his messages for Africa when, to support his analysis in this case, he cites the example of the African slave Josephine Bakhita, who became a nun and then a saint? In any case, it is indeed the quintessence of the same analysis which comes back as if in a refrain, in particular in his speech at the presidential palace in Cotonou, on November 19, 2011: "God alone purifies hearts and intentions. The Church does not provide any technical solution and does not impose any political solution. She repeats: do not be afraid! Humanity is not alone in facing the challenges of the world: God is present. This is a message of hope, a hope that generates energy, which stimulates the intelligence and gives the will all its dynamism."[16]

The Ecclesiastical-Community Dimension of Hope

Pope Benedict XVI clearly emphasizes that Christian hope cannot be perceived in an individualistic way as it will have been the case following a certain modern perversion. In Christian hope, there is no question of *"working out one"s salvation"* in a selfish search that refuses to serve others. In a very synthetic approach, where he refers in particular to Kant, Adorno, and even Marx, the pope denounces the individualistic perversion of hope by the moderns in the name of reason, freedom, and the progress of science. As a result of this perversion, salvation then seemed reserved for scientific progress, with hope finally remaining only the task of caring for souls when science could no longer do anything for them. This, moreover, sheds light on the Marxist reaction, which then tried to bring a materialist salvation to help all those left behind. But, says the pope, "its real error is materialism:

man, in fact, is not merely the product of economic conditions, and it is not possible to redeem him purely from the outside by creating a favourable economic environment."[17]

Otherwise, however useful it may be, progress cannot save man: "It is not science that redeems man. Man is redeemed by love."[18] The Pope also pleads for "a self-criticism of the modern era" in dialogue with Christianity and its conception of hope. A dialogue in which Christianity must also constantly relearn what its hope really consists of, what it can offer the world, and what it cannot. So that the self-criticism of the modern era is accompanied concomitantly by a self-criticism of Christianity which must always be understood afresh from its roots. Roots of which, it (Christianity) rightly holds that:

> Our relationship with God is established through communion with Jesus—we cannot achieve it alone or from our own resources alone. The relationship with Jesus, however, is a relationship with the one who gave himself as a ransom for all (cf. 1 Tim 2:6). Being in communion with Jesus Christ draws us into his "being for all"; it makes it our own way of being. He commits us to live for others, but only through communion with him does it become possible truly to be there for others, for the whole.[19]

The pope cites for this the example of Augustine—his mentor—who after his conversion wanted to withdraw into a contemplative life, but things turned out differently. While participating in Sunday Mass in the port city of Hippo, he was called out of the crowd by the Bishop and forced to allow himself to be ordained for the exercise of the priestly ministry in that city. Looking back on this moment, he writes in his Confessions:

> Appalled by my sins and the heavy mass of my misery, I had, in my heart, agitated and hatched the project of fleeing into solitude: but you prevented it, and you strengthened me with these words: Christ died for all

> so that the living may no longer have their lives cen-
> tered on themselves, but on him, who died and rose
> again for them. (2 Cor 5, 15)[20]

Christ died for everyone. To live for Him means to allow oneself to
be associated with his "being for." And this prevents Christians from
living for themselves and pushes them to transmit their common
hope. In the same vein, the pope develops a kind of communion
mystique that makes hope possible even in the heart of suffering.

> In the history of humanity, it was the Christian faith that
> had the particular merit of bringing forth within man a
> new and deeper capacity for these kinds of suffering that
> are decisive for his humanity. The Christian faith has
> shown us that truth, justice and love are not simply ideals,
> but enormously weighty realities. It has shown us that
> God—Truth and Love in person—desired to suffer for us
> and with us. Bernard of Clairvaux coined the marvellous
> expression: *Impassibilis est Deus, sed non incompassibilis—*
> God cannot suffer, but he can *suffer with.* Man is worth so
> much to God that he himself became man in order to suf-
> fer with man in an utterly real way— in flesh and blood—
> as is revealed to us in the account of Jesus's Passion. Hence
> in all human suffering we are joined by one who experi-
> ences and carries that suffering with us; hence consolation
> is present in all suffering, the consolation of God's com-
> passionate love—and so the star of hope rises.[21]

And as if to invite all Christians to enter into this communal mys-
ticism in suffering, the pope highlights in a paradigmatic way
how the saints for their part have made themselves "collaborators
of God" in their solidarity and their compassion for those who
suffer. This ecclesiastical-community dimension of hope, Pope
Benedict will address in Africa in particular in his speech of November 19, 2011, at the presidential palace in Cotonou: The
Church accompanies the State in its mission; it wants to be like

the soul of this body by tirelessly pointing out to it the essential: God and man. She wishes to carry out, openly and without fear, this immense task of one who educates and cares, and above all of one who prays without ceasing (cf. Lk 18, 1), who shows where God is (cf. Mt 6, 21) and where is the true man (cf. Mt 20, 26 and Jn 19, 5). Despair is individualistic. Hope is communion. Isn't this a splendid way that is proposed to us?[22] And as if to testify to his own involvement in the aforementioned mystical communion, he expressed his solidarity and compassion in the name of Christ with those who suffer in these terms:

> Brothers and Sisters, this passage of the Gospel is truly a word of hope, because the King of the universe has made himself very close to us, servant of the smallest and most humble. And I would like to address with affection all those who suffer, the sick, those affected by AIDS or other illnesses, all those forgotten by society. Keep courage! The Pope is close to you in prayer and thought. Keep courage! Jesus wanted to identify himself with the little one, with the sick; he wanted to share your suffering and recognize you as brothers and sisters, to free them from all evil, from all suffering! Every sick person, every poor person deserves our respect and our love because through him God shows us the way to heaven.[23]

Hope in the Eschatological Perspective

For Pope Benedict XVI, the eschatological dimension of hope derives from the certainty of the Christian faith "that heaven is not empty," that "above everything there is a personal will, there is a Spirit who, in Jesus, revealed himself as Love." It was then that Pope Benedict XVI made a clear difference between "small hopes" and "great hopes," represented by God alone, he who embraces the universe and who can propose and offer us what we cannot achieve by ourselves, namely eternal life. This eternal life whose contours are rationally all the more elusive in that the pope himself can only define it in rather poetic language as being the "plunging into the ocean of infinite love, a moment in which time—the before and after—no longer exists."[24] This implies for the pope that we can only reach by ourselves the "small hopes" which, in daily life, come to comfort us. On the other hand, there is only great hope to comfort us in the assurance that, when there is nothing more to expect from life, when all horizons seem to close in, when all seems lost, we can still hope. In short, Christian hope is not limited to this world, its ultimate aim is eternal life.

This is moreover why, as Frédéric Louzeau so opportunely points out in his contribution to the seminar on what could be called the Christological trilogy of Joseph Ratzinger/Pope Benedict XVI, Jesus of Nazareth, organized by the Schülerkreis Joseph Ratzinger and the Center Notre Dame de l'inculturation from September 16 to 21, 2013, in Cotonou, Benin, that for Benedict XVI "Christians, like other citizens, need to be delivered from the myth of 'eschatologies within history'."[25]

And it is with reference to this eschatological dimension of hope that Pope Benedict XVI invited the Christians of Africa, in his aforementioned homily of October 4, 2009, to turn, in the light of the Word of God, towards their spiritual and cultural heritage, in order to be an immense spiritual lung for humanity. The same is true of his exhortation in his speech at the presidential palace in Cotonou. After having evoked hope in socio-political and economic life, the pope formulates the exhortation to make interreligious dialogue a field conducive to the flowering of hope, let us say the "great hope."

Conclusion

Thus, apprehended under the bright light of its theological anchoring which is the encyclical letter *Spe salvi*, the theological virtue at the heart of the message of Pope Benedict XVI vis-à-vis Africa, appears under the triptych Christologico-soteriological dimension, ecclesiastical-community, and eschatological, as a true utopian model, different from the utopian hope of Ernst Bloch[26] and the anthropological optimism of Jürgen Moltmann,[27] one of his former colleagues from his time at the University of Tübingen. In Benedict XVI, hope is rather given to be read as a utopian model capable of awakening in the faithful, members of the portion of the people of God who are in Africa, the desire for the "true life" which can only come of communion with God (Jn 17:3), source of life. It follows that it is by entering into an authentic relationship with Christ Jesus that they participate with the spiritual and cultural genius that is their own in his way of being for others and discover the true Christian hope that turns to all. However, two questions are fundamentally stuck in my throat, and I cannot finish my remarks without freeing myself from them.

Firstly: Pope Benedict XVI, by giving the impression of minimizing the importance of the transformation of structures in his approach to the performative dimension of hope, does he not risk exposing himself to criticism of theological politics, in particular that of Jean Baptiste Metz,[28] one of his former colleagues from his time at the University of Münster, and to the Latin American liberation theology? Isn't Benedict XVI thus in danger of opening the floodgates to their criticism against a certain bourgeois theology taxed with distilling only intimate and individualistic bigotry?

Secondly: does not too great an insistence on the eschatological character of Christian hope risk leaving the African faithful indifferent, living in a context where, as Jean-Marc Ela puts it so well, "all the salvific potential of the God of Christians (can only) be accessible in the face of the concrete and daily problematic where the radical questions of faith and reason, of nature and grace, of sin and redemption do not come to the minds of people who wonder what God is for them from other situations, other human experiences"?[29]

Charles Moukala
Professor of Theology at the Faculty of Theology,
Catholic University of Central
Africa, (UCAC, Yaoundé, Cameroon)

The Theological Point of View

Apparently, following most of the analyses, the underlying design of the entire theological work of Joseph Ratzinger, Benedict XVI, is his quest for truth. According to him, the real purpose of theology is to be at the service of the truth in the very place of truth which is the Church. Inscribed in this perspective, his theological thought has its roots first and foremost in the theology of the Patristics, as his first two works on the church doctrine of St. Augustine and the theology of history in St. Bonaventure attest, if proof were needed. Like St. Augustine, who, according to almost all experts, has remained his principal mentor, the theologian Ratzinger has never ceased to reconcile faith and reason, meditation and analysis. As a correlation to this central concern of his theological thinking are the questions of the relationship between the city of God and the earthly city, between the "God of faith" and the "God of the philosophers," between the "historical Jesus" and the "Jesus of faith," between the Church and the personality of Mary, between the unique covenant of God and the plurality of religions. All these themes are likely to constitute the "menu" of fruitful discussions within the framework of an academic-scientific exercise, to inspire the development of African theological research which also wants to be an *intellectus fidei* in the African context.

During his eight-year papacy (2005–2013), Benedict XVI brought about important norms in the canonical legislation, some of which constitute real mild reforms. These legislative acts can be seen in the context of the essential concerns expressed by Benedict XVI when he occupied Peter's throne. Indeed, we know this Pope's concern for unity among Christians, for the improvement of the quality of ecclesiastical studies, for the accountability of ordinary persons in punishing the perpetrators of sexual abuse of minors within the Church, etc. His legislation has thus focused on various areas that can be the object of a historical and prospective review in order to better understand and appreciate them in the current African religious context. It would then be necessary to find in Benedict XVI's main legislative measures, the main line of his thought, based on some points such as: The modifications of the law concerning the election of the Pope, the reform of the studies of canon law and philosophy, the search for Christian unity, the contribution to the canonical management of sexual abuse of minors, and the reform of the Roman Curia.

God's Word and Exegesis in Benedict XVI: What Heritage for Africa?

Patrice Mekana, SAC[1]

Introduction

Like other popes, Benedict XVI preaches the Word of Christ, a Word that heals, liberates, and reconciles the entire world, and to Africa in particular. Evangelisation to him consists in announcing Jesus, the Word of God incarnate, dead and risen, always present in the lives of Christians, in the Church, and in the world. Evangelisation therefore aims at the knowledge of Jesus, in the literal sense of the term. One of the privileged channels of this knowledge is an adequate and authentic interpretive approach, which aims to deepen the mystery of God and to foster for believers the growth of a relationship with Jesus. An African perspective of Benedict XVI's philosophy must take into account—if not start from there—the place the pope gives to the Word of God and to theology, whether in eminently exegetical-theological works[2] or in teaching documents.[3] In fact, everything revolves around the Word of God and Jesus.

This contribution, therefore, aims on the one hand to highlight the place of the Word of God and the study of scripture in the teaching of Benedict XVI, and on the other hand, to highlight the echo of his teaching for Africa through three biblical references that emerge from his apostolic exhortation *Africae Munus*. Ultimately, it will be a question of seeing how Benedict XVI's approach can still impact the life of the Church in Africa.

The Place of the God's Word
in the Live of the Church and Christians

As a theologian and more so as a pastor, Benedict XVI gives a central place to God's Word in his ministry. He considers the Bible to be a Dialogue between God and man. Thus, the Bible is the Word of God addressed to every man:

> In this light, each man appears as a recipient of the Word, challenged and called to enter into this dialogue of love through free will. God made each of us capable of listening and responding to the divine Word. Man is created in the Word and lives in it; he cannot understand himself unless he opens himself to this dialogue.[4]

Besides its divine dimension, Benedict XVI insists on another very important dimension of the Bible, namely its historical dimension. Indeed, although it is the Word of God, the Bible was written by God's people and for God's People, inspired by the Holy Spirit. It is therefore not just simply a literary piece; it was born of a living subject, God's people. The Bible developed and lives within God's people. This is a clear insight into the main theme of inspiration of the sacred texts. According to Benedict XVI:

> One could say that the books of the Scripture refer to three interrelated subjects acting on each other. First, there is a particular author or a group of authors, to whom we owe this or that writing. But these authors in the modern sense are not autonomous writers; they are part of a common subject, God's people, from whom they speak and to whom they address themselves. It is this subject, then, that is really the deeper 'author' of the writings. And on the other hand, this people is not isolated; it knows that it is guided and challenged by God himself, who in depth is the one who speaks, through men.[5]

We can then understand the place of this word of God in the Church. Indeed, the Church is founded on the Word of God; it is born from it and lives from it. Throughout centuries of its history, the Church has always found its strength in it, and even today the Church community grows and is nourished by the personal relationship with the Holy Scriptures, by their interpretation in the Liturgy and in the catechism, as well as in scientific research. In this way, the Church does not regard the Bible as a Word of the past, but as a living and present Word.[6] This central stage for the Word of God does not mean, however, that the Christian faith is a "book religion." According to the Pope, Christianity is the "religion of the Word of God," not of "a written and mute word, but of the incarnate and living Word."[7]

Moreover, the Bible, as the Word of God, has a considerable impact on human life. In fact, to the Pope, he who knows the divine Word also fully knows the meaning of every creature:

> He who sets up his life on his Word really builds in a solid and durable way. (...) We need this especially in our era, when many of the things we rely on to build our lives, on which we are tempted to put our hope, turn out to be ephemeral. Having it, sooner or later it is realised that fulfilling the deepest aspirations of the human heart cannot come through pleasure and power. Indeed, in order to build one's life, there is need for solid foundations, which remain even when human certainties fade.[8]

By opening up to the Word of God, man understands himself and finds the answer to the deepest questions that inhabit his heart. Benedict XVI thinks that the Word of God does not oppose man, nor does it mortify his authentic desires. On the contrary, it illuminates them, purifies them, and brings them to fulfilment:

> It is important for our generation to discover that only God responds to the thirst that is in the heart of every man. (...) It is therefore decisive, from a pastoral point

of view, to present the Word of God in its capacity to responding to the problems that man has to face in daily life. Jesus presents himself to us as the one who came so that we might have life in fullness (cf. Jn 10, 10). For this reason, we must make every effort to ensure that the Word of God appears to each person as an opening to his or her problems, an answer to his or her questions, a broadening of values and, at the same time, as a satisfaction to his or her aspirations.[9]

The Interpretation of the Word of God

How does Benedict XVI view the interpretation of the Bible in the Church? First of all, his openness to modern and critical study must be emphasized. He insists on the necessity of the historico-critical method of interpreting the Bible, because it is the very essence of theology and faith. According to Benedict XVI:

> It is essential for the biblical faith that it can refer to truly historical events. It does not tell legends as symbols of truth that go beyond history, but is based on a history that took place on this earth. The *factum historicum* is not for her an interchangeable symbolic figure, it is the soil of which it is made: 'Et incarnatus est'—'And was made flesh'—with these words we profess God's actual entry into real history. The Christian faith would be abolished as such and merged in another form of religion, if we dismiss this history. Indeed, since history, the factual, is part of the very essence of the Christian faith, it must confront the historical method. It is the faith itself that demands it.[10]

In a second stage, Benedict XVI brings out the limitations of critical preaching, which we summarize in three points. Firstly, its nature: the historical approach places Scripture in the past. It studies the event-driven context in which the texts were written, in order to reconstitute what the author could and wanted to say at that particular time, in the context of his reflection and the events. In order to remain true to itself, the historical method must not only seek out the word as belonging to the past, but it must also leave it in the past.[11] Then its purpose: the historical method postulates the regularity of the context in which the historical events took place. Therefore, it handles the words it deals with as human words. Even if it can perceive the "added value" of the word and sense a higher dimension in it, its proper object remains the word of man as human word.[12]

It is obvious that these two elements constitute a real risk in the interpretation of the Bible. Joseph Ratzinger, then Prefect of the Roman Congregation for the Doctrine of the Faith, in the foreword of *Interpretation of the Bible* in the Church, writes:

> The search for the original meaning can lead to relegating the Word completely to the past, so that its present significance is no longer perceived. It can lead to the appearance of only the human dimension of the word as real; the true author, God, escapes the grasp of a method that has been developed for the understanding of human realities.[13]

One important thing that must be considered is the following: In the Bible, human and divine words, the peculiarity of historical event, and the constant validity of the eternal word are intertwined. Indeed, "the origin of biblical word is in a real past, but not only in a past; it comes from God's eternity. It leads us into God's eternity, but it does so by way of time, which includes the past, the present, and the future."[14]

And lastly, a third limitation of the historical method, is that by looking at the different books of the Bible in their historical period and dividing them up according to their sources, historical-critical exegesis ignores the main determinant of the unity of all these scriptures as "the Bible."[15] Another issue is how Benedict XVI proceeds in interpreting the biblical text. The pope starts from the fact that the "historical Jesus" sought and proposed by explanation is too insignificant in content to have been able to engage in any great historical impact; he is too distant in the past to make a personal relationship with him possible.[16] On the basis of this observation, he proposes to go beyond the historico-critical method, applying new methodological criteria, which allow for a properly theological interpretation of the Bible. These criteria require, among other things, faith and the unity of the Scriptures, without, however, being willing or able to renounce historical rigor.

Faith and Interpretation

Benedict XVI views the Bible as "the voice of the wandering People of God," and it is only in the faith of this people that we are, so to speak, in the right tone to understand Holy Scripture. An authentic interpretation of the Bible must always be in harmony with the faith of the Catholic Church. Therefore, any approach to the sacred text which disregards the faith, although it may suggest interesting elements, would inevitably be only a preliminary, structurally incomplete one.[17]

In this regard, the American biblical philosopher, Sandra Schneiders, believes that in order to be correct and appropriate, a hermeneutical theory must ultimately embrace the whole reality of the object to be interpreted. From one point of view, the biblical text is a human text, and one can develop a hermeneutical theory that grounds its interpretation as a human text. From another point of view, this text is Holy Scripture, and an adequate hermeneutical theory will have to take full account of the reality of the Bible, which is that this human text is a privileged mediation of the encounter between God and man. The Bible has more than one text. We are dealing with the revealing text.[18]

The reader can discover something greater behind the human word in the Bible, through faith; this is also the Word of God. In the case of the Gospels, for example, the reader discovers the character of Jesus best when he looks at him through the eyes of faith and in his relationship with his Father. It would therefore make much more sense, from a historical point of view, to consider that the historical Jesus broke all available categories, that he could only be understood from the mystery of God. This goes beyond the scope of the historical method.

Benedict XVI therefore recommends reading the Bible in general, and the Gospels in particular, in the light of this faith-based conviction, obviously relying on the historical method, but opening up to something greater.[19] This approach also rejects another argument often put forward by some scholars, according to which the Gospels want to clothe the mysterious figure of the Son of God who appeared on earth in flesh. In this regard, Benedict XVI writes, the Gospels did not need to "clothe" Jesus in flesh, since he actually took on flesh. The challenge being to truly find that flesh.[20]

In more concrete terms, exegesis, cut off from faith, cannot anchor Jesus in God and would render him schematic, unreal, and unexplainable. This would run the risk of making Christians uncertain about the possibility of keeping faith in Jesus Christ as Saviour of the world. Benedict opts instead to look at Jesus from the point of view of his communion with the Father, which is the core of his personality; without this communion, nothing is understood, and Christ is still present to us today, thanks to it.[21]

Exegesis and Unity of the Scripture

Benedict XVI also emphasizes on the need to read the Scriptures in their unity, because this gives them a completely new light. This is a basic principle of any theological exegesis: "Whosoever wants to understand Scripture with the same spirit that made it written must consider the content and unity of the whole of Scripture."[22] As he explains, the process by which the words transmitted in the Bible become Scripture is a process of constant readings: in a new situation, the ancient texts are the object of a new reception, a new understanding, a new perusal. Through readings and reviews, corrections, in-depth studies, and amplifications, the progressive elaboration of a Scripture unfolds like a process of speech that gradually opens up its inner potentialities, which have been lying dormant as seeds, waiting to bear fruit until they are strongly encouraged by new situations, experiences, and sufferings.[23]

The principle of the unity of the Scriptures also makes it possible to bear in mind that every word of a man of a certain importance contains from the outset much more than what may have come to the author's immediate awareness. This word acquires added value when it matures in the process of the history of faith, in the process of rereading and amplifications.[24] It is therefore necessary to read the different texts of the Bible as a whole. In fact, what Benedict XVI is aiming at in his exegetical approach is to foster for the reader and the believer the growth of a living relationship with Jesus.[25] This should be the goal of all biblical exegesis as a theological discipline. In fact, "If scientific biblical exegesis does not want to exhaust itself in the constant search for new hypotheses that become theologically insignificant, it must take a further methodological step and recognize itself again as a theological discipline, without relinquishing its historical character."[26] He summarizes his exegetical approach as follows:

> In my opinion, a proper interpretation requires two steps. First, we must ask ourselves what the authors of these texts meant in their time—this is the historical component of the exegesis. But the text must not be left in the past, storing it among events that happened long ago. The second question must be: Is what is being said true? Does it concern me? And if it concerns me, in what way? In the face of such a biblical text, whose ultimate and most profound author, according to our faith, is God himself, the question of the relationship of the past to the present is inevitably part of the interpretation itself. In this way the seriousness of historical research is in no way diminished but increased.[27]

Benedict XVI's Legacy to Africa

Benedict XVI's emphasis on the Sacred Scripture and his exegetical approach are undoubtedly a legacy for Africa. This can be seen, on the one hand, in his invitation to the Church in Africa to give a central place to the Word of God, and on the other hand, in the biblical references he uses in his Apostolic Exhortation *Africae Munus*.

The Place of the Word of God in Africa

From the outset, the pope recalls the truth of faith: Africa is no stranger to divine revelation in Jesus Christ. Addressing the members of the Special Council for Africa of the Synod of Bishops, he states:

> Two thousand years ago, through Jesus, God himself brought salt and light to Africa. Since then, the seed of his presence has been sown in the depths of the hearts of this dear continent and is gradually germinating beyond and through the ups and downs of the human history of your continent.[28]

This assertion is a response to the view that the Bible is imported and alien to Africa, and that reading it is an alienation. It is necessary to reiterate beyond any ideology, that the Word of God is not the property of anyone: not of the Jews, and certainly not of the Western missionaries. The Word of God contained in the Bible is humanity's heritage, it is our common heritage and Africa is part of this heritage.[29] A quotation of Father Engelbert Mveng's inaugural lecture at the Jerusalem Congress in April 1972 is an appropriate response to this question:

> The message of the Bible is our message, because we are the people of the Bible, because Africa is the Land of the Bible and the second river of Paradise is called Geon which surrounds the land of Kush, that is, Black Africa. From Genesis, Africa and Black Africans are present in the Bible; the message of the Bible is our message and the People of the Bible are our People. We too are the heirs of the Bible and responsible for its message yesterday, today, and tomorrow.[30]

It is obvious that the Bible, as humanity's heritage and more so as the Word of God, does not take anything away from Africa, neither does it impoverish nor alienate it. Neither does it aim at any kind of "cultural imperialism." In fact, just as it was sown in the land of Israel and in the pagan lands of the West and the East, the Word of God was sown alike in Africa. The Bible opens Africa to hope and an experience of God. Not because the African did not know God, but because the Bible makes us know the true God, brought by Jesus. Indeed, while it is irrefutable that Africa is a continent with a distinct religious background, it should also be recognized that the newness of biblical revelation comes from the fact that God makes himself known in the dialogue he wishes to establish with us.[31] It is to this novelty that the Bible in general, and Jesus in particular, opens Africa. Jesus also brought God to this religious Africa:

> He brought the God whose face was slowly and progressively being revealed from Abraham through Moses and the Prophets to sapiential literature—the God who had shown his true face only in Israel and who had been honored in the Gentile world under obscure avatars—it is this God, the God of Abraham, Isaac, and Jacob, the true God that he brought to the peoples of the earth. He brought God: from then onward we know his face, from then onward we can call upon him. From then on, we know the path that, as men, we must follow in this world. Jesus brought God and with him the truth about our origin and destiny; faith, hope, and love.[32]

Like all the peoples of the world, the peoples of Africa can and must make this good news theirs. The Bible is a message of life, a gift from God to the peoples of Africa. In the words of St. John, it is what was from the beginning, what has been heard, what has been seen and contemplated, what has been touched by the Spirit of life, that is what the Bible proclaims to Africa so that its sons and daughters may be in communion with other Christians and with Christ. (cf. 1Jn 1, 1–3) Through the Bible, the

Church opens today the way to God for the African, to the God who speaks and who communicates his love to us so that we may have abundant life (cf. Jn 10,10).[33]

Furthermore, Benedict XVI recognises the fact that Africa's memory is painfully scarred by slavery, colonisation, and fratricidal ethnic struggles. Even today, the continent is confronted with rivalries, new forms of slavery, and colonisation.

> The Pontiff believes that in order for Africa to stand with dignity, she needs to hear the voice of Christ, who today proclaims love for the other, even for the enemy, to the point of giving his own life, and who prays today for the unity and communion of all men (cf. Jn 17, 20–21).[34]

For this reason, based on St. Jerome's motto—" ignorance of Scriptures is ignorance of Christ"—Benedict XVI advocates reading and meditating on the Word of God. Indeed, they not only give us the eminent knowledge of Jesus Christ, but also root us more deeply in Christ and guide our service to reconciliation, justice, and peace.[35] In other words, "it is the Word of God that can help us to know Jesus Christ and bring about the conversions that lead to reconciliation, since it sifts 'the feelings and thoughts of the heart' (Hb 4, 12)."[36]

The Word of God must, therefore, have a central place in the mission of the Church's, because every process of (new) evangelization must incorporate the intellectual dimension of faith into the living experience of the encounter with Jesus Christ present and acting in the Church community. The knowledge of Christ the Holy Scriptures revealed appears to be one of the answers to the religious ignorance often deployed in the African continent. In fact, E. Messi Metogo states in many cases there is a withdrawal of reason and a search for the marvelous, which leads to the practice of magic, the misuse of prayer and the sacraments, and which is largely responsible for the proliferation of sects and the development of popular credulity. Many Christians know nothing about their religion apart from their first holy communion catechism, in case they have not forgotten it.[37] The words of Benedict XVI's successor seem to us more relevant than ever for the African continent:

Faith, without truth, does not save, does not make our steps safe. It remains a beautiful tale, the projection of our desires for happiness, something that satisfies us only when we want to be deluded. Or it is reduced to a beautiful sentiment, which consumes and delights, but which is linked to our states of mind, to the variability of the times, incapable of sustaining a constant march through our lives.[38]

The Word of God: a Word that Lifts and Renews

In his apostolic exhortation *Africae Munus*, Benedict XVI makes reference to several biblical texts. We have highlighted the three most important ones, because they summarize his proclamation of Christ to Africa.

"Have faith! Get up, he is calling you!" (Mk 10:49)

This ends the Exhortation: a true word of hope. This extract is taken from the Markan parable of Bartimaeus the blind man (Mk 10:46–52). Jesus on his way to Jerusalem passes through the city of Jericho. He is accompanied by his disciples and a large crowd as he leaves the city. When Bartimaeus hears that it is Jesus who is passing by, he starts crying out loud: "Jesus, Son of David, have mercy on me!" Bartimaeus shouted even louder, despite the fact that the crowd rebuked him. Jesus stops and calls him. Until then, the crowd that had been trying to stifle Bartimaeus told him: "Have faith! Arise, he is calling you!" Bartimaeus leaps, abandons his cloak and goes to Jesus who gives him back his sight.

This is the last healing narrative in Mark's Gospel before Jesus' triumphal entry into Jerusalem. While everyone else (Jesus, his disciples, and a large crowd) is on the move, on their way to Jerusalem, Bartimaeus remains still, sitting at the side of the road. Blind and reduced to begging, he is an outcast, sitting outside the city by the roadside. All these features indicate his disgraceful condition and social exclusion.[39] Why it is true that Benedict XVI does not explicitly compare Africa to Bartimaeus in his exhortation (he uses only the words of the crowd in Bartimaeus to address Africa), we would not hesitate to do so.

The Africa to which Benedict XVI addresses himself is likened to Bartimaeus. It seems to be immobile, sitting on the edge of the path of development, truly marginalized in a dishonorable condition. John Paul II and the Synod Fathers already compared it in *Ecclesia in Africa* to the man who went down from Jerusalem to Jericho, who fell into the hands of robbers who stripped him, beat him, and went away, leaving him half dead: "Africa is a continent where countless human beings—men and women, children and young people—lie somehow by the roadside, sick, injured, helpless, marginalized, and abandoned. They are in dire need of good Samaritans to come to their aid."[40] What Bartimaeus expects from the one he recognizes as the son of the messianic king David is pity and a little attention.[41] Commenting on this parable, Camille Focant issues a very interesting remark:

> *Jesus does not go to the blind man, as he did with Jairus* (Mk 5:24). Nor do others bring him, as they did with the paralytic (Mk 2:3–4) or the blind man of Bethsaida (Mk 8:22). Jesus only stops and asks that the cripple be called (Mk 10:49). In this way, he shows both his availability and his refusal to let the blind be called Bartimaeus, locked in his passiveness. His desire for healing must not only be expressed in words, but also in action.[42]

By calling Bartimaeus and restoring his sight, Jesus gives him life. He who was socially marginalized at the roadside becomes a connected man, a disciple who follows his master on his path, irrespective of how difficult it may be.[43] Benedict XVI invites Africa to listen to Jesus' word of hope, for it uplifts and gives life in the same way that Bartimaeus sprang up, full of hope, at Jesus' call:

I reiterate: Arise, Church in Africa [...] the heavenly Father is calling you, He whom your ancestors called the Creator, before they knew his merciful closeness, revealed in his only Son, Jesus Christ. Embark on the journey of a new evangelization with the courage that comes to you from the "Holy Spirit."[44]

The Pope in these words reiterates to the Christians of Africa, the dignity of their vocation as children of God, a vocation which consists in spreading the light of the Gospel, the splendor of Jesus Christ, the true light that enlightens every person, in this world that is often darkened.[45]

"Get up, pick up your mat and walk" (Jn 5:8)

These are words used in the second part of the exhortation to deepen certain points in the accomplishment of the mission of the Church in Africa. These words of Jesus are taken from the Johannine parable of the healing of the crippled man at the pool of Bethesda (Jn 5:1–18). After his journey through Samaria and Galilee (Jn 4), Jesus goes up to Jerusalem on the occasion of a Jewish festival. Under the porch of the pool of Bethesda lay a multitude of cripple, blind, lame, and impotent people who were waiting for an angel to make the water bubble so that they could throw themselves in and be healed. Jesus sees a paralyzed man who has been suffering for thirty-eight years but has no one to help him get into the pool for healing. Jesus says to him: "Get up, pick up your mat and walk!" Immediately the man is healed: he takes up his mat and starts walking.

As in the Markan parable of Bartimaeus, we would like to focus attention on this man who benefits from Jesus' action. He is a cripple, he cannot walk, he is lying there among the others. Talking of the length of his illness—thirty-eight years— underlines the seriousness of his condition and, in turn, the power of Jesus.[46] His response to Jesus' question—" Sir, I don't have any one here to put me in the pool when the water is stirred up" (Jn

5:7)—shows that his situation is hopeless.[47] In short, lying down and cut off from others, this man is like an outcast from life. His desperation of—"I have no one…"—contrasts with the presence of Jesus.[48]

Jesus portrays his authority by healing this man with his one word, made up of three imperatives issued: "Get up, pick up your mat, and walk." The expression "lying"—(cf. *"katékeito," "katakeimenon"* (v.3–6), is contradicted by Jesus' command, "get up," in Greek "egeire," an expression traditionally used to denote resurrection.[49] The man gets up and walks. He is standing; he is now alive. Jesus has given him full life, for he has come that people may have life, and have it in all its fullness (cf. Jn 10:10.) This life, he gives through his word, which is life-giving.

As was the case with Bartimaeus the blind man and the man who fell into the hands of robbers on the road to Jericho, Africa can be compared to the cripple in Bethesda whom Jesus heals. The Pope invites him to arise, take up his mat, and walk. We can compare Africa's plight not only to all the mentalities, burdens, realities, and conditionalities that keep it paralyzed, but also to all its possibilities for emergence that are not properly exploited, notably its human resources, the dynamism of its youth and its diaspora, the richness of its soil and subsoil, etc.

Above all, Benedict XVI invites Africa to embrace Jesus and his teachings, as its source of healing. Unlike the crippled man of Bethesda who had no one to plunge him into the pool and who did not know who Jesus was and that he was able to heal him, Africa has a partner who does not intend to exploit him or keep him paralyzed: He is Jesus. In other words:

> Receiving Jesus offers Africa a more effective and pro-found healing than any other. As the Apostle Peter declared in the Acts of the Apostles (3:6), I repeat that Africa needs neither gold nor silver first; it desires to stand upright like the man in the pool of Bethesda; she desires to have confidence in herself, in her dignity as a people loved by its God. It is therefore this encounter

with Jesus that the Church must offer to the broken and wounded hearts, in need of reconciliation and peace, thirsting for justice. We must offer and proclaim the Word of Christ that heals, liberates and reconciles.[50]

"And now, I make all things new" (Rev 21:5)

This statement is the title of the first part of the Exhortation. It is the statement of the One who sits on the throne in the Revelation of St. John. Being the last book of the Bible, the book of Revelation was written against a backdrop of unrest, hostility, and violent persecution of the nascent Church by Rome and the Roman Empire. The book has a twofold purpose: to console Christians in their suffering and to exhort them to persevere in faith in order to reign with Christ on the day of his impending coming.

The book of Revelation is therefore centered on the knowledge of Jesus Christ and in the messianic gifts he brings: peace, consolation, joy. In this light, far from being the book of catastrophe, terror, or the end times, the book of Revelation is rather the biblical book par excellence of hope, for it vigorously attests that at every moment in human history, even the most desperate, which pushes men to despair, God is present.

Chapter 21, from which the statement of the One who sits on the throne is taken, has two main themes, namely the new world and God's dwelling among men. Concerning the new world, it speaks of the vision of a new heaven and a new earth, of the disappearance of the old things including the sea, of the disappearance even of death, since the first things have passed away and God makes all things new.[51]

The prophets are those talking of the theme of the regeneration of the world. It is sometimes conceived in the context of a purification that happily removes all that is defiled and affected by and sin. Sometimes, however, it is a new beginning, new genesis, where God intervenes in a way that is as totally creative as in the first creation.[52]

In Rev. 21 the author is not interested in bringing out a realistic description of the End and specifying its time, conditions, and modalities. Instead, "He repeats on every page that God's intervention in the world cannot but upset all data, be it temporal or spatial (...) All that is marked by the old conditions is swept away. God will therefore create anew. It is the renewed framework of men who live by the new life."[53] The peak of the text is thus the proclamation of a new way of life in which faithful Christians participate.

By proposing the renewal of all things to the African Christians, Benedict XVI invites them to invent a new Africa. This brings reconciliation to the forefront: reconciliation with God and with others. The Pontiff sees reconciliation with God as the source of all purification and inner maturation of man. Indeed, it is God's grace that gives us a new heart and reconciles us to him and to others. Reconciliation thus taps from the Father's love manifested in Jesus; it is born out of the Father's initiative to renew His relationship with humanity that was broken by man's sin.[54] In other words, reconciling with God is the condition for genuine reconciliation among the sons and daughters of Africa. It is therefore important now and, in the future, to purify the memory in order to build a better society where such tragedies are not repeated.[55]

Making the new universe for Africa also means reinventing fraternal service, synonymous with the creation of a just order in line with the beatitudes. Benedict XVI believes that no society, even a developed one, can do without fraternal service animated by love:

> He who wants to free himself from love prepares to free himself from man as man. Suffering, which demands consolation and help is always bound to occur. There will always be loneliness. Similarly, there will always be situations of material need, for which help is indispensable, in the direction of a concrete love for one's neighbor. It is love that soothes wounded, lonely, abandoned hearts.[56]

Africa doing new things means making a real "metanoia," an authentic conversion. If it is true that Christians are marked by the spirit and habits of their era and environment, by the grace of their baptism they are invited to drop the dominant harmful tendencies and to go against the current. This "metanoia" is experienced in a special way in the sacrament of reconciliation, a real "school for the heart," where the disciple of Christ is shaped into an adult Christian life and becomes capable of facing the difficulties of everyday life with a life imbued with the spirit of the Gospel.[57]

Making a new world is about promoting and protecting family life. In concrete terms, this means among other things, combating all violence against women, and denouncing and condemning those violences.[58] More than ever, in Africa, "the equal dignity of men and women must be recognized, affirmed, and defended: they are both persons, unlike any other living being in the world around them."[59] This also means protecting human life, which is under heavy threat of drugs and alcohol, which destroy the human potential of the continent and afflict mostly the youths.[60]

Benedict XVI thinks that the Church has a crucial role to play in bringing about this new Africa. She must make the voice of Christ heard, by being present where the sons and daughters of Africa know and recognize the face of Christ in a child, the sick, the suffering, or the needy. It must, therefore, be ready to give an account of the hope that it carries within it (cf. 1 Pt 3:15), for a new dawn is on the horizon.[61] The word of God is capable of raising up and renewing Africa.

Conclusion

The central place of the Word of God and its authentic Christian interpretation is undoubtedly Benedict XVI's legacy for the Church in Africa. Indeed, Africa, like the other continents, also needs the Word of Christ. This Word is not foreign to her and is in no way a form of cultural imperialism, because Christ does not take anything away from Africa. It instead brings to her the true face of the God whom her children have always sought and wor-shipped. In view of the distressing situation of many of the sons and daughters of the continent, the knowledge of Christ in his Word is able to bring about a new Africa. In order to do this, African exegetes and biblical scholars can tap from Benedict XVI's approach: an authentic and profound exegesis that nurtures a re-lationship with Jesus, that touches the African in his or her lifestyle and daily life, and that presents Jesus as the one who re-sponds to the expectations and questions of Africans.

Pope Benedict XVI's View on the Liturgical Reform in the Face of the Challenge of Inculturation in the Churches of Africa

Rev. Pr. Antoine Essomba Fouda[1]

Introduction

The reform resulting from the second Vatican Council has opened new horizons to give a more dynamic and intelligible paschal content to liturgical celebrations. This requires an ever deeper knowledge of the liturgy of the Church and the desire to promote it in its twofold dimension of interior and collective participation. This is why Pope Benedict XVI insists on the *ars celebrandi* which "flows from faithful obedience to the liturgical norms in their entirety" and are "the primary means of fostering the participation of the people of God in the sacred Rite."[2]

Moreover, inculturation, which is "a priority and an emergency in the life of particular Churches for a real implantation of the Gospel in Africa,"[3] must never be considered as a disintegration of the liturgy of the Catholic Church in order to make a new one.[4] This would be exposing it to the dangers of syncretism, juxtaposition, too easy transposition—in short, to acculturation or even to a total break with the secular tradition of the liturgy. This is, therefore, a major challenge which calls for a liturgical hermeneutic and a rigorous methodology in the long process of inculturation. The question is, therefore, whether in the explicit presentation of the liturgy in our African churches, the Christian is aware of what he is celebrating and why? How and in what spirit should he celebrate? With whom should he celebrate to express the church as family of

God? When and for how long should he celebrate in order for the liturgical celebration to bear fruit? To answer all these questions, our presentation will be divided into three parts:

In the first part, we will bring out the theological foundations of the liturgy according to Vatican II. This insight will enable us in the second part to involve the hermeneutics of Pope Benedict XVI's reform for a liturgical Christology in line with the authentic cultural values of the various African peoples. With all this in mind, we shall see concretely in a third aspect, what are the key elements of the liturgy that may continuously be updated in the African Churches. It is with this in mind that on the basis of its steadfast source, the appropriation of the liturgy by the African Churches cannot be understood even less without taking into account, for example, the two Post-Synodal Apostolic Exhortations *Ecclesia in Africa*[5] and *Africae Munus.*[6] Our conclusion will focus on proposals and perspectives.

The Theological Foundations of the Liturgy According to Vatican II: The Context of the Development of the Constitution De Sacra Liturgia Sacrosanctum Concilium[7]

At the outset, it should be noted that for many centuries the Christian liturgy was seen and understood, wrongly, as a set of signs and words harmoniously arranged under the vigilant authority of persons assigned by their ministerial priesthood, namely bishops, priests, and deacons. To this must be added the elitism of the Latin liturgical language, which constitutes a no less significant barrier for the people. This juridicism and linguistic exoterism create a great gap between the so-called "masters" of the liturgy, the ordained ministers, and the people, who no longer understand anything about the liturgical phenomenon and turn to the numerous popular devotions as a sign of parallel participation in the celebration.

The gradual loss of the nature of the liturgy celebrated fortunately triggered circles of reflection for decades aimed at restoring the true meaning of the liturgy in its theological and ministerial content as well as in its various forms of expression. If some members of the liturgical movement, in their reflective boldness, draw rather hasty conclusions about the interchangeability, transposition, or even assimilation of baptismal and ministerial priesthoods, the encyclical *Mediator Dei* of Pope Pius XII in 1947,[8] restructured the reflection on the level of its Christological and ecclesiological foundations.

Pope Pius XII specifies that liturgical worship is above all "the continuation of the priestly function which Jesus Christ, our Redeemer, rendered to the Father as Head of the Church (Christological perspective), but also and inseparably, the liturgy is also worshipping of the Head, performed by the community of the faithful, and by Him to the Father, that is to say, in a word, the integral worship of the Mystical Body of Christ, that is to say, of the Head and of the parts"[9] (ecclesial perspective). This clear doctrinal stance of the Church on the liturgy was a prophetic sign that led to the announcement of the Second Vatican Council by Pope John XXIII in 1959 with the setting up of a preparatory liturgical commission. This announcement was the fulfilment of a dream to bring the liturgy to the people and to bring the people to the liturgy. The encyclical *Mediator Dei*, which provides certain answers to the most legitimate expectations of the liturgical movement, also served, with caution and commitment, as a beacon for the Constitution De Sacra Liturgia Sacrosanctum Concilium, which opens up an avenue for a liturgical *aggiornamento* and, by the same token, allows the Christian to make his celebrated faith comprehensible.

The Key to the Theological Reading
of Sacrosanctum Concilium (SC)

If the review of this very first conciliar document, approved and promulgated in the Vatican on 4 December 1963, leads us to divide it into seven chapters, sub-divided into 130 numbers,[10] our reflection will focus above all on its theological reading key, which is elucidated from "l'histoire du salut"[11] (*The history of salvation*).

SC explains that God's plan to save humanity is fulfilled through Christ and in Christ "especially through the paschal mystery of the blessed passion, resurrection of the dead and glorious ascension."[12] With this assertion, Christ's Passover, or the reality of Christ's redemption (man's reconciliation with God and God's perfect glorification), is placed not only at the center of salvation history but also at the heart of the Church's liturgy.

Indeed, the history of salvation expressed in the mystery of Christ gets its fulfilment, its accomplishment and its center in Easter not only as a historical moment, but also as a ritual fulfilment of this historical event.[13] This is why "the liturgy is considered to be the exercise of the priesthood of Jesus Christ; in it, through sensitive signs, the sanctification of man is signified and in its own way, the integral public worship is exercised by the Mystical Body of Jesus Christ, that is to say, by the head and by its members."[14] The Church as Mother and Teacher has received the mission from Christ to perform this saving act to the extent that the liturgy becomes "the work of Christ the priest and of his Body, which is the Church."[15] The ecclesiology that emerges here is therefore an ecclesiology of communion that puts the nature of the Church as an ontological, supernatural, and sacramental communion of divine life in the foreground, to the point that "liturgy and Church are one and the same precisely because the Church by its nature is a liturgical assembly."[16] In short, it is a theological reality "at a time human and divine, visible and rich in invisible realities."[17]

If the liturgy is "the summit to which the Church's action is directed, and at the same time the source from which all her virtue flows,"[18] then this communion invites us to take a fresh look at the liturgy in order to discern in it the unchanging elements linked to the secular liturgical tradition of the Church and those elements which are a matter of cultural contingency and therefore liable to change. *Sacrosanctum Concilium* therefore calls for the renewal of liturgical texts and rites to express "the holy realities they signify, and that the Christian people, as far as possible, may easily grasp them and participate in them through a full, active and communal celebration."[19] Only then will the liturgical celebration, expressed in a language accessible to all, fulfil one of the conditions for a "full, intelligent and active participation"[20] of the people of God and bear the expected spiritual fruits. But if the Christology and ecclesiology of Vatican II seem clear, it is actually their concrete application that is still problematic, to the point that since the Reformation, two more or less clear-cut positions have been taken: On the one hand, are found the progressives who, as Ratzinger rightly notes, are "fierce defenders of the reform" and advocate a discontinuity with the past in order to achieve a concrete break with the past by eliminating all the liturgical barriers that could hinder its progress towards real novelty, including the official language of the Church, which is Latin. On the other hand, the traditionalists who, as Benedict XVI once again points out, "criticize not only its practical application, but also its conciliar foundations—and who see salvation only in a total rejection of the reform."[21] In the face of these two almost diametrically opposed positions, the theologian, liturgist, and pastor advocate what he calls "reforming the reform" which shall pass through a rigorous hermeneutic.

The Hermeneutics of the Liturgical Reform of Pope Benedict XVI: Hermeneutical Principles of the Liturgy

In the post-synodal apostolic exhortation, the *Sacramentum caritatis* which dwells on the *fons et culmen* of the Church's mission, the Eucharist, Pope Benedict XVI gives the key to the hermeneutic reading of the liturgical reform when he declares that "the changes willed by the Council within the unity that characterizes the historical development of the rite itself" must take place "without introducing artificial breakages."[22] This means that the liturgy, expressed through a verbal language composed of speaking formulae and a non-verbal language, i.e. signs, symbols, gestures, etc., is the bearer of an ecclesial patrimony which links it not only to its founder, Christ, but also to the whole tradition and

58

to the Magisterium. The method therefore consists in making changes from within in an organic manner "so that the healthy tradition is maintained, and yet the way is open to legitimate progress."[23] It is not about a revolution that demolishes everything, upsets everything, and creates a new liturgy. It is rather an issue of the restoration and progress of the liturgy.[24] Thus, as Ratzinger so aptly states, it would be "similar not to technical equipment that can be produced, but to a plant, that is to say, to something organic, therefore, something that grows and whose laws of growth determine the possibilities of further development."[25] We can consider this organic view of the liturgy as the first principle to be retained.

The second principle is that of the full, active, and conscious participation of all the Christians in celebrating the liturgy. It can only really bear all its spiritual fruits if it blends the external and internal factors as mentioned above. For, as Cardinal Joseph Ratzinger forcefully points out, "the survival of the liturgy as such is at stake."[26]

The third principle insists on the simplicity, sobriety and solemnity of the liturgy expressed in the Constitution *Sacrosanctum Concilium* in these words: "the rites shall manifest a noble simplicity, shall be remarkably brief and void of unnecessary repetition; they shall be adapted to the capacity of understanding of the faithful and, in general, there shall be no need for many explanations in order to understand them."[27] This is what Pope Benedict XVI calls a conformity to the Logos in the Christian liturgy.[28]

The fourth principle insists on the centrality of the Eucharist. Saint John Paul II already underlines this strongly when he writes: "the Eucharist thus appears as the summit of all the sacraments because it brings to perfection communion with God the Father, thanks to identification with the only-begotten Son through the action of the Holy Spirit."[29] The form of Christ's presence is thus manifest par excellence in this sacrament,[30] which is the "hic et nunc" update of the memorial of the passion, death and resurrection of Christ. Moreover, the Eucharist contributes to the reinforcement of the incorporation of the faithful into Christ acquired at baptism through the gift of the Spirit (Cf.1 Co 12:13–27). This is why it is considered the center and summit of the Church, which has the duty to perpetuate it until the end of time. This is what leads Saint John Paul II to state forcefully that: "The Eucharist is too great a gift to be able to bear ambiguities and reductions."[31] Pope Benedict XVI follows suit when he shows in his post-synodal apostolic exhortation *Sacramentum caritatis* that inasmuch as all the other six sacraments each celebrate the Lord's Passover from a very specific angle, in truth all converge towards the Eucharist *fons et culmen* of the liturgy.

Moreover, the Eucharistic liturgy is divided into two tables: the table of the word and the Eucharistic table. Benedict XVI insists on the sacramentality of the Word, which should be given its full importance during the celebration.[32] Hence the preponderant role of the homily, which must always be of a high profile. And because it is an explanation of the proclaimed word of the Lord to the people, "it must help them in understanding the mystery that is being celebrated, appealing to the mission, preparing the Christians for the profession of faith, for bidding prayer and for the Eucharistic liturgy."[33] Pope Francis continues that, for this reason, "The homily has a special value that comes from its Eucharistic context, which surpasses all catechisms because it is the highest moment of dialogue between God and his people, before sacramental communion."[34]

It should be noted that the homily, which is linked to the sacrament of Holy Orders, can only be delivered by a priest or a deacon.[35] It is not a matter of great eloquence or theological erudition; but of "a function reserved for those who are consecrated by the sacrament of Holy Orders."[36] It is therefore not appropriate or advisable to entrust the homily to anyone other than the minister of the Eucharist. The homily is obligatory on Sundays and feasts of precept with the participation of the people, except for a serious reason. It is recommended on other days, especially during the feasts of Advent, Lent, and Easter, as well as on other feasts and occasions when the people of God flock to the Church.[37]

A fifth principle is called eschatology. The action of Christ in the Church is directed towards the eschatological fullness in fact, as SC states, "in the earthly liturgy we participate, having a fore-taste of the heavenly liturgy, which is celebrated in the holy city of Jerusalem, towards which we tend as pilgrims, where Christ sits at the right hand of God. Let us wait for the Saviour, our Lord Jesus Christ, until he appears in our lives, and we shall appear with him in glory."[38] In this text, the idea of the contemporary presence of the Lord in the moment and of the communion between the pil-grim Church and the triumphant Church prevails, but always in the dimension of expectation; the link is made by the presence of the Lord: "He is always present in his Church and in a special way in the liturgical actions,"[39] but he has yet to come in glory.

The sixth principle is that of silence, which is an integral part of the liturgy. Indeed, interior life is fostered by a recollection: one must know how to be silent in oneself and around oneself. It is also in the silence of recollection that people can make personal prayers or meditations on the word of God. As Pope Benedict XVI points out, "the great Patristic Tradition teaches us that the Mys-teries of Christ are linked to silence."[40] Then the soul that listens to God can receive all that God wants to inspire in it.

After this explanation of Benedict XVI on the hermeneutics of the reform against the backdrop of the Christological primacy in the liturgy, what lesson can be drawn for the Churches of Africa in their reception for an in-depth assimilation of the liturgy of Vat-ican II with this necessity of inculturation?

Important Factors of the Liturgy in Its Continuous Updating in the African Churches Definitive Approach

The Magisterium, after having spoken for a long time of adapta-tion, for the sake of a true and profound liturgical renewal, has spoken of inculturation to designate "the inculcation of the Gospel in the indigenous cultures and at the same time the intro-duction of these cultures into the life of the Church."[41] The em-bodiment in the civilization of peoples is thus the theological reason for inculturation. Indeed, the Church in its evangelizing mission enters into a dialogue with peoples. The fruitful exchange that is established results in a dynamic assimilation of the cultural models of these nations. "Inculturation therefore means, an intimate transformation of authentic cultural values through their integration into Christianity, and the rooting of Christianity in the various human cultures."[42] This undertaking, which can be described as "urgent and necessary, even a priority," is an imperative for the Church in our time. Indeed, "because it was integral and concrete, the incarnation of the Son of God was a cultural incarnation."[43] Saint John Paul II considers inculturation as "a priority and an emergency in the life of particular Churches for a real rooting of the Gospel in Africa."[44] To him, it is therefore "an evangelization requirement."[45] He continues by saying "a journey towards full evangelisation"[46] is "one of the major challenges for the Church at the beginning of the 3rd millennium."[47]

This goes in line with a major concern of the Church, which is to respect and above all to promote the cultural values of the various peoples.[48] But rooting the Gospel in the habits and customs of African peoples is not an easy task. What is required of the ecclesiastical community is faithfulness to the Gospel message in its entirety, and at the same time respect for the authentic cultural values of these peoples. Faced with this observation, we must acknowledge the fact that if much has been done, much still has to be done in the process of the New Evangelization. We are going to make some proposals, based on *Ecclesia in Africa* by John Paul II and *Africae Munus* by Benedict XVI.

Proposals

a) The liturgy can only positively transform the person who celebrates if it reaches him in his daily life. Hence the urgent need for inculturation. In fact, "it is the entire Christian life that needs to be inculturated" so that it is transformed by the values of the Gospel in the light of the paschal mystery.

For "a faith that does not become culture is not fully accepted, fully thought out, faithfully lived."[49] It is in this respect that African liturgies will always be centered on reconciliation, justice, and peace. For this to happen, it will be necessary, for example, to inculturate the sacraments of healing, such as penance, reconciliation, and the sacrament of the sick, by emphasizing their communal dimension.

b) Festive tone. Liturgies in African Churches often have a very festive tone and in order to encourage "a full, intelligent, active and conscious participation,"[50] they are accompanied by songs of praise and dancing, a bodily expression of joy. Meanwhile, it is also "necessary today to educate the people of God on the value of silence which breeds recollection and inner peace."[51] This will undoubtedly help to rediscover the central position of the Word of God in the life of the Church. Christ's mysteries are linked to silence. Mary Mother of God, woman of the Word of God and of silence, serves as a paradigm for us: "Verbo crescente, verba deficiunt."[52] This silence for example, is being observed at different moments, during the celebration:

- The silent entry into the Church;
- silence before the collect;
- silence after the proclamation of the Gospel;
- silence after the homily; and
- silence after communion.

c) Acquiring the notion of what is sacred. God is a mysterious being: "I am who I am" (Ex 3, 14b), a being set apart, not to be touched; and everything that belongs to God, everything given to him, belongs to him alone: it is sacred. God is to be feared, respected, and venerated; what belongs to God must also be respected and venerated:

- People consecrated to God;
- Objects reserved for worshipping God;
- Places of worship; and
- Signs and symbols of God's worship.

d) Pious gestures and attitudes. It is recommended that the faithful be helped to deepen their understanding of the traditional gestures and attitudes that promote individual or community piety, such as:

- The sign of the cross at the entrance into the church or at the beginning of prayer;
- Genuflecting or kneeling before the Blessed Sacrament. However, in front of an altar where there is none, one may just make a deep and pious bow;
- Silence and calmness in the Church and during the celebrations; and
- Clean, correct and decent dressing.

The Eucharistic celebration is therefore the place and object of the greatest care and veneration. Hence the need to put away all levity, improvisation, negligence, or vulgarity. Finally, everything takes place in perfect harmony between all those involved in the celebration. For this to happen any Eucharistic celebration shall require order and the respect of the rules set by the competent authorities. It is then that all the qualities thereto pertaining are highlighted, namely to be "simple, solemn, and sober."[53]

e) Liturgical books. The dignity of the liturgy and respect for the Word of God demands decent, good quality liturgical books (Missal, Lectionary, Book of the Gospels, etc.) for the celebrations. The use of leaflets and brochures especially for the altar and the ambo is to be avoided.

f) The Liturgy of the Word. The proclamation of the Gospel constitutes the summit of the Liturgy of the Word during the Eucharistic liturgy. The same liturgy teaches that it should be given the greatest veneration in order to distinguish the Gospel from other biblical texts. This is why the deacon or priest has to prepare himself well by prayer, blessing, and the burning of incense. The congregation recognises and professes that Christ is present and is speaking to them through the acclamations. They also listen to this proclamation of the Gospel standing. The Pope recommends solemnising this proclamation of the Word, especially the Gospel, by using the Evangeliary carried in procession and placed on the Ambo. In fact, the proclamation of the Gospel constitutes the summit of the Liturgy of the Word.[54] Therefore, it is good to sing the initial announcement "The reading of the Holy Gospel accord to..." and at the end "The Gospel of the Lord" to emphasise the importance of what is being read. But in our African liturgies the problem of the inculturation of the procession of the Evangelium arises.

g) The problem of inculturation of the Gospel. Today, for the purpose of inculturation, the procession of the Word is sometimes being accompanied by rites inspired by the ceremonies at Fon's palaces or royal courts. These are rites that should not be introduced into the liturgy without first passing through the sieve of evangelical illumination and purification. This would avoid falling into syncretism and folklore. Furthermore, the rite of the procession of the Bible at the beginning of the Liturgy of the Word should be abolished in favour of the procession of the Evangelical for the reasons mentioned above.

Christians listen to the Gospel standing. For purposes of education, some pastors think that the proclamation of the Gospel should be listened to, while sitting. This is a mistake, for it is never the culture that is primary but the Gospel.

h) The translation of liturgical texts. One of the novelties of Vatican II is the importance of the Word of God in liturgical celebrations. Therefore, one of the important and urgent tasks for the Churches in Africa in order to start the process of inculturation, is to translate the liturgical texts into the local languages which are the sure vehicles of the culture of a people. It is therefore necessary to avoid making either transpositions or *ad litteram* translations of biblical, catechetical, or ritual model texts. One must either adapt or inculturate. The method is to start from the principle that the update of a biblical culture in the language of faith and liturgy is the sure method for evangelising cultures. The spirit of the Bible, the language of the Bible, and the biblical imagination must therefore be sought and inserted into the language of a people. This would require following the norms laid down by the Holy See (Liturgiam Authenticam). The texts translated and used in the lectionary, the Evangeliary, and the Divine Office must receive the *recognitio* of the Congregation.

i) Liturgy and Life. It is clear that the liturgy aims to praise God and sanctify men. A healthy and authentic liturgy must therefore be encouraged in order to help the people to move from the celebrated liturgy to the lived liturgy, i.e., from the *lex orandi* to the *lex vivendi* or *ars vivendi*. The liturgy is not just a celebration, it requires a liturgical catechesis beforehand. *Lex orandi, lex credendi. Ecclesia celebrans* is at the same time *ecclesia docens*.

j) Inculturated rituals in the light of *Africae Munus*. The sad fact in most African families is that they are very divided and there is no peace. Starting from the Ritual on the Sacrament of Penance and Reconciliation, it is necessary to adopt rituals adapted or even inculturated for the reconciliation of families. In this light, the Christian will have the possibility to be truly and authentically reconciled with God and especially with his neighbour by giving and receiving forgiveness for a lasting peace. May the sacrament of penance and reconciliation become a "sanctuary of life" for Christian families and a vital cell of the society and of the Church a true "school of the heart."[55] The choice of biblical texts on reconciliation, justice, and peace should not be neglected in liturgical celebrations and the catechism of divided families.

A culture of reconciliation and peace proves to be important for children. For this reason, the virtues of truth, justice and reconciliation must be inculcated in children from an early age in the family, in order to "nurture consciences that are upright and receptive to the demands of justice, so that they grow up to be men and women concerned about and capable of realising this just social order through responsible behaviour."[56] Adopting memory purification rites centred around Christ in situations where injustice has led to conflicts that have bred bloodshed and brought about wanton suffering and hatred sometimes stretching to generations, so as to build a better society where such tragedies do not repeat themselves.[57]

If rites, as stressed by the bishops of Congo, are expressions of a communicated divine truth and a human truth addressed to God, action for reconciliation and peace must be handled with care by the pastors of the African churches.

Pope Benedict XVI recommends the celebration in each African country and on a yearly basis, "a day or week of reconciliation, especially during Advent or Lent."[58] This will make the liturgy a real **school of spirituality**, of communion through reconciliation, so as to help the Christian move from celebrated liturgy to lived liturgy. Thus, the *lex orandi* will form a harmonious whole with the *lex vivendi* or *ars vivendi*.

Pope Benedict XVI also recommends "that SECAM, in agreement with the Holy See, promote a Year of Reconciliation at the continental level to ask God's special forgiveness for all the wrongs and sorrows that human beings have inflicted on each other in Africa, and to reconcile individuals and groups who have been wounded in the Church and in society as a whole." This is in fact an extraordinary Jubilee Year.[59]

During liturgical celebrations homilies and sermons are used to continue to educate Christians and awaken their conscience about their civic responsibilities.[60]

Conclusion

Inculturation should establish a continuity between Christianity and the Christian faith. It is in fact the invitation of African cultures in the domain of evangelisation. This is certainly a difficult question that as in daily Christian life requires effort. This entails causing an existential and incarnate encounter between Christ and the African culture as a whole. The transfiguring power that emanates from the risen Christ is expected to shed light on every culture, including the African culture.

Pope Benedict XVI provides two answers. The African Church is expected above all to be Catholic, that is to say, the content, the message of Christ; the identical and essential patrimony, the same constitution of the doctrine of Christ, the same faith, the same Creed as a universal Church. This is fundamental and indisputable.

Keeping the faith and the apostolic tradition, to follow the example of the martyrs who are witnesses of the Christian faith.

On the other hand, Pope Benedict XVI makes us understand that as far as faith is concerned, the Church is conservative. This is about a real and radical encounter of African Christians with the Gospel message. The constitutive elements of the Christian faith, such as the Creed, Canon Law, the Word of God, the liturgy, and the sacraments, must be based on Christ. All this is to prevent divisions and to keep the message of revealed doctrine intact, even though it is mediated by cultures. Mother Church and Teacher has laid down certain conceptual and verbal guidelines which are the treasures of truth and which are sometimes difficult. It is not therefore about inventing another celebrated faith, of crafting another Christian liturgy according to cultures, but of proceeding by an organic transformation. This price consists of the preservation of the faith bequeathed by the Apostles. This is why the word of God and the liturgical rites must be harmoniously interpreted with the Apostolic Magisterium.

The Place of Africa in Benedict XVI's Social Teachings

Dr. Thomas Bienvenu Tchoungui[1]

Introduction

Although one might be tempted to make systemic and spiritual theology in Pope Benedict XVI's teaching more prominent, the significance of his contribution in the sphere of ethics should be noted as well. This is the objective of our research, which intends to focus on Benedict XVI's social teaching by examining some major texts addressed to the churches and peoples of Africa. Why must we not ask about the contribution of his social doctrine in the face of socio-political challenges such as the management of public assets in our "democracies in the making," the mastery of violence-producing mechanisms, and the implementation of peace in an Africa torn by wars of interest and fratricidal conflicts? Why don't we take seriously the emergence of an African identity in this increasingly global culture? Can we remain indifferent to the ecological threats in an Africa devastated by the exploitation of multinational companies and subjected to the dictatorship of a liberal and essentially capitalist economy? These are all areas of interest that deserve our attention in dialogue with the social doctrine of Benedict XVI.

However, in order not to get stuck in a very narrow reasoning at the risk of grasping Benedict's social magisterium in a one-sided way with regard to Africa, we believe that it is just and appropriate to discuss the multidimensional personality of Joseph Ratzinger the theologian. This brief look into history will help us to understand the interest that Benedict XVI constantly shows for Africa and for the spread of theological thought in the African context. This opening leads us to structuring our reflection in three main points: Joseph Ratzinger's encounter with Africa, Africa in Benedict XVI's social magisterium, and managing a heavy legacy.

Joseph Ratzinger and Africa:
Prelude to a Double Theological Encounter

Born on 16 April 1927 in Marktl, the Free State of Bavaria, as the third child of the union of Joseph and Marie Ratzinger, Josef Aloisius Ratzinger (in German), the man who later become Pope Benedict XVI by succeeding Saint John Paul II's papacy on 19 April 2005, is no stranger to Africa. It can be said as well, without the need for a rhetorical twist, that Africa is no stranger to him either. Indeed, Joseph Ratzinger's interest in African issues dates back to the dawn of the Second Vatican Council II.[2] Invited as a young conciliar expert alongside Cardinal Frings, the Archbishop of Cologne, the young Bavarian theologian got to know some distinctive persons of the African episcopate who were remarkable for their vision of the Church and, more so, for the new perspective they intended to give to its mission in the world of that time, following the example of Archbishop Jean Zoa, the young archbishop of Yaoundé.

Africa on the Horizon of Ratzinger's Theological
Research in Regensburg

This first encounter with Africa at the Council aroused in this eminent theologian a certain curiosity. What is Africa? How can we consider the impact of its historical experience in the process of its post-colonial development? What is its place in the Church and what role can it play in the Church of tomorrow? These are certainly the first questions that dominated Joseph Ratzinger's mind after the Second Vatican Council.

In spite of the sad turbulent moments that he had to go through in Tübingen in the hot years after 1968, by accepting the stance of dogmatic theology at the University of Regensburg in the 1970s,

Professor Joseph Ratzinger was engaging in what should be described here as a "love affair" with Africa. The first action manifested when he agreed to supervise the doctoral research of the young Beninese student, Barthélémy Adoukounou, who proposed to confront the stakes of the Christian faith and the challenges of African socio-cultural traditions. This close encounter between faith and culture under the auspices of Ratzinger led to a major publication in two volumes by Barthélémy Adoukounou, which became a landmark in the history of African theology: *Milestones for an African Theology. Essay on a Christian Hermeneutic of the Dahomean Vodun.* T.1: Theological Criticism, T. II: Ethnological Study. Recalling with nostalgia his memories as a former student of the Pontifical Urban University (Rome) as he moved to Regensburg, B. Adoukounou does not fail to underline what marked him most in the intellectual personality of Professor Joseph Ratzinger:

> During the years of the Second Vatican Council, I was fascinated by both him and Rahner. When I went to Regensburg afterwards, I discovered a brilliant theologian who did not read the lesson he had prepared from the pulpit, but gave the impression that he was reading it in heaven. He had a panoramic, historical and synthetic vision, profound as befits a German and clear as that of a Latin. I was thrilled by the Christocentrism of his thought: it was found in all the themes he tackled, with his rare articulation capacity.[3]

On becoming Prefect of the Congregation for the Doctrine of the Faith, Joseph Ratzinger integrated the African theologian Adoukounou into the restricted college of theologian members of the International Theological Commission. Upon becoming pope, Benedict XVI appointed him secretary general of the Pontifical Council for Culture under the direction of Cardinal Ravasi, then made him a bishop in October 2011. Why such a review, one might ask? This anamnesis makes it possible to highlight Joseph Ratzinger's closeness to Africa, to which he intends to offer the possibility of deepening the great richness of its socio-cultural identity in order to better assume its role as the "spiritual lung of humanity." In his interview with *L'Osservatore Romano*, the new Secretary General of the Pontifical Council for Culture interpreted Benedict XVI's openness towards Africa as:

> A decisive step in the recognition that human nature in Africa is endowed with the same expressive dynamism defined as culture by the Second Vatican Council in *Gaudium et spes*. The black man, like any other man, is capable of the Gospel, because he too is endowed with this expressive natural drive called culture in the deepest sense. With my appointment, a step has been taken forward in the recognition of African theology as an expression of faith that becomes culture. Faith becomes culture to prevent culture from suffocating it and thus suffocating man. The inculturation is done by the man of faith.[4]

Joseph Ratzinger's encounter with Africa also took a decisive turn during his time as Prefect of the Congregation for the Doctrine of the Faith and President of the International Theological Commission. This leads us to saying a word about the memorable meeting in Kinshasa.

The Kinshasa Meeting

On 21 July 1987, Cardinal Joseph Ratzinger organised an important meeting in Kinshasa between the Congregation for the Doctrine of the Faith and the representatives of the Episcopal Conferences of Africa and Madagascar, especially their respective Doctrinal Commissions. In order to give some effect to the Vatican II spirit, aiming at deepening the meaning and the requirement of Catholicism, Cardinal Ratzinger thought that it was time to make "the reciprocity between the universal Church and the particular Churches" effective.[5] This intention was clearly stated in his opening remarks:

We have come above all to listen, for a fraternal dialogue, to better understand the realities of the Church
in Africa, and thus to prepare an ever deeper and more
fruitful collaboration between the young African
Churches and the Holy See, which is the centre of the
unity of the Church, for a meeting, therefore, in true
Catholicism, which embraces unity and multiplicity
equally, a true collegiality of the Successors of the Apostles in communion with the Successor of Peter.[6]

The new spirit that Joseph Ratzinger intends to instill in the
relations between the universal Magisterium and the particular
Churches of Africa is clear. The new terminology chosen on purpose underlines its significance: *reciprocity, fraternal dialogue, center
of unity, and collegiality*. It is, therefore, time to move away from
the unilateralism of a mother church that thinks and dictates its
will to the rest of the world. The new tendency is to open up to
others and being humble in the steps that lead to the truth commonly sought and assumed. As he himself highlights, the new
challenge is to break down those "almost impassable distances,
closed societies and cultures that hardly interacted with others.
At the time of the great religious upheavals, it was almost impossible to talk about dialogue. In religion, as in military tactics, the
'City of God' closed its doors and became like a besieged city."[7]
It is in this almost revolutionary spirit that Joseph Ratzinger
comes to affirm that: "Rome is no longer an enclosed city but has
once again become the meeting point of all nations."[8]

The new stance adopted by the Church here makes it possible
to better integrate the contribution of those of the new Christianity by accepting to engage in a theological and cultural dialogue
with them. Hence the unavoidable challenge of inculturation.
Such a dialogue is essential if the evangelising mission of the
Church is to escape from any assimilation and any reduction of
cultural and religious imperialism of the West under the banner
of the Judeo-Christian faith. This concern for clarity was borne
for a long time by the young professor from Regensburg who,

noticing the reluctance of Adoukounou, the young student, to integrate the Christianity universality in the face of the hegemonic tendencies of certain currents manifested by their disdain for cultures still alien to Christianity, confided in him, saying:

> You know, Bartholomew, that we Germans also had difficulty finding food after the war and that the Americans had to help us with the Marshall Plan. He who does not have the simplicity to receive, neither has the right to give. It was then that I understood that life was about giving and receiving, about sharing. A thought of communion expressed from this, as a theology, could not be imperialistic.[9]

What place should be given to Africa in this *crossroads of nations*? Pope Benedict XVI is a logical, coherent, and consistent theologian. His vision of the Church is deeply rooted in the Vatican II ecclesiology, which he personally helped to develop. His Magisterium cannot therefore be exclusive, let alone Eurocentric, as some people wanted us to believe. This is why in the life and mission of the Church, Africa and Africans cannot be marginalised. He says it clearly:

> In baptism, the universal Church continually precedes and constitutes the local Church. From then on, […], in the Church, everyone is at home everywhere and is not just a host, no one is a stranger: It is one Church, one and the same. Someone who is baptized in Berlin feels same in the Church in Rome or in New York, or in Kinshasa, or in Bangalore, or in anywhere else; he feels at home as in the Church where he was baptized. He does not need to register again to belong, it is the same Church. Baptism comes from her and it is the Church that begets him.[10]

It is in this spirit of universality of the Church that Benedict XVI opens himself to Africa to make of its worries and sufferings, the worries and sufferings of the whole Church, God's people. Hence the special place that Africa occupies in his social Magisterium.

Africa at the Centre of Benedict XVI's Social Magisterium

We will start from two considerations to deal with Benedict XVI's social teaching regarding Africa. The first is, not understanding Africa's position in a peripheral manner, as if the pope should make it his duty to pronounce an original and a very special address on Africa. It would be tempting to reiterate the speeches, reflections, and other presentations essentially reserved for Africans. Such an approach appears to be reductive and difficult. In order to avoid this, we believe that Africa should be included among the universal recipients of Pope Benedict XVI's social teaching. However, we can read and interpret this teaching from the historical experience of the peoples of Africa. This approach would then make the African reception of Benedict XVI's social teaching more visible.

The second consideration, however, without any contradiction to the first, would be to analyse the social dimension of the post-synodal apostolic exhortation, *Africae Munus*. This choice is based on the major importance of this text, which is the result of the deliberation of the Second Special Assembly of the Synod of Bishops for Africa.

African Reception of Benedict XVI's Universal Social Teaching

In order to talk about Benedict XVI's social teaching and the place given to the Black continent, it is appropriate to begin by recalling some presuppositions that help to define the theological posture of this great thinker. The first is the basic unit that links faith and reason, the natural order and the supernatural order, man and God, the spiritual world and the physical world, anthropology and theology, history and eschatology. This unity gives a predominant place to the vitality of faith and theology, which itself is illuminated and clarified in the light of the incarnation of the Son of

God, true God and true man. Christology thus appears as the point of truth where the mystery of God and the enigma of man are revealed. This is the core of the message that Benedict XVI intended to address to Africa and that he revealed so clearly in the homily he gave during his Mass at the Yaoundé omnisport stadium:

> One needs to be very careful today, as so many un-scrupulous people seek to impose the rule of money at the expense of the poor. Africa in general and Cameroon in particular, are in danger if they do not recognise the True Author of Life! Brothers and sisters of Cameroon and Africa, you who have received so many human qualities from God, take care of your souls! Do not be deceived by false glories and false ideals! Believe, yes, continue to believe that God, Father, Son and Holy Spirit, is the only One who truly loves you as you expect, that He is the only One who can bring you fulfilment and stability to your lives. Christ is the only way to Life.[11]

The warning Benedict XVI sounds to Africa in general, and to Cameroon in particular, highlights the great danger that threatens us, namely the disconnection from God that is increasingly observed among the African elite, who have become more inclined to secret societies and esoteric sects. This resignation from the life of faith is reflected in the fact that we abandon our lives into the hands of illusion peddlers by allowing ourselves to be "fascinated by false glories and false ideals."[12] Indeed, a great conviction runs through Benedict XVI's teaching. By associating the history of the world in its ups and downs with the historical experience of Jesus of Nazareth, the whole of human life regains its splendour and, at the same time, the historical itinerary of peoples, nations, and human cultures takes on its consistency and also discovers their authentic meaningful horizon. In his homily in Luanda, Benedict XVI proposes that Africans follow the Pauline model to enrich their experience of faith and draw substance from it for their spiritual and material growth.

The encounter with Jesus [...] was crucial in Paul's life: Christ appeared to him as a dazzling light, spoke to him, and conquered his heart. The apostle saw the risen Jesus, that is, the man in his perfect stature. Paul's shift in focus occurred in him, and he began to see everything in terms of the final state of man in Jesus Christ: what originally seemed too crucial is now worth no more to him than "rubbish"; it is no longer a gain but a loss, because now only life in Christ counts (cf. Ph 3:7–8). It is not a simple maturity of Paul's "self," but a death to self and a resurrection in Christ: in him a certain form of existence has died; and with the risen Jesus a new form is born.[13]

From this follows a second premise that allows us to redefine the challenges of development and the relevance of social action as works of faith and its transforming force. For if we unravel from this point, the fight against poverty and the fight against underdevelopment risk degenerating into a class struggle; to the point where we end up assuming a Marxist position of liberation based more on immanence than on transcendence. Hence the social stakes of the dogma. This key to interpretation allows us to interpret the social action and social teaching of the Church as the fruits of the active presence of God at work in the world of men.

True liberation, as Benedict XVI shows in his meditations on Jesus of Nazareth, begins with what sets man free from the power of sin. This programme is already apparent in the very name of Jesus, *Jeshua* in Hebrew, which means JHWH is salvation. And the angel immediately clarifies: "He will save his people from their sins" (Mt 1:21).[14] Therefore, it is only when man is connected to Christ that he can be a promoter of progress or of acts of human salvation. It is he who makes every man capable of taking his destiny into his own hands in order to walk and promote a standing humanity. The healing of the paralysed man who was brought to Jesus through the roof of a house testifies to this. After forgiving him his sins, Christ restored his full physical health. "I tell you, get up, pick up your mat and go home" (Mk 2:11). In this light, evangelisation and human promotion are inseparable, as Paul VI demonstrated in *Evangelium Nuntiandi*:

> For the Church, Evangelisation means bringing the Good News to all parts of humanity and, by its impact, transforming from within, making humanity itself new [...]. The aim of evangelisation is therefore this interior transformation and, if it had to be expressed in one word, the most accurate would be to say that the Church evangelises when, by the sole divine power of the Message she proclaims, she seeks to convert at the same time the personal and collective conscience of men, the activity in which they engage, the concrete life and environment which are theirs.[15]

Having defined these presuppositions, let us move to the contents of Benedict XVI's social magisterium. In fact, in the course of his rich eight-year papacy (2005–2013), Benedict XVI produced numerous texts of different kinds. These include encyclicals, apostolic exhortations, decrees, and many other papal documents. With regard to the issues at stake in our topic of reflection, we will focus on two encyclicals: *Deus caritas est* (2005) and *Caritas in veritate* (2011). Looking at these documents through the eyes of an African theologian, we would like to dwell on some points of Benedict XVI's social theology.

Charity as a Diaconia and the Preferential Option for the Poor

The first teaching that is drawn from Benedict XVI's social philosophy revolves around love. Since "God is love" (1 Jn 4–16), as his first encyclical reminds us, every person's life must be imbued with it:

> Love of neighbor, rooted in the love of God, is first of all a task for each Christian, but it is also a task for the entire Christian community, and this at all levels: from the local community to the particular Church to the universal

78

Church as a whole. The Church, too, as a community, has to practice love. Consequently, love also needs organisation as a prerequisite for an ordered community service.[16]

The duty of love is, therefore, not a mere exhortation, but a commandment that must be taken seriously by every Christian. Benedict XVI draws two main implications from this. The first recalls the three fundamental missions of the Church: The "proclamation of the Word of God (*kerygma-martyria*), celebration of the Sacraments (*leitourgia*), and service of charity (*diakonia*). These are three tasks that appeal to each other and cannot be separated from each other. For the Church, charity is not a kind of social assistance activity that could also be left to others, but it belongs to her nature, it is an expression of her very essence, which she cannot abandon."[17] The second implication is ecclesiological in that it posits the Church as "God's family in the world" in which "no one should suffer for lack of what is necessary."[18] The universality of the commandment of love must therefore be applied in a particular way to the Church, and this obliges her to take the challenge of diakonia very seriously as a ministry of charity. In this sense, Benedict XVI exhorts the entire Church institution to appropriate Apostle Paul's teaching to the Galatians: "So then, as often as we have the chance, we should do good to everyone, and especially to those who belong to our family in the faith" (6:10). *Caritas* has a deep stake in Christian solidarity, in which the preferential option for the poor deserves special attention.

The Role of the State:
Between Charity and the Duty of Justice

Focusing on historical references that highlight a tumultuous past, Benedict XVI refers to a certain confusion that prevailed in the past regarding social justice and the way in which certain States believed they had to resolve the problem. This was the case with Marxism, which "presented the world revolution and its preparation as a panacea for the social problem: with the revolution and the subsequent collectivity of the means of production— In this doctrine, it was asserted that everything should immediately go differently and better. This dream has vanished."[19] The new world economic situation has changed the course of history and the globalisation of the economy dictates new rules. It is here that the Church's social doctrine regains its importance as a basic reference point to provide valid guidelines and propose reliable criteria of judgement far beyond its limits. According to Benedict XVI, "these guidelines—in the face of growing development—must be understood in a dialogue with all those who are seriously concerned about man and the world."[20]

However, the Marxist criticism that the Church is responsible for making people dormant as she encourages charity rather than stimulating states and citizens to fight for social justice, must be addressed. Benedict XVI's response is incisive and unequivocal: "Justice first. *Ubi societas, ibi ius."*[21] In other words, there is no human society without justice. This principle justifies the duty of every political society or state governed by the rule of law to elaborate its own appropriate justice system. Benedict XVI, therefore, states:

> That the basic norm of the state must be the pursuit for justice, that the aim of a just social order is to ensure that each person, in accordance with the principle of subsidiarity, gets his or her share of the common good. This is what the Christian doctrine on the State and the Church's social doctrine have always emphasised.

However, charity implies going beyond the order of justice.

> Charity goes beyond justice, because to love is to give, to offer something of mine to another; but it never exists without justice, which leads to giving the other what is his, by virtue of his or her being and action. Justice demands that; I cannot "give" another what is mine, without having first given him what is his. He who loves others with charity is first of all just towards them. Not

only is justice not foreign to charity, not only is it not an alternative or a parallel path to charity: justice is "inseparable from charity," it is intrinsic to it.[22]

In the Christian sense, charity is a perfection of justice, which it also demands by encouraging "the recognition and respect of the legitimate rights of individuals and peoples." But since "man's city is not only constituted by relationships of rights and duties, but even more, and first of all, by relationships of gratis, mercy and communion," charity goes beyond justice "and completes it in the logic of gift and forgiveness." In this way it is a reflection of God's love for humanity. "It gives a theological and salutary value to every commitment to justice in the world."[23]

However, the great upheavals that occurred with the industrial revolution in the nineteenth century cannot be overlooked or ignored. One of the consequences of that was the breakdown and disappearance of the old social structures which, together with the mass of wage earners that had to be managed, "brought about a radical change in the composition of the society, in which the relationship between capital and labour became a decisive issue, an issue which, in this form, had hitherto been unknown." As *Caritas in veritate* so aptly notes, "the structures of production and capital now became the new power which, placed in the hands of a few, resulted in a disenfranchisement of the working masses, against which they had to rebel."[24]

This clarification, therefore, makes it possible to remove the misunderstandings concerning a conflicting or antithetical approach between justice and charity. Charity does not exclude or swallow up justice; it presupposes it and brings it to perfection. This is why the Church's social doctrine advocates integral development and an economy of solidarity.

The Need for an Economic Ethic

Another major concern of Benedict XVI's social teaching is how to give a new meaning to economic ethics. As can be observed today, there is a kind of inflation of the term ethics, which is intermingled in all the discourses and practices relating to the economic domain, finance, and even in the industrial realm. "However, it is good to develop a valid discernment criterion, because there is a certain misuse of the adjective 'ethics' which, when used generically, lends itself to designating very diversified contents, to the point of passing under its cover decisions and choices contrary to justice and the true good of man."[25] This clarification is essential for Benedict XVI insofar as the response to "the deepest moral demands of an individual also has important and beneficial repercussions on the economic level. Indeed, *the economy needs ethics in order to function properly; not just any ethics, but ethics that are people-friendly.*"[26]

Justice and the Common Good

Writing the encyclical, *Caritas in Veritate,* in the context of a bewildering global financial crisis, Pope Benedict XVI makes no secret of the underlying purpose of his project. To him, it is a matter of proposing to the Church, the people of God, and men of good will a summary of social morality on justice and the common good.

> "*Caritas in veritate*" is a principle on which the Church's social doctrine is based, a principle that takes on an operational form through the criteria for guiding moral action. I wish to recall two of these in particular; they are dictated primarily by the commitment to development in a globalising society: justice and the common good.[27]

For this, he proposes the enhancement of justice through charity and the building of the modern State on a stable and solid foundation of the common good. This renovation therefore requires the rediscovery of the benefits of the principle of gratis in a world where the dictatorship of liberal capitalism has made profit the only law that governs exchanges and even relations between men, peoples, and nations. Benedict XVI advocates prioritising the common good, the scope of which he makes explicit:

> Loving someone means wanting his or her good and doing everything possible to achieve it. Alongside the individual good, a good is linked to life in society: the common good. It is the good that belongs to "all of us," made up of individuals, families, and intermediate groups that form a social community. It is not a good sought for its own sake, but for the people who are part of the social community and who, in it alone, can achieve their good more effectively. *It* is a requirement of justice and charity to desire the common good and to seek it.[28]

The Pope does not merely define the common good. He gives further explanations as to the very manner of its realisation. Moreover, he highlights the need to watch over this good, insofar as it constitutes the good of the community of "us all." Hence the responsibility of institutions and even of the whole community to care for it.

To work for the common good means, on the one hand, to take care of and, on the other hand, to make use of the set of institutions that legally, civilly, and culturally structure social life, which thus takes the form of the pólis, the city. The more we work for the common good, which also meets our real needs, the more we love our neighbour.[29]

Environmental Conservation and Human Rights

This new vision of the common good also calls for the reshaping of our relationship with the environment. This is why chapter 4 of his encyclical is devoted to "The development of peoples, rights and duties, environment": The great originality that arises here lies in the inseparable link that Benedict XVI establishes between man and the environment. He states that:

The manner in which man treats the environment influences the manner in which he treats himself, and vice versa. This is why today's society really needs to reconsider its lifestyle, which in many parts of the world is inclined towards hedonism and consumerism, remaining indifferent to the damage that results from this.[30]

It is clear from this that there can be no environmental ecology without human ecology, since "environmental degradation is closely linked to the culture that shapes the human community." Hence the need for a real change of mentality "that leads us to adopt *new lifestyles*" in which the factors that determine consumption, savings, and investment choices are "the search for the true, the beautiful, and the good, as well as communion with other men for a common growth."[31] The message is therefore clear:

When "human ecology" is respected in society, ecology itself also benefits. Just as human virtues are related, such that weakening one endangers the others, so too the ecological system is based on the respect of a project that concerns both healthy coexistence in society and a good relationship with nature.[32]

It is to this extent that nature should be considered a universally common good that calls for collective responsibility. In this same light, universal solidarity is imposed on all humanity as a benefit and a duty at the same time.[33] "This is why it is important to stimulate a new debate on the fact that rights presuppose duties without which they become arbitrary."[34]

From Environmental Ecology to Human Ecology

In a context where the dictatorship of a certain globalisation imposes its law everywhere in order to defend its interests and subject the rest of humanity to the domination of powerful lobbies of doubtful morality, Benedict XVI distinguishes himself by taking a stand in favour of the Third World countries, dominated by African countries. One can note in particular this remarkable criticism of the Malthusian solutions adopted at the famous Cairo conference in 1994, the implementation of which consisted of making development aid conditional on the fight against demographic growth in Africa. Benedict XVI's response is unequivocal:

> The concept of rights and duties in development is dramatically challenged by the problems of *population growth*. This is a very important limit for true development, because it concerns the primary values of life and the family. Considering population growth as the primary cause of underdevelopment is incorrect, even from an economic point of view.[35]

He points to two main arguments for this: on the one hand, the positive reduction in infant mortality and the average life expectancy in economically developed countries, and on the other hand, the signs of crisis in societies where there is a worrying drop in the birth rate. He therefore advocates for a balanced approach that promotes "responsible reproduction, which constitutes, among other things, an effective contribution to integral human development."[36]

For this to happen, it is also necessary to give full consideration and importance to human sexuality, which cannot be "reduced to a purely hedonistic and playful fact, just as sex education cannot be reduced to technical instruction, with the sole aim of protecting those concerned from possible contamination or the 'risk' of reproduction. This would be tantamount to impoverishing and ignoring the profound meaning of sexuality, which must instead be recognised and accepted with responsibility, both by the individual and by the community."[37] This reasoning leads Benedict XVI to remind everyone of the need for good education and good moral behaviour in society as the best way to preserve nature. This also requires that human and environmental ecology be maintained in balance. He affirms, in fact, that:

> If the right to life and natural death is not respected, if human conception, gestation and birth are made artificial, if human embryos are sacrificed for research, the common conscience ends up losing the concept of human ecology and, with it, that of environmental ecology to demand that the new generations respect the natural environment becomes a contradiction when education and laws do not help them to respect themselves.[38]

According to Benedict XVI, modern man, governed by the power of techno-scientific reason, must never lose sight of the fact that "the book of nature is unique and indivisible, whether it concerns the environment or life, sexuality, marriage, the family, social relations, in a word, integral human development." It also implies a set of links that people, nations, and states must hold together to preserve human life in its dignity and to safeguard nature, our common home, as Pope Francis puts it. In other words, "the obligations we have towards the environment are linked to the obligations we have towards the person considered in himself and in his relationship with others. One cannot demand the one and trample on the other. This is a serious antinomy of the current mentality and approach that degrades the person, upsets the environment, and deteriorates society."[39]

The New Social Movement Promoted by Africae Munus

Focused on the challenges of justice, reconciliation, and peace, the main message of the post-synodal apostolic exhortation *Africae Munus* can be understood as a summary of the essential element of the Church's social teaching as we have just gone through it with the Social Magisterium of Benedict XVI. Having already sufficiently substantiated the concepts of justice and the common good, what is left is for us to highlight two other aspects that deserve our attention: the need to promote a culture of peace and the importance of reconciliation.

Indeed, in a continent saturated with sad news, everywhere is war, a constant and permanent ally. Yet its presence assumes its gruesome role of sowing destruction and division everywhere.

> It is true to say that war can destroy all that is precious (cf. 2 Ch 36:19): families, whole communities, the fruits of men's labour, the hopes that guide and sustain their lives and work! Such an experience is unfortunately too familiar to the whole of Africa: the destructive power of civil war, the dizzying fall into the vortex of hatred and revenge, wastage of the efforts of generations of honest people.[40]

This is the sad experience paralysing the development of the black continent. Benedict XVI believes that this can only be avoided by accepting and listening to the Word of God which calls man to conversion. This was the important message delivered in Angola during the Mass celebrated in Luanda:

> The Gospel teaches us that reconciliation—a genuine reconciliation—can only be the fruit of conversion, of a change of heart, of a new mindset. It teaches us that only the power of God's love can change our hearts and make us stronger than the power of sin and division.[41]

The Responsibility of a Heavy Legacy

Carrying the hope of humanity in faith and oxygenating the world in charity summarises in a few words the great heritage that Benedict entrusts to Christians and to the African Church. During his first apostolic journey to Africa as successor of St. Peter, Benedict XVI clearly outlined the purpose of his mission.

"I have come to Africa particularly to announce this message of forgiveness, hope, and new life in Christ."[42] He, therefore, came to urge Africans to forgive in order to get out of the yoke of violence and vengeance caused by the crimes and atrocities of fratricidal wars and geo-strategic positioning conflicts, often to the benefit of foreign powers. Above all, he came to give hope to a desperate Africa, which the fathers of the first African synod, not without reason, likened to that man who fell in the hands of bandits.[43]

In an Africa where young people are constantly rushing into the waters of the Mediterranean in search of greener pastures, Benedict XVI appeals to the African *intelligentsia* to become aware of its potential, of its cultural heritage rich in values, of the strength of its youth, and even of its spirituality, to shape a new future. The encounter with Christ is therefore a unique opportunity that has changed the destiny of other peoples and can do better for the black continent. For it is in Jesus Christ that God "makes all things new" (Rev.)

Reminding Africa of the heavy burden of being the "spiritual lung" of humanity, the Magisterium of Benedict XVI thus assigns to the black continent a great mission: that of keeping the lamp of faith burning until the glorious return of Christ, Lord of the created universe and Saviour of the human race. Adherence to such a responsibility implies the radical necessity of a change of life, since we are henceforth called to integrate the missionary process of the Church in which each baptised person is called to become a living pillar in the salvation venture bequeathed by Christ for the happiness of the human race. Benedict XVI is, therefore, not wrong when he says:

> If we are convinced and experience has proven that without Christ life is incomplete, that it lacks a reality—
> the fundamental reality—we are also convinced that we do no injustice to anyone if we present him Christ and give him the possibility of finding in this way to not only his true identity, but also the joy of having found

life. Indeed, it is our duty to do so; it is a duty to offer
to all this possibility on which their eternity depends.[44]

The challenge now for African peoples, and in particular
every Christian, is to work so that faith becomes culture in Africa
and that our culture becomes a leaven of faith for the nations. This
seems to me to be the obligatory passage towards becoming the
spiritual lungs that can oxygenate humanity. To do this, we must
accept bringing Christ to the centre of our lives, in the face of our
daily challenges, and even to position him as a vector of meaning
on the horizon of our history in this world. This position allows
us to better assume our faith and our own identity to the extent
that it helps us to get out of the yoke of ideological impostures as
well as the various enslavement mechanisms that paralyse Africa
today.

Conclusion

The personality of Joseph Ratzinger-Benedict XVI that emerges
from this journey is that of a great man of faith deeply rooted in
Christ and "that of a very attentive humanitarian, concerned to
build relationships with others in truth."[45] It is this attachment to
truth that is reflected in his episcopal motto *Cooperatores Veritatis*.
It is also in the name of this truth that Benedict XVI has focused
his pontificate in the fight against the "dictatorship of relativism"
that globalisation is increasingly gaining ground today, and Africa
is not left out of its assaults. B. Adoukou emotionally recalls that
"The black continent, which appeared to be the most exposed,
was pleased to salute in him [...] the Pastor who could defend it
in what is most essential for man: his living relationship with the
truth."[46] This truth, in which an operational and transforming
charity of the world order is expressed and revealed, is founded
by Ratzinger in the theology of the cross, where humanity has a
concrete experience of the love that is given in Jesus of Nazareth.
This is why the cross of Christ becomes the source of benevolent
love that nourishes and transforms the world through a diakonia

of service, an economy that reconciles profit and gratis, and a development that unfolds in a logic of solidarity with all social strata and with all parts of the world.

In a *sequela Christi* logic, which challenges our humanity today more than ever, Benedict XVI gives us as a human model the example of Simon of Cyrene, the African, whom he praises:[47]

> Simon of Cyrene, you are a small, poor, unknown peasant, about whom the history books do not speak. And yet you make history. You have written one of the most beautiful chapters in human history. You carry someone else's cross; you lighten his heavy burden and prevent him from suffocating under the sacrifice. You give dignity to each one of us, a dignity in which you remind us that we are ourselves then, when we no longer think of ourselves (Lk 9,24.) You remind us that Christ is waiting for us on the road, in public places, in hospitals, in prisons,...and in the outskirts of our cities. Christ is waiting for us (Mt 25:40).

Through this testimony of love for Christ, Simon of Cyrene opens us up to the theology of otherness in order to flush us out of our withdrawal into identity, our struggles for self-assertion, our self- centred imperialisms, our policies of excessive exploitation of others, and most dramatically, of the poor. What a beautiful message for our world! But also, what a heavy and exalting mission for our fellow Africans. As far as I am concerned, I see in this message a testament of faith from Benedict XVI and I welcome it as a mission and a responsibility. May we therefore become those Simons of Cyrene who can revolutionise the face of this old world so that a new world may finally spring up.

Joseph Ratzinger and the Universality of Logos in Cultures: The Preference for Interculturality over Inculturation

Maurice Ashley Agbaw-Ebai

Introduction

When on September 12, 2006, Joseph Ratzinger/Benedict XVI delivered what is now known as the Regensburg Lecture at the Magna Aula of the University of Regensburg, the storm that followed the lecture resulted from a narrative of the dialogue, as recounted by Benedict, that took place in 1931 by the erudite Byzantine emperor Manuel II Paleologus and an educated Persian on the subject of Christianity and Islam, and the veracity of both.

The needle of the tempest lay in the unacceptable brusqueness of the challenge put forth by Manuel Paleologus to his Persian interlocutor: *"Show me just what Mohammed brought that was new, and there you will find things only evil and inhuman, such as his command to spread by sword the faith he preached."*[1] Benedict goes on to cite the explanation by Paleologus why violence in the name of religion was unacceptable then, and unacceptable now: *"Violence is incompatible with the nature of God and the nature of the soul.* God is not pleased by blood and not acting reasonably is contrary to God's nature. Faith is born of the soul, not the body. Whoever would lead someone to faith needs the ability to speak well and to reason properly, without violence and threats."[2]

"The decisive statement in this argument against violent conversion is this," Benedict says: *"Not to act in accordance with reason is contrary to God's nature.* (...) For the emperor, as a

Byzantine shaped by Greek philosophy, this statement is self- evident. But for the Muslim teaching, God is absolutely transcendent. His will is not bound up with any of our categories, even that of rationality."[3]

"At this point," declares Benedict, "as far as understanding of God and thus the concrete practice of religion is concerned, we are faced with an unavoidable dilemma. Is the conviction that acting unreasonably contradicts God's nature merely a Greek idea, or is it always and intrinsically true?" I believe that here we can see the profound harmony between what is Greek in the best sense of the word and the Biblical understanding of faith in God. Modifying the first verse of the Book of Genesis, the first verse of the whole Bible, John began the prologue of his Gospel with the words: "In the beginning was the *Logos*. This is the very word used by the emperor. God acts with *Logos*."[4] In the theological worldview of Ratzinger, *Logos* means several things: Creative Reason, Person, Son, Word, and Unity of Love.[5]

Heraclitus, the Philosopher of *Logos*

The Greek philosophical tradition of *Logos* is traceable to Heraclitus, the philosopher of the *logos*. In the 131 surviving fragments from Heraclitus, the concept of *logos* takes on multiple roles of meaning that very well serve a Ratzingerian appropriation and reading, at least from a theological point of view: Firstly, we have the sense of *logos* as the verb *legein* on which the noun *logos* is built. In this context, *logos* connotes the sense of picking up, laying down, lay by, to collect, to count up, to tell as in a tale, and hence, to give account.[6] These largely are related to speech, which, from a philosophical perspective, is the vehicle for human rationality, in that thanks to speech, we can get to know what the mind was thinking in and by itself.

As Heraclitus pointed out in antiquity, therefore, everything happened in accordance with the *logos*,[7] thereby giving the *logos* a universal import and application. Following this Heraclitean reading, it is on target to conclude that the "failure to understand the *logos* results in an epistemic state that is both child-like and apparently not significantly different from sleep."[8] If ignorance of the *logos* is likened to being asleep, then knowledge of the *logos* is awakening. It means *logos* provides a sense of epistemic cognition of things, of the truth of things.

Logos in the Thoughts of the Fathers

Justin Martyr (AD 100–165)—Logoi spermatiko: The treatment of *logos* takes on a sense of historical fulfilment. Justin sought to expose the similarities between Christian thought and Greek philosophy, with the ultimate goal of showing Christianity as the true and safe philosophy worth adhering to. In terms of the *Logos*, Justin's point of departure is first of all the transcendence of God, who as God, is an ineffable Father who is without origin or beginning. There is, therefore, an insurmountable wedge between God and creatures. Only the *Logos* is capable of bridging this abyss between finite creatures and an infinite and transcendent God. In this sense, the same *Logos* who revealed himself to the Hebrew prophets, as we find in the *First Apology*, likewise manifested himself in seeds of truth in Greek philosophy, especially in Socrates. Hence, "the doctrine of the *Logos* is the most important doctrine of Justin, because it forms a bridge between pagan philosophy and Christianity."[9]

Though Justin disputed Greek philosophy and its contradictions, and although Justin affirms that the fullness of the *Logos* only took form in Christ, Justin maintains that the seed of the *Logos* was already very much present in much of humankind, long before the arrival of Christ on the historical scene, for all humans possess a seed of the *Logos* in their rational faculty. Justin is therefore decisive in orienting all philosophical truths to the *Logos*, thereby making a claim regarding the universality and veracity of the Christian religion. The Old Testament and Greek philosophy are, therefore, two paths pointing to Christ, and this happens thanks to the presence of seeds of the *Logos* in these historical antecedents to the Christian era.

Irenaeus of Lyons (AD 130–202): In Irenaeus, one finds the appropriation of the *Logos* as a *Recapitulation*, in which the *Logos* is identical with the Son of God, with the God-man Jesus, with our Saviour and Our Lord. The heart of Irenaeus' claim is that since by the fall of Adam the whole human race was lost, the *Logos* had to become man in order to effect a recreation of humankind.[10] Christ is thus the true prototype of the human person, for it is in Christ that humanity becomes liberated from the condition of sin and oriented towards becoming more and more like God.

Thus, the Incarnation of the *Logos* is the singular event that brought about not only the divinization of the human being, but likewise, the entry into divinity of human nature, for the glory of God is a living man and the life of man consists in beholding God.[11] This is the perspective, that is, of the divine-human meeting in Christ, that one can understand in Irenaeus' doctrine of recapitulation (*anakephalaiosis*), in which the whole of reality is gathered into Jesus Christ.

Given this perspective, Christianity transcends all borders and ethnicities. It addresses all peoples and nations (Mt 28:19) bringing the gospel "to the ends of the earth" (Acts 1:8) as the New Testament enjoins.

Origen of Alexandria: (AD 184–253): This historical trajectory of the theological understanding of the *Logos* will be incomplete without mentioning Origen, head of the Catechetical School of Alexandria. Benedict says about Origen: "He was a true 'maestro,' and so it was that his pupils remembered him with nostalgia and emotion: he was not only a brilliant theologian but also an exemplary witness of the doctrine he passed on."[12]

Benedict characterizes Origen as the "most prolific author of Christianity's first three centuries."[13] In terms of Origen's theology, one could point out that with language reminiscent of Platonism, Origen maintains that just as the soul dwells in the body and gives life to the body, so does the *Logos* dwell in the Church, the mystical Body of Christ. In other words, the *Logos* is the life-giving principle that not only brings about the Church, but animates and sustains the Church in being.[14]

In all, the concept of *Logos* that emerged from Greek philosophy found a home in the Fathers, as seen in Justin, Irenaeus, and
Origen, sampled above. To Ratzinger, that the Fathers and the Johannine tradition took up this concept of *Logos* marked the beginning of what one might describe as an initial "inculturation"
of the Gospel, understood as employing a Hellenistic category or
concept to communicate the essential truth of the incarnation of
the Second Person of the Trinity (Jn 1:1–5).

Given all that has been said above, at this point, it is important
to highlight a significant difference in the usage and application
of the concept of *logos*: From a philosophical perspective, *logos* is
strictly a principle of reason, a rational concept, connoting multiple meanings such as speech, word, reason, discourse, *et cetera*.
From a theological perspective, on the other hand, *logos* under-
goes a transition, from a principle to a person, Jesus of Nazareth,
following above all, the Johannine tradition: In the beginning was
the Word, and the Word was with God, and the Word was God;
(…) and the Word became flesh and dwelt amongst us (Jn 1:1 &
14). Ratzinger offers this incisive reflection on the Prologue of
John, worth citing here at length:

> The Logos becomes flesh: we have grown so accus-
> tomed to these words that God's colossal synthesis of
> seemingly unbridgeable divisions, which required a
> gradual intellectual penetration on the part of the Fa-
> thers, no longer strikes us as very astonishing. Here lay,
> and still lies, the specifically Christian novelty that ap-
> peared unreasonable and unthinkable to the Greek
> mind. What this passage says does not derive from a
> particular culture, such as the Semitic or the Greek, as
> is thoughtlessly asserted over and over again today.
> This statement is opposed to all the forms of culture
> known to us. It was just as unthinkable for the Jews as
> it was (although for altogether different reasons) for the
> Greeks or the Indians or even, for that matter, for the
> modern mind, which looks upon a synthesis of the

phenomenal and the noumenal world as completely unreal and contests it with all the self-awareness of modern rationality. What is said here is 'new' because it comes from God and could be brought about only by God himself. It is something altogether new and foreign to every history and to all cultures; we can enter into it in faith and only in faith, and when we do so, it opens up to us wholly new horizons of thought and life. (Hans Urs Von Balthasar and Joseph Cardinal Ratzinger, *Mary, The Church at the Source*, trans. Adrian Walker, San Francisco: Ignatius Press, 2005, 90).

To Ratzinger, therefore, the novelty marking the transition of *logos* from a concept to a person is much more than an evolutionary leap, for it defied all that unaided reason could have conceived or brought about. It is necessary to keep this difference in mind. In other words, the unicity of the Incarnation lies in its origins— it came from God—and only God could have initiated such an act in which the Eternal Son who is also the Creative Word, Logos, in a singular event, enters time and by so doing, make history *his-story*. There is, in this singular event, an intervention into the horizontal character of human history by a vertical dynamism that forever changes how we must read the historical. To Ratzinger, therefore, the sheer power of this event, the transition of logos from concept to person in history, is a reality that is foreign to all cultures and hence, can only be received as a gift by all cultures. No one culture can claim any chronological privilege regarding the entry of God's Logos into human history. And if cultures allow this event to touch them, it is because cultures, given the transcendental principle that shapes them from within, already possessed, albeit in an *a priori* fashion, an entelechy placed in cultures by the Creative Logos.

Taking its cue from the Prologue of the Gospel of John, as I have already pointed out, in the thought of the Fathers, *logos* was not just adopted. It was translated, moving from an impersonal principle to a concrete singular individual, the second person of the Trinity, God's Eternal Son. This translation, this inculturation is a pointer that at its most inner core, Christianity is a religion of reason, for in translating *logos* from a principle to a person, the Fathers did not leave behind the rational heritage and character of philosophical *logos* of Greek philosophy. On the contrary, with the consciousness of God as the Ordering Mind, that creation is an act of a rational God, the Fathers saw in the Greek concept of *logos* an inner quality of God's reasonableness that points to the reasonableness of creation, so much so that, in their reading of John's Gospel in particular, the Creator God of Genesis becomes the Redeeming God of the New Testament.

Opposition to Dehellenization as a Service to the Universality of *Logos* in All Cultures

This is the patristic context in which we could situate and understand Benedict's forceful defense of the inner rapprochement between philosophical rationality and biblical faith, between the God of philosophy and the God of religious faith, between Athens and Jerusalem, in his Regensburg lecture. Much has been said about the Eurocentric character of Ratzinger's outlook, especially from the perspective of his liturgical theology and his forceful criticism of certain strands of Latin American theologies of liberation. This is not the space to engage such criticisms. To Ratzinger, the vision of Paul of Tarsus wherein he is barred from going to Asia and rather goes to Macedonia (Acts 16:6–10), "(…) can be interpreted as a 'distillation' of the intrinsic necessity of a rapprochement between Biblical faith and Greek inquiry."[15] Ratzinger sees this event as Divine Providence bringing about a synthesis between faith and reason that could not have been the case, had Paul rather gone into Asia, dominated by a religious culture of mythology.

What is particularly illuminating are *the three stages that Ratzinger identifies in terms of the historical evolution of this dehellenization*: Firstly, the rejection of the Medieval Metaphysical Scholasticism as alien to the spirit of Christian thought by the

Reformers in the sixteenth century, following Luther's *sola scriptura*. Secondly, the nineteenth and twentieth century liberal movements in theology that, following Pascal's distinction between the God of faith, of Abraham, Isaac and Jacob as distinct from the God of philosophers, pushed to an extreme the former, arguing for a return to the simple Jesus of the Gospels, a Jesus without the layers of human tradition and reason. And finally, the argument that today, the inner rapprochement that came about between Biblical monotheism and Philosophical monotheism, culminating in the Hellenism of the New Testament, is not binding in nature. We must return to New Testament anew in order to inculturate it in our own context.[16]

To Ratzinger, this process of dehellenization "is not simply false, but it is coarse and lacking in precision (...) The fundamental decisions made about the relationship between faith and the use of human reason are part of the faith itself; they are developments consonant with the nature of faith."[17] But is defense of Hellenization not synonymous with defending the Europeanization of the Christian faith?

This is certainly not the case, at least, for Ratzinger, for in a 1960 article, Ratzinger wrote that "there exists no legitimate philosophical or theological grounds for setting the occidental expression of Christianity exclusive."[18] For Ratzinger, the Christology of the *Logos* provides the fundamental orientation thanks to which all cultures are open to the Christ-event, and this is the theological context thanks to which one must understand Ratzinger's argument, not against the usage of the term "inculturation" per se, but perhaps in a much more nuanced manner, a movement beyond inculturation to interculturality.

Inculturation and Interculturality

The History of a Term: We cannot do justice to the question of the historical evolution of the term "inculturation" given the limits of this presentation. However, it suffices to note that the term "inculturation" was first coined by the Jesuit missiologist, Joseph

Masson S.J., in the 1950s. The noun "inculturation" occurs for the first time in the 32nd General Congregation of the Society of Jesus (1974–1975). In a 1978 letter to the Society of Jesus, then Jesuit Superior General Pedro Arrupe (1907–1991), writing on the subject of inculturation, provided a since oft-quoted definition:

> It is the incarnation of Christian life and of the Christian message in a particular context, in such a way that this experience not only finds expression through elements proper to the culture in question, but becomes a principle that animates, directs, unifies the culture, transforming it and remaking it so as to bring about a "new creation.[19]

Turning to the Papal Magisterium, the first time one finds the term "inculturation" being used is in *Catechesi Tradendae* (# 53), and in *Redemptoris Missio*, both issued by St. John Paul II in 1979 and 1990 respectively. In *Redemptoris Missio*, the term occurs no less than thirteen times. Pope Francis uses the term as well in *Veritatis Gaudium* (#2). These usages point to the understanding of inculturation as the discerning of the points of contact between cultures and the Gospel message of Jesus Christ, in such a way that, while respecting the good found in cultures, purifies these cultures from elements that are not in conformity with the Gospel. Inculturation, in this context, seeks to place the person of Christ at the center of all cultures.

Turning to Ratzinger, a proper understanding of his nuanced treatment of "inculturation theology" necessitates a close study of three key texts that, in my opinion, are significant and even indispensable. The first text is an essay which Ratzinger wrote in 1963, first published for the Festschrift in 1964, on the occasion of Karl Rahner's 60th birthday. In this essay, Ratzinger argues that human culture is an anthropological datum oriented towards the expectation of an ultimate truth that is not of human making. Ratzinger maintains that this *orientation* of all peoples and cultures towards a transcendental truth that is not self-created or self-generated, is a universally defining character of a sociological and theological assessment of what constitutes culture at its deepest levels. To Ratzinger, "each particular culture not only lives out its own experience of God, the world, and man, but on its path, it necessarily encounters other cultural agencies and has to react to their quite different experiences."[20] In effect, cultures are not closed in on themselves, in a kind of suffocating staticity, but are innately dynamic, taking on new values and shedding off others. As Ratzinger points out, Culture develops along the way, through the encounter with new realities and the assimilation of new perceptions. It is not closed up in itself but is affected by the impetus of time's onward flow, in which the confluence of different currents, the processes of union are important. The historical character of culture signifies its capacity for progress, and that implies its capacity to be open, to accept its being transformed by an encounter.[21]

Dynamism is therefore a characteristic element of the unfolding of culture in the historical processes that mark human history. In other words, there is no insular culture, from Ratzinger's perspective. And the encyclical *Fides et Ratio* offers a concurring affirmation when St. John Paul II writes:

> Inseparable as they are from people and their history, cultures share the dynamics which the human experience of life reveals. They change and advance because people meet in new ways and share with each other their ways of life. Cultures are fed by the communication of values, and they survive and flourish insofar as they remain open to assimilating new experiences. How are we to explain these dynamics? All people are part of a culture, depend upon it and shape it. Human beings are both child and parent of the culture in which they are immersed. To everything they do, they bring something which sets them apart from the rest of creation: their unfailing openness to mystery and their boundless desire for knowledge. Lying deep in every

culture, there appears this impulse towards a fulfilment. We may say, then, that culture itself has an intrinsic capacity to receive divine Revelation.[22]

Central to this perspective of *Fides et Ratio* is its anthropological understanding of culture. It is the human being, created in
the image and likeness of God and endowed with intellect and
will, capable of loving and responding to love, that builds, shapes,
and influences culture. In this light, a proper understanding of
culture demands a thoughtful consideration and assessment of
the origin, mission, and destiny of the human person and humanity's place in the grand scheme of things in God's good earth.

Returning to Ratzinger's lecture on Rahner's birthday anniversary, it is important to note that while Ratzinger in no way sub-
scribes to Rahner's "anonymous Christianity," Ratzinger points out
that this human capacity for truth is one that is primordially,
though inchoately oriented ultimately towards Christ, "the *Logos*
who has become man, the self-revelation of truth itself. It is then
clear that truth is the sphere within which everyone can find and
relate to one another and, in so doing, lose nothing of his own value
or his own dignity."[23] In other words, becoming a Christian does
not deprive one of the best and good found in one's own culture.
Christianity does not estrange a person from the valuable roots of
one's own culture. Clearly, Ratzinger is refuting the Marxist critique
of the Christian faith as a producer of self-alienation. Christianity
does not alienate its adherents from culture, because, at least for
Ratzinger, self- transcendence is already obliquely envisioned by
all forms of human culture, for all cultures are ultimately oriented
towards truth, that is, an inner entelechy for the transcendentals of
the true, the beautiful, and the good, residing in all cultures.

The second pertinent text is an address that Ratzinger delivered to the Presidents of the Asian Bishops' Conferences on March
5, 1993, titled, "Christ, Faith, and the Challenges of Culture." This
address marks the first instance in which Ratzinger argued for
the replacement of the term "inculturation" with that of "interculturality." To Ratzinger, interculturality is the meeting of

cultures on an equal footing.[24] Notice how this is substantially different from the definition of inculturation by Pedro Arrupe in GC 32. Inculturation, in the Arrupean sense of the term, calls on the missionary or evangelist to find expressions in a given culture that could serve as points of entry of the Christian faith into that culture, hoping all the while to animate, inspire, and transform the given culture from within. With interculturality, the emphasis moves from entry into equal engagement. How does Ratzinger justify this shift? Because, as Emery de Gaál points out, to Ratzinger, "in *concreto*, a faithless culture or a cultureless faith are oxymorons and hollow edifices of ideas. Both realities thrive on mutual interpenetration and, in fact, exist necessarily in the mode of interdependence."[25] To Ratzinger, therefore, a thinking divorcing religion from culture "is basically Manichean: it reduces culture to a merely interchangeable embodiment; faith is materialized into a mere spirit, ultimately lacking in reality. Such a conception is of course typical of post-Enlightenment spirituality. Culture is relegated to more outward form, and religion to more inexpressible feeling or to pure thought. Thus, the productive tension, which ought normally to arise from the coexistence of two cultural entities, disappears."[26] And we can see this reduction of faith or religion to thought in Hegel and Feuerbach, for example.

In this sense, inculturation might convey an understanding of a singular route that eliminates a dialogical approach to the question of religious faith. Ratzinger writes:

> Accordingly, faith would always have to live from borrowed cultures, which remain in the end somehow external and capable of being cast off. Above all, one borrowed cultural form would not speak to someone who lives in another culture. Universality would thereby finally become fictitious. Such thinking is at root Manichean. Culture is debased, becoming a mere exchangeable shell. Faith is reduced to disincarnated spirit ultimately void of reality. To be sure, such a view

is typical of the post-Enlightenment mentality. Culture is reduced to mere form; religion, to inexpressible mere feeling or pure thought.[27]

Clearly, for Ratzinger, the interpretation of faith that came with the Enlightenment led to a disintegration of the harmony of faith and culture.

In a word, Ratzinger's argument is that faith and culture can mutually enrich and interact with each other owing to his conviction that they are not utterly different to each other, that there is some interiority between them, and that they naturally draw near to each other and unite, in their concern for the question of God and the question of the human being. To Ratzinger, a cultureless faith is an existential impossibility: "In all known historical cultures, religion is the essential element of culture, indeed it is its determining core. It is religion which determines the structure of values and thereby forms its inner logic."[28] Faith and culture are therefore, not separate entities, as implied by the term "inculturation," for faith itself is culture.

The third text is the 1999 lecture on the foundation of the Archdiocese of Paderborn, Germany, 1,200 years ago: Ratzinger argued that Jesus Christ, as the *Universale Concretum et Personale*, dignifies everything human and good. In Christ, therefore, truth is universal and cross-cultural. In other words, Christ as the *Universale Concretum*, is the guarantor against a closed-cultural mindset. Christ is the unifying *humanum* of the differences of cultures, and hence, the locus for the meeting of cultures, given that self-transcendence, realizable in Christ, *universale et personale*, is the central nexus of culture. Foreshadowing this universality of Christ is the God of the Old Testament's constant challenge to Israel to transcend Israel's own culture towards an openness to a universally common truth. Conclusively, that which was specific is now owned by all (Lk 15:31).

Seen together, De Gaál points out that "the arguments Ratzinger advances are remarkably consistent—from 1964, via 1993 to 1999. Not only is he faithful to his own previous statements on the relationship between faith, mission, and culture. He is at the same time loyal to the consistent Church teaching on this matter."[29] And this consistency is remarkable because the Early, Middle and Later Ratzinger is not just a static categorization, but are each indicative of what captured Ratzinger's theological imagination, especially from the perspective of his interlocutors, which, regarding the question of Christ and the cultures, has to do with how we can meaningfully proceed with interreligious dialogue today, given the unicity and salvific universality of Jesus Christ and the Church.

Logos Christology as the Hermeneutical Key to a Theology of Inculturation and Interculturality

In the first five points of this lecture on the universality of *Logos* in all cultures and the implications for the meeting between faith and cultures, we have examined, firstly, the philosophical and theological understanding of *Logos*. Secondly, we have also studied the historical trajectory of Ratzinger's theology of inculturation and interculturality. At this point, what would constitute the link between *Logos* theology and inculturation or interculturation theology?

It is significant to note that the event of the incarnation is not extrinsic to the inner contours of history. It is *Logos*, Creative Reason, that is behind the start of history, entering history to bring history unto a new level of being, shaped by the humanizing and concomitant divinizing of history thanks to the *Gestalt* of the Eternal *Logos*, Jesus Christ. This is the Christology that emerges from Ratzinger's trilogy on Jesus, that is, *Jesus of Nazareth*, volumes I-III. As Benedict himself maintains in *Verbum Domini* when talking about *Logos* and historical consciousness, the *Logos* has been "abbreviated," that is, it has become "shorter" in that it has become historical in order to be apprehended and understood by human beings.[30] And as Benedict puts it again in his Christmas homily of 2006, "the eternal word became small—small enough to fit into a manger. He became a child, so that the Word could be grasped by us."[31]

Given this understanding, that is, that the *Logos* as Creative

Reason is the foundation for history and all of culture, the essential Ratzingerian synthesis on faith and culture will amount to the following arguments:

Firstly, Jesus Christ as the *Logos, Universale Concretum et Personale*, makes it possible for us to speak of interculturation and not of inculturation, with the former understood as the meeting of cultures, while the latter "presupposes that, as it were, a culturally naked faith is transferred into a culture that is indifferent from the religious point of view, so that two agents that were hitherto alien to each other meet and now engage in a synthesis together."[32] In effect, interculturality levels the playing field not only for the encounter between cultures, but more especially, between cultures and religions, given the entelechy of all cultures towards metaphysical self-transcendence. And Ratzinger does not only acknowledge this equality which interculturality presupposes and presents, but likewise highlights why he thinks interculturality offers a more compelling account of the encounter between faith and culture. Ratzinger argues:

> But this depiction (that is, of a culturally naked faith presupposed by inculturation), is first of all artificial and unreal, because there is no such thing as a culture-free faith and because—outside of modern technical civilization—there is no such thing as religion-free culture. But above all one cannot see how two organisms that in themselves totally alien to each other should, through a transplantation that starts by mutilating them both, suddenly become a single living whole. Only if it is true that all cultures are potentially universal and have an inner capacity to be open to others can interculturality lead to new and fruitful forms.[33]

The argument being made here by Ratzinger is based on his conviction that both the position of a culture-free faith and a religion-free culture are existential anomalies. In other words, culture will always be an expression of faith, for culture displays a people's understanding of self-transcendence. Faith and culture are, therefore, not separate entities. Culture and faith communicate a people's self- consciousness in time and space, and how the transcendental orients and shapes the present-ness of any given people. Furthermore, Ratzinger believes that the synthetic relationship between culture and faith is grounded on that a priori entelechy of universality that is latent in both culture and religion, and entelechy that is the capacity for openness to transcendence. And given this potential for universality and this inner symbiosis between faith and culture, we have grounds to speak of interculturality rather than inculturation.

Secondly, inculturation leaves untouched the presumptive character of the designation of the so-called "non-Christian cultures." All cultures are opened to the transformative power of the Gospel. While it is the case that certain cultures have long been exposed to Biblical faith and hence, could be described as Judeo-Christian, it remains true that in the light of the Gospel, there always remains an ongoing tension between the *zeitgeist* and religious faith, seen as well in the religious development of Israel. Ratzinger employs the image of the Call of Abraham in Genesis 12, to explain that for all cultures, faith always implies a movement from the "surrounding culture." Ratzinger takes as a paradigm God's call to Abraham to leave the land of his Fathers (Gen 12). Another image that corroborates the dynamism that eschews a complete identification between faith and culture is the significance of the death of Christ outside the walls of Jerusalem, on the Hill of Calvary. As with Abraham who is called to leave the land of his ancestors, Christ, as it were, stands outside the gates of culture of Jerusalem, on the hill of faith, that offers an aerial view of reality, to be seen now through the lenses of Jesus' death and resurrection. In the light of this movement that "leaves culture behind," all cultures are thus invited to undertake a conversion that is demanded by the call to faith based, certainly, in the transcendental character of culture, that is, the capacity for culture to go beyond the mere empirical and positivistic.

Ratzinger repeatedly reminds his readers of the quote from

Tertullian, "Christ calls himself truth, not custom," in demonstrating the limits of cultural Christianity, very different from Christian culture. The former elicits a flow with the rivers, while the latter demands a conscious and responsible yes to the gift of faith, that comes with a price of letting go of the certainties of culture to embrace a reality that is wider, deeper and mysterious, namely, the God of Jesus Christ. In this light, faith in Christ imposes a new way of being and of coming into consciousness for all cultures, for in introduces a new principle, an utterly different hermeneutic in the apprehension and comprehension of all cultures, namely, the Incarnation of God in history, who, as the Second Person of the Trinity, stands as the principle of evaluation of all cultures. Thus, it is not just a case of a culture opening up to a transcendent reality, but more specifically, a culture opening to the specific reality and manifestation of the God-Man, the Everlasting Man, to use a Chestertonian appellation. Seen from this perspective, the particularity of Jesus Christ becomes a stumbling block for cultural presumptuousness and classicism, precisely because of who Jesus Christ is, the God-Man who, by fully revealing God to all cultures, not only brings into sharper focus the inadequacy of a "culture" that seeks to exclude God, but more precisely, invites all cultures to embrace the new height and breadth, the new possibilities that the Incarnation offers to all cultures, Christ in all cultures, Christ beyond all cultures.

Thirdly, inculturation tends to eliminate the vagueness that must be and must remain the outcome of the meeting between cultures and faith, in the sense that it presumes an already-decided line of action from the part of the antecedent Christian culture to the recipient culture of the Christian faith. To Ratzinger, such a structuralizing of the encounter between two cultures brings about a restrictive impulse in a process that ought to be marked by a necessary vagueness and openness; all the more so, because as Ratzinger believes, there is always an inner rapprochement between cultures and faith, and the two are never completely foreign to each other.

Fourthly, the relationship between faith and culture, in the

Ratzingerian understanding of things, always demands a movement, what one could refer to as an *exitus*. Herein enters the Christological reading of faith and culture by Ratzinger. This exitus of the starting point of faith is crucial because though it is helpful to articulate the inner relationality and representationality of faith and culture, one cannot simply articulate a comfortable rapprochement between the two, as close in expression of a worldview as they might be and that we might desire them to be. Ratzinger takes the call of Abraham to leave the land of his kindred (Gen 12:1), which marks the beginning of Israel's faith, to be a significant and normative pedagogy on the relationship between culture and faith: Faith begins with a cultural break. Ratzinger writes:

> There will always be such a break with one's own prehistory, such a setting forth, at the beginning of a new moment in the history of faith. Yet this new beginning then proves to be a force for healing, creating a new center with the ability to draw to itself all that is true to the measure of humanity, all that is true to the measure of divinity.[34]

Faith, therefore, cannot simply fit perfectly with the cultural ethos or cultural *Weltanschauung*, even if it expresses the culture. Faith always asks for the more, demands a movement which in the final analysis, becomes a healing and liberating experience for culture, for it opens culture up to a new reality coming from revelation. For Ratzinger, the theological fulcrum of a break with culture that returns to heal culture is the Cross: Calvary is a breaking forth from the earth. Jesus is lifted from the earth.[35] But from this lifting forth, from this hill of Calvary, comes a new gravity that heals the world, for Calvary draws a divided world into the unity of love with God's Son (Jn 12:32) —"I, when I am lifted up from the earth, will draw all to myself."

Finally, besides the Christological aspect of faith and culture, there is also an Ecclesiological component to the Ratzingerian understanding of faith and culture, that is, the Church herself has her own culture "with her own many-layered intercultural character that has grown up in the course of her history. Without a certain exodus, a breaking off with one's life in all its aspects, one cannot become a Christian."[36] Ratzinger's assertion here is that the living tradition of the Church gives the Church her own distinctive culture. In other words, the experiences of faith, hope and love; of worship; of listening to the scriptures; of discerning the will of God in the midst of the world; of the apostolic witness and the life of the saints; of faith seeking understanding; and finally, of the normative historicity of the Jesus of Nazareth, have, over time, built a distinctive Christian culture that shapes the Church from within as a people of God and differentiates her from without, even if the Church lives her life in the midst of the world. Ratzinger asserts:

> Faith is no private path to God; it leads into the people of God and into its history. God has linked himself to a history, which is now also his history and which we cannot simply erase (…). We cannot repeat the process of the Incarnation at will, in the sense of repeatedly taking Christ's flesh away from him, so to speak, and offering him some other flesh instead. Christ remains the same, even according to his body. But he is drawing us to him.[37]

This implies that catholicity is the first cultural element of the Church, for the people of God who stand before the Lamb are taking from every nation, tribe, people, and tongue (Rev 7:9). In effect, while we seek to articulate Christian faith from the perspective of the cultural forms as Africans, we should not lose sight of the universality of the cultural textual of the Church, so much so that the "Jesus of Africa" becomes an isolating and an insulating Jesus that shuts us off from the universal Church. In other words, African theological reflections on the Christian faith should not become a channel of an exaggerated and an unwarranted amplification of Africo-centricism, an us-against-them mentality, that subtly constructs a hermeneutic of suspicion towards what we as African Christians have received from the living tradition of the universal Church. That will transform African theology from an endeavor of a faith seeking understanding along the lines of the Church of Jesus Christ to a party of Christ, governed by a certain ideological activism that is anything but Christian, or precisely, Roman Catholic. Christ, the *Logos*, is for all and encompasses all, and it is helpful to remember that.

Conclusion: The Programmatic Significance of Ratzinger's Theology of Interculturality for African Theology: African Theology Beyond Inculturation and Black Liberation Theology Quo Vadis, African Theology?

Summarily, it remains to be seen how much impact Ratzinger's argument for interculturality, as the concept that captures in a more profound manner the inner dialogue between culture and faith, will have on future theological reflections in the *memoria ecclesiae*, that is, the living memory of the Church. Perhaps after decades of African theology focusing on the twin facets of liberation and inculturation theologies, Ratzinger's treatment of the *Logos* as the basis of interculturality can offer a fresh and new perspective.

This does not imply that the focus of African theologians on liberation and inculturation have been futile. Certainly not, for especially in the area of the liturgy, inculturation of the Roman Rite has made many an African to feel at home in the Church, while worshiping God. And it is also the case that African theologies of liberation especially from colonialism and neo-colonialism have given African theology a particular idiom of struggles, pain, hope, and freedom that have likewise enriched the global theological edifice. However, it clearly is the case that a continuous emphasis on these two aspects keeps African theology in a lockdown mode of a certain parochialism, often concerned about relative needs and missing out on the big picture of the *Logos* and its universal breadth. What is often overlooked is the fact that African cultures, like all other cultures, bears within it and is sustained by the *Logos*. For African Christianity in particular, the inner unity between culture and religion can provide an impetus that must be continuously tapped into, if African cultures must provide an attractive alternative to the enticements of Western liberal culture, especially in the light of the constant threat of ideological colonialism. Hitherto to the modern era, the transcendental principle constituted a life source to Western culture.

The religious dimension of the human being provided a welcomed resource that shaped Western thought on social, political, and economic questions. Tracing to the Enlightenment, the West, particularly Europe, has increasingly marginalized religion, consigning it to the sphere of the private cult. References to religion in the public square are often met with suspicion and hostility, all in the name of secular pluralism and tolerance. The link between culture—a word etymologically linked to *cult*, that is, worship—and religion, appears irreversibly broken in large sectors of the Western world today. As scholars like Josef Pieper and Christopher Dawson have prophetically and rightly pointed out, when worship is taken out of culture, what we are left with is a tree without its roots, so much so that culture *qua* culture, disappears and in its place, entertainment and unbridled hedonism sets in. As Blaise Pascal pointed out centuries ago, namely, the dominant characteristics that are defining the modern man and woman in the West are diversion and indifference.

With the dynamism of transcendence increasingly excluded in the name of progress, there appears in the human reality a truncation of the spiritual dimension of human beings. If the West must save its culture from total annihilation and collapse, it is imperative to rediscover, once again, the life-giving force that comes with a transcendental outlook of reality, an outlook that pays attention to the gift of interiority. Attention must be paid to this consciousness because as Dawson points out, cultures are bearers of religious truths. This does not imply that culture is religion. Nevertheless, as bearers or transmitters of religious truths, cultures contain Divine revelation, capturing the historical workings of grace in the unfolding of human history. In a word, the West must rediscover its religious roots, for the death of religion is the death of culture. The West needs its own exodus from relativism, hedonism, leisure, and atheism, for as Pieper correctly argues, cut off from the worship of God, leisure metamorphosizes into laziness, while work becomes inhuman. Boredom sets in, due to the absence of the spiritual power. In effect, for the sake of its own cultural survival, especially given the changing demographics currently underway in many Western nations, the West will need, once again, to see religion not as a problem to be solved but as a legitimate interlocutor in the public square. And this relationship between culture and faith is a witness that Africa can and should offer the West. But Africa will be able to do that on condition that she keeps the dynamism of culture and the dynamism of faith or the supernatural in an ongoing living relationship. And this testimony on the part of African Christianity, to be precise, will not appear completely foreign to the West, for, as has been argued in this lecture, all cultures have an inner presence and capacity for Logos. All cultures possess an inner entelechy towards the Logos that at the fullness of time, became man in Jesus of Nazareth (Gal. 4:4).

If African theology can open itself all the more to *Logos* interculturality, African theology will not only be entering evermore into the breadth of *Logos*, of reason, but will find within its inner self the resources that will make African theology capable of engaging a post-Enlightenment world of rational positivism, offering, especially the Western Church, a faith-affirming and faith-living witness of the inner rapprochement between faith and culture that provides a convincing alternative to the Hegelian, Nietzschean, and Marxist reading of culture and history. And this will be no small achievement on the part of African theology, especially in the service of the world Church, which clearly needs the enthusiasm and energy of the Church in Africa. Such is the case because all cultures are *logos*-capable, all cultures have an inner orientation to *logos*, to rationality.

Personally, it comes across as symbolic that during his apostolic visit to Cameroon and Angola in March 2009, Benedict, in his address to the Bishops of Africa, called for a reopening of Origen's Catechetical School of Alexandria, albeit in a different form today.[38] Conclusively, therefore, African theology does not need a dehellenized theological orientation for the twenty-first century. *Logos* is not only not foreign to African cultures, but *Logos* is not a private property of Western theology and the Western Church. Perhaps the theological orientation of this new School of Alexandria, if it ever comes to be which will be Benedict's dream for African Theology in service to the world Church, could begin with and follow the pedagogy of *Logos and Interculturality*, which, while paying attention to the concrete and the particular, does not close itself in, but rather, in finding what is truly African and Christian, offers that witness in the universality and interculturality of *Logos* to all cultures of the living Church.

The Philosophical Point of View

Benedict XVI represents a model of intellectual rigor. Benedict XVI's philosophy revolves around the relationship between faith and reason. He affirms the high value of human reason, the rationale of faith and the autonomy of reason and faith. He reminds us that the true greatness of reason is to seek the truth, including the truth about religion. Truth can only be sought through dialogue, through work, in an atmosphere of respect and freedom. It is then that human reason wholly appears and reveals its potential. This is a challenge not only for Christians, but also for everyone in a secularized society that may no longer ask itself the essential metaphysical questions. However, the fact that the Church is going through a turmoil is regretted. It is essentially due to the "Pyrrhonism doctrine" that has taken hold of current mentalities. Pyrrhonism is a denial of reason as the faculty of reaching the being of things and their meaning as well as of adhering to them by will. It is a kind of illogic on which what Benedict XVI called "the dictatorship of relativism" lies: nothing should be considered as definitively true anymore.

"Love" and "Truth" in the Thought of Joseph Ratzinger/Benedict XVI

Fabrice N'semi[1]

"The meeting of Love and truth. Justice and peace embrace each other; truth will spring up from the earth and justice will lean from heaven" (Ps 84, 11–12).

Introduction

If we go through the lexicographical repertoire of Joseph Ratzinger/Benedict XVI's philosophy we see that the concepts of "love" and "truth" occupy a prominent place. At the beginning of his academic career, Professor Ratzinger published an anthology in 1968, the French version of which is entitled *La foi chrétienne hier et aujourd'hui*. In the book, he addressed, among other things, the essence of Christianity and laid down six principles of Christianity, the synthesis of which is love. As Prefect of the Congregation for the Doctrine of the Faith, he signed the instruction *Donum veritatis* on the ecclesial vocation of the theologian (24 May1990). The first encyclical of his pontificate, *Deus caritas est* (2005), will bring out this supreme principle in a prominent way, while the latest, *Caritas in veritate* (2009), brings this principle into a dialogical relationship with truth. It goes without saying that his episcopal and pontifical motto is *Cooperatores veritatis*, with inspiration from the third epistle of St. John (3 Jn 1:8).

Augustinian Roots

These elements, although not exhaustive, are sufficient proof of constancy and the roots of these two concepts in Joseph

Ratzinger/Benedict XVI's philosophy. Thus, starting from the epistemological aspects that emerge in his approach to these two concepts, we shall examine their relevance in the African context, which is faced with enormous challenges related to reconciliation, justice, and peace, in line with the post-synodal apostolic exhortation *Africae Munus* of the same Pope Benedict XVI.

If one traces the theological journey of Joseph Ratzinger, it is clearly observed that his "first intellectual investigations [...] took the form of a study of St. Augustine."[2] His dialogue with this great teacher from North Africa undoubtedly marks the starting point of his love for the truth. However, while dialoguing with Augustine, Ratzinger remained a son of his time, as he himself states: "St. Augustine kept me company for over twenty years. I have developed my theology in dialogue with Augustine, even though I have tried to conduct this dialogue as a man of today's world."[3] These Ratzinger observations are all the truer because his approach to the concepts of "love" and "truth" are Augustinian in their essence and expression.

Augustine's ideology centers around the concept of "love." In the supplementary notes to his *magnum opus*, *The Confessions*, Solignac points out that "Augustine is the first to provide the elements of a Christian doctrine of love: in any case, on this point, he neither depends on Plotinus nor Ambrose, the two great masters of his ideology, on this point."[4] He defines love through several metaphorical expressions: the "hand of the soul," i.e., that by which it holds something that occupies it, the "foot of the soul," i.e., that which sets it in motion and leads it, that which gives it strength and life, by leading it to its natural place.[5]

Much more than these metaphors, Augustine emphasizes that love is the very weight of the soul: "*Pondus meum amor meus*," that is to say, "My weight is my love."[6] He clearly thinks that the value or unit of measurement of existence is love. Moreover, he specifies that the object of love is God. By emphasizing this theological or theocentric dimension of love, Augustine stresses that he who loves is engaged in a beautiful impulse towards God and will thus be divinized and eternalized. He points out that such love is genuine.

He calls this *caritas* or *dilectio*. It is *agapè*, which he contrasts with *eros*, the inauthentic love which he calls *cupiditas* or *libido*.[7]

Augustine thinks that, as much as love is linked to God, so is truth linked to God. In his approach, God is Love and *Logos*. Based on this assumption, the relationship between "love" and "truth" is articulated around a process in which the one who loves always desires to know more about what he loves.

This Augustinian theory of love has greatly influenced Western philosophy to the point of being the absolute reference. As Solignac rightly points out, "we find in it a phenomenology, a psychology, but also, a spirituality, a theology and a metaphysics of love."[8] It is precisely for this reason that Pope Benedict XVI's encyclical *Deus caritas est* releases a perfume concocted from the Augustinian sources.

Ratzinger's View of Love: A Language Problem

Benedict XVI's approach, based on the Augustinian theory of love, goes beyond the antagonism between *eros* and *agapè*, which is very much in keeping with Anders Nygren's approach.[9] Under the theological view of the Bavarian pope, a process of love purification emerges.

From the beginning of *Deus caritas est*, Benedict XVI identifies language as the first place for the purification of love: "God's love for us is a crucial question for life and raises decisive questions about who God is and who we are. In this regard, we encounter above all a problem of language. The word 'love' has become one of the most used and overused words today, a word to which we give totally different meanings."[10] In this process of purifying language, he analyses the terms *eros* and *agapè* in Greek philosophy first, then in biblical revelation.

Among the Ancient Greeks

Generally speaking, the ancient Greeks used the term *eros* to refer to the love between man and woman.[11] But, as Benedict XVI stresses, this term referred above all to drunkenness, a kind of "divine madness" which had as mediators the sacred prostitutes in vogue in many of the temples of the time.[12]

From this point of view, *eros* is thus identified with instinct. Not only does it exclude reason, which it "overcomes," it also deprives the one who celebrates it of freedom, since it is "drunkenness." This is why Benedict XVI states that, "in the temple, prostitutes, those who give Divine intoxication, are not treated as human beings or as persons, but are only instruments to arouse divine madness: in reality they are not goddesses, but human persons who are abused. This is why the drunken and unruly *eros* is not an elevation, an ecstasy towards the Divine, but a fall, the degradation of man."[13]

He continues saying, consequently, "it thus becomes obvious that *eros* needs discipline, purification, to give man not a moment's pleasure, but a certain foretaste of the summit of existence, of the beatitude towards which our whole being tends."[14] But how can *eros* be disciplined if it already bears the seeds of imperfection? Is it not easier to destroy it completely or to put it on the cathexis? It is on this particular point that the approach of Benedict XVI is innovative and original. This originality does not manifest itself in the pure and simple exclusion of *eros*, still less in its categorical refusal or "its poisoning, but in its healing in view of its true greatness.[15] The biblical interpretation that he proposes for this purpose further clarifies this originality.

In the Old Testament

The Old Testament, faithful to the faith in one true God, distances from the Greek conception that we have just elucidated, criticizing it vigorously. It does not question *eros* as such, but its "false divinisation."[16] Among the books of the Old Testament, the *Song of Songs* is undoubtedly that which makes the most extensive reference to love, especially conjugal love. Two words are used to speak of it: "First we have the word *'dodim,'* a plural which expresses love as yet uncertain, in a situation of indeterminate search. This word is then replaced by the word *'ahabà'* which, in the Greek translation of the Old Testament, is rendered by the like-sounding word *'agape,'* which [...] becomes the defining expression of the biblical conception of love."[17] As *agapè*, love turns away from its self-referentiality and resolutely turns towards the other, towards the search for his or her happiness. This turning of the self, which is at the same time a re-centering of the other, becomes the vector of a peaceful coexistence and a search for the collective good.

By enriching its vocabulary with the term *agapè*, does the Old Testament sign the death certificate of the term *eros*? Is God's love for Israel exclusively *agapè* and not *eros*? According to Benedict XVI, "the one God in whom Israel believes loves personally. Moreover, his love is a love of election: among all peoples, he chooses Israel and loves it, yet with the intention of healing all humanity through it. He loves, and his love can undoubtedly be described as *eros*, which is, however, at the same time and totally, agape."[18] With such a statement, Benedict XVI follows the line of Pseudo-Dionysius the Areopagite who refers to God as *eros* and *agapè* at the same time. This is especially true since some Old Testament books, such as the books of prophets Hosea and Ezekiel, describe the relationship between YHWH and Israel using erotic imagery. YHWH loves Israel with a passionate love, and in spite of her infidelity to the Law, her prostitution (idolatry), he still forgives her. It is thus in this form of bipolar tension between *eros* and *agapè* that God's unconditional love for Israel unfolds.

Jesus Christ: Love Incarnate

In the light of Old Testament revelation, there is *eros* and *agapè* which, paraphrasing the title of a book by Raniero Cantalamessa,[19] are the "two faces of love." But in reality, Benedict XVI points out, "God's *eros* for man [...] is, at the same time, totally *agape*."[20] This reconciliation is more explicit and concrete in New Testament revelation, where God's love transcends all speculative categories in that it is incarnated in Christ. Indeed, Benedict XVI emphasizes that, "the newness of the New Testament does not consist in new ideas, but in the very person of Christ, who gives flesh and blood to the concepts."[21] Through the mystery of his incarnation, God's love becomes a face and thus visible to every man and woman. And at the top of the cross, this face reveals the alphabet and grammar of God's love.

In the end, it is in staring at the cross of Christ that the real face and the very truth of God's love is revealed. His cross is the most radical form (in the etymological sense of the word *radix, -icis*, root) and therefore, the most perfect of love. It reveals to us love in its vertical and horizontal dimensions, that is, love of God and neighbor. And since it is the supreme expression of love in its substance and form, it becomes the *Logos* that draws us into Christ's act of offering: "And I, when I am lifted up, I will draw all men to myself" (Jn 12:32).

Thus, Christ's act of offering on Calvary—of which the Eucharist is the memorial—assumes a universal and paradigmatic value. As such, it constitutes the unit of measurement and the reference par excellence of love. Henceforth, Love is to imitate Christ who died on the cross for us and for our redemption.

Truth as Seen by Ratzinger:
Basics

Closely related to love, truth is one of the key concepts in the theology of Joseph Ratzinger/Benedict XVI. He has made it not only his episcopal and pontifical motto, but also his flagship on the theological front to the extent that he has always defended "the primacy of truth in the face of consensus and group convenience."[22]

In his philosophical and theological approach to truth, Joseph Ratzinger relied essentially on two references: Socrates and John Henry Newman.[23] The former (Socrates) because of his fundamental option for truth, (against the sophists), thus becoming the "prophet of Christ"[24] and his philosophy "a vessel adapted to the Christian *logos*, announcing liberation through truth and towards truth";[25] the latter, (John Henry Newman) because he "places truth before goodness in the order of virtues."[26]

The Truth of Christianity

In 2002, the highly influential Prefect of the Congregation for the Doctrine of the Faith, "the one whom the media and the vast majority of public opinion insist on portraying as the *Panzer-Kardinal,* the Grand Inquisitor,"[27] published a book entitled *Glaube-Wahreit-Toleranz* (Faith, Truth, Tolerance[28]) on Christianity and the world's reigions. After addressing the unity and diversity of religions (chapter one), the interaction of faith, religion, and culture (chapter two), and the new questions that have arisen in the 1990s (chapter three), Ratzinger points the cursor at a fundamental question, which undeniably constitutes the very heart of this book: "What is the truth of Christianity?" (chapter four), before concluding with the triptych truth, tolerance, and freedom (chapter five).

To tackle the theme of the truth of Christianity, Ratzinger in fact takes up a theme dear to his master Augustine who, in *De vera religione,* associates the question of true religion with that of true philosophy. Revising this intuition, Ratzinger highlights as one of the major specificities of Christianity "the combination of faith and reason."[29] As Pope, Benedict XVI constantly referred to this combination in his speeches at the Sorbonne (27 November 1999) and at Regensburg (2 September 2006) to mention only these prominent cases which have caused much ink and spit to flow. And according to him, this synthesis is already present and realized in biblical revelation itself. De facto, while opening up reason or the *Logos* to the truth and love of God, biblical revelation, as he stipulates, "entrusts the world to man's reason, without handing it over to plundering."[30] Two reasons account for such a statement being crucial, bold, and original. First of all, because it makes it possible to reconcile two variables (faith and reason) that were opposed in the extreme by illuminism, and secondly, because it helps to justify "the claim to universality of the Christian fact, based on the universality of truth."[31]

However, does not talking about the universality of Christianity imply in a certain way a total and full belonging? In what manner can Christianity really claim to be universal? What theological basis justifies this claim?

To answer these questions, Ratzinger draws from St. Paul who, in his letter to the Ephesians (2:14) posits Christ himself as the principle of universality in that he destroyed—by his death and resurrection—that which separated, the wall of hatred between the chosen people and the pagan nations. From then, he became the universal bridge that unites men and women of all peoples, languages, nations, families, and tribes of the earth. Through him, with him, and in him, "blood ties to one's ancestor are no longer necessary, because the relationship to Jesus brings about true belonging, true kinship: everyone can now fully belong to God, all men must and can become one people."[32]

The Incarnate Logos

We have just elucidated how, for Ratzinger, Christianity is the bearer of a greater truth, one that transcends all forms of human knowledge and is universal. But far from being an abstract idea or a doctrinal code, the truth of which Christianity is the bearer, it is a Person: Jesus Christ, the *Logos* of God made flesh (Jn 1, 14.) The mystery of his incarnation is linked to two realities, invisible and visible. Thus, Jesus unites these two realities in himself, as attested by the Gospels. The Gospels, especially the Synoptic gospels, present the origin of Jesus from his space-time connection, while St. John affirms that his true origin is the Father (Jn 7, 27. 28.) With this in mind, Benedict XVI insists that in Jesus Christ, the *Logos* of the Father, "God has spoken his eternal word in a human way."[33]

By uniting to himself the invisible and visible reality, Jesus reveals to us the very truth of being human and of being in the world. He reveals the truth of being man because he is, as St. Paul says, the "last man" (1 Cor 15:45) and as such, "he introduces man into a future that is his, a future that consists in not just being man, but in being one with God."[34] In the same way, he reveals the truth of being in the world in that he is, as St. Paul puts it, "the first-born of all creation" (Col 1, 15.) It is for all these reasons that he is the incarnate, living, and inclusive Truth: he includes everything and excludes nothing; in short, he "recapitulates everything" (*anakefalaiosis*) to use a word inspired by Paul and dear to Saint Irenaeus of Lyon.

Moreover, for Ratzinger, truth is also a gift from Christ to the Church, his mystical body. Thus, he points out, the Church, the Holy Magisterium, and the hierarchy are the bearers of divine truth revealed and incarnated in the person of Christ.

Relationship Between Love and Truth

In Ratzinger's approach, there is an intrinsic relationship between "love" and "truth." He illustrated this in the most beautiful way in his 2009 encyclical *Caritas in veritate*. The title of this encyclical is provocative in a particular manner in that it evokes the opposite of the *"veritas in caritate"* spoken of by St. Paul (Ep 4, 15). True to his theological line, Benedict XVI emphasizes that this intrinsic link is embodied in the very life of Christ who reveals to us that God is both Love and *Logos*. In fact, he says, "in Christ, love in truth becomes the face of his Person."[35] Consequently, he continues that, "it is our vocation to love our brothers and sisters in truth following his plan. For he himself is the Truth (cf. Jn 14, 6)."[36] The correlation between these two concepts is necessary to strengthen not only personal or particular relationships, but also public relationships in the social, economic, and political domains. This implies that without this correlation, both concepts lose their real substance and degrade. Indeed, "without truth, love becomes sentimental. Love becomes an empty vessel that can be arbitrarily filled. This is the deadly risk that love faces in a culture without truth. It falls prey to the emotions and contingent opinions of human beings: it becomes an overused and distorted term, to the point of meaning its opposite."[37] Likewise, without love, truth is a path that leads nowhere. This is why Benedict XVI insists that, "truth must be sought, discovered and expressed in the economy of love, but love in turn must be understood, verified and practiced in the light of truth."[38]

In arguing throughout his encyclical *Caritas in Veritate* for the interdependence or indissoluble link between "love" and "truth," Benedict XVI leads us to understand that Christianity is a perfect synthesis of orthodoxy and orthopraxy.

For "Love and Truth to Meet" in Africa

After this overview of Joseph Ratzinger/Benedict XVI's idea on the understanding of the concepts of "love" and "truth," we can now sketch out a reappropriation of his intuitions in the African *issue*. In this undertaking, two basic questions of equal importance will serve as our guideline. The first is: what is the language of love in Africa? The second is: what is the truth of Christianity in Africa?

Purifying the Conception of Love in Africa: From the Love of Power to the Power of Love

Benedict XVI in the very first lines of *Deus caritas est* emphasizes "the vast semantic field of the word 'love': we speak of love of country, love of work, love between parents and children, between brothers and sisters and between relatives, love for one's neighbor and love for God."[39] Without excluding or minimizing this list, we can, in the African context, highlight several variables to indicate the semantic field of the word "love": the land, the language, the family, the tribe, etc. Thus, one can speak of love of one's own country, of love for one's own language, of love of one's own family, of love of one's own tribe, of love of one's own clan, etc. Georges Lebrun-Keris states that, "in Africa, the sacred comes first and the group is the second, inseparable from it. Man cannot conceive of himself without the group."[40]

This observation is widely shared by most sociological and anthropological studies on Africa. The two special assemblies for Africa of the Synod of Bishops have even echoed it. In this regard,

Monsignor Barthélémy Adoukounou states that "the first synod compiled what could be called the richest anthropological background of African culture: the family. Man is a family and society only really exists if it has as its cells healthy families that are deeply rooted in the values that have constituted humanity since its most ancient days."[41] This is why in the post-synodal apostolic exhortation *Ecclesia in Africa*, John Paul II consecrated the family as the model of the family.[42]

As for the second synod, taking the right measure on the tragic situation prevalent in many countries on the continent that is plunged in a vicious circle of violence and in the whirlpool of fratricidal wars, it defined the mission of the Church-Family of God in Africa in terms of commitment to the service of reconciliation, justice, and peace. "Promoting reconciliation, justice, and peace means assuming the mission of a prophet."[43] Thus, this synod has contributed to awakening and strengthening the prophetic consciousness of the Church in Africa.

On what can we rely on to build a harmonious living together, in a continent where belonging to a land, to a language, to a tribe, to a family, and other such attachments constitute, in many respects, factors of division, armed conflict, violence, and war? How can *"eros* and *agapè* be removed from the shadow of *Thanatos (the death instinct)"*[44] in Africa? Taking up the contribution of the synod fathers, Benedict XVI proposes "a commitment to the Lord." This is the opening sentence of his post-synodal apostolic exhortation *Africae Munus*:

> Africa's commitment to the Lord is a precious treasure which I entrust, at the beginning of the third millennium, to the bishops, priests, permanent deacons, consecrated persons, catechists, and laity of this dear continent and her neighboring islands. This mission pushes Africa to deepen her Christian vocation. It urges her living, reconciliation between persons and communities in the name of Jesus and the promotion of peace and justice in truth for all.[45]

Talking about commitment, the Congolese theologian Léonard Santedi Kinkupu, during a conference to present *Africae Munus* held in December 2011 at the Foyer Abraham in Brazzaville, spelt out the difference between the words "commitment" and "involvement" by making a double analogy on the pig and the chicken. He said, in the production of sausage, the pig is committed in that it gives its flesh and blood, while in the process of laying of eggs, the hen is simply involved. Above this familiar example, the invitation is not just becoming committed, but to become truly committed for the Lord in what is at stake. For Ratzinger, among the six principles of "Christian being" developed in *La foi chrétienne hier et aujourd'hui*, "the principle of the for"[46] exists and explicitly underpins the commitment for the Lord, but also the commitment to one's neighbor.

He sees Christian life as essentially a pro-existence, that is, a life totally dedicated to the service of God and the neighbor. Without this requirement of commitment, the Church-Family of God in Africa loses the good sense of the Gospel, turns away from its prophetic vocation, sinks piteously into tribal dictatorship, and finds itself caught in the "dreaded trap of ethno-dioceses and ethnomaniac communities."[47] The presence of these figures, antithetical to the evangelical spirit, is a symptom of the state of "deprophetisation" of our particular Churches and communities, which have lost their sense of direction. Hence the urgent need to rethink the mission in terms of prophetic commitment.

By engaging on the prophetic front, the Church-Family of God in Africa reinvests the existential ordeals that abound on the continent and displays the hope of salvation that Christ came to bring to the whole human race. With this decisive orientation, "the objectives of the mission are no longer to perform the greatest number of baptisms possible, to ensure accountability of Easter communions, to settle wedding ceremonies, or to play, as a priest, to the village notable. [...] Specifically, it is not as much a question of doing a lot of things as per being and living."[48] Africa's commitment to the Lord is therefore an invitation to rediscover the essence, meaning, beauty, and truth of being a Christian.

Rediscovering the Truth of the Name "Christian" in Africa

The name "Christian" bears a particular mystery in that it reflects the identity, the deep and dynamic being of one who has received Jesus Christ as Lord and Saviour. Benedict XVI thinks that a Christian identity stems from an experience, a personal encounter with the Risen One: "at the origin of being Christian there is not an ethical decision or a great idea, but the encounter with an event, a Person, who gives life a new perspective and thus its decisive orientation."[49]

Ratzinger believes that[50] rediscovering the truth of the name "Christian" is first and foremost delving into one's origins. In this regard, the Book of Act of the Apostles (11, 26) attests that this name was given for the first time to the Disciples of Christ in Antioch.

It goes without saying that the background to this name was ironical. In the early centuries of the Church, and in accordance with the Roman law at the time, the name "Christian" was synonymous to a punishable offence because it was considered a conspiratorial sect. This state of affairs worsened from Hadrian, under whose reign being a Christian clearly meant being guilty. Despite the potential danger of the name, Christians of the time of St. Ignatius of Antioch took it for granted, not without pride and dignity. Hence their attachment to "spirituality of martyrdom" as the perfect form of imitating Christ.

Hatred for mankind and debauchery are among the serious crimes *(flagitia)* of which the Christians of the time were accused. In his defence of the Christian community, "Ignatius plays with words, long preserved in Christian apologetics. According to Greek phonetics, the word 'chrestos' (good) was, and still is, pronounced with 'i': christos. Ignatius uses this pronunciation when, to the phrase 'let us learn to live in accordance with Christianity' (christianismos), he proposed these words: 'we are not insensible to his goodness' (chrestotès, pronounced as christotès). The conspiracy of 'christos' is a plot to be 'chrestos,' a conspiracy to do good."[51] "Following this reasoning, Tertullian, the Carthaginian, a century later affirmed that the word Christ is derived from the expression to be good."[52]

In fact, to get the truth of the name "Christian" in Ratzinger-ian theological hermeneutics is to learn to know and to know how to learn that "Christianity is a conspiracy for good."[53] All those called "Christian" in Africa are called upon to live this commit-ment for good. The strength of Christians in Africa depends not on their numbers, let alone on their lively and sophisticated ritu-als, but on their ability to "reject that which is unworthy of the name and to seek that which does it honour,"[54] that is, to practice good relentlessly in all spheres of social, political, and economic life. This is how they will fight the corruption syndrome and other negative values whose metastases are eating up our societies and our banana democracies governed by life presidents. This is how they will contribute to building "new heavens and a new earth" (Rev 21:1) on the continent. For Africa to truly become—as Bene-dict XVI says—"the spiritual lung of the world," she is therefore called to conspire for good and breathe love; otherwise she will get tired and expire. Love in truth remains the only power to achieve this.

Conclusion

Ultimately, in the Joseph Ratzinger/Benedict XVI approach, the concepts of "love" and "truth" have an unprecedented theologi-cal depth. They are rooted in the mystery of the incarnation and are illuminated in the mystery of redemption. They are gifts from God and as such they constitute a mission entrusted to all hu-manity, to the whole Church, and to all those who declare them-selves Christians. These two concepts are so connected that their real value, or the theological density of which they are bearers, lies precisely in this interaction. Love without truth degrades sub-stantially into pure emotionalism with all that this entails in terms of counter-production on a relational, social, and political scale, while truth without love is sterile in every respect. In the center of a continent balkanized by narrow-minded individualisms, engulfed by the venom of tribalism, caught in the clutches of political, economic, and ideological monsters of all kinds, the Christians of Africa are called to take the right measure of their natural and supernatural responsibilities. This demand requires the efficient rediscovery of the mystique of the name they bear, that is to say, conspirators for good, for love in truth.

Benedict XVI and Hope:
From a Forgotten Africa to an Africa
of Authentic Hope

Pr. Stephen Kizito Forbi, S.J.

"Go the opposite direction; do not listen to the many voices that propagate models of life based on arrogance and violence, success at all costs, appearance and material possessions."
(Benedict XVI)

Introduction

In the course of his trips to Africa, Benedict XVI has been examining the ups and downs of Africa in order to better map out a future for the continent. The future at stake concerns, among other things, the future of the family, the future of the priesthood, and, in particular, the future of the African as a man. Benedict XVI makes hope the guiding principle of the historical dynamics of this future. During the *ad limina* visit of the Central African Bishops on 2 June 2007 Benedict XVI asked for hope for Africa, "I strongly hope," the pope said, "that Africa will no longer be forgotten in this world of profound change, and that an authentic hope will arise for the peoples of this continent." (Zénit, edition of 5 June 2007) In the history of humanity, philosophers like Nietzsche and his nihilism have considered it a great illusion. However, in the face of rising despair in the world in general and the challenging, debilitating, and dehumanizing situation of weakness in Africa, in particular, there is a renewed zeal for the priority of hope.

This presentation handles the following issue: Is Africa a forgotten land or a land of authentic hope? In a world where Africa is in the spotlight when things go wrong, *Africae Munus* is an invitation and a challenge to have an alternative look at Africa. It is in this sense that one should review its introduction which, far from being the Afro-pessimism to which the media have accustomed us, presents a positive image of Africa. *Africae Munus* moves away from the traditional approach of presenting only a battered Africa, "a humanity that seems to be in crisis of faith and hope." (AM, §13)

It takes the path of the "vision" that calls out to Africa: "*Africa, rise up and live actively in hope!*" *Africae Munus* portrays a positive view that recognizes the maturity of the continent (AM, §4) and sees it as a land of promise (AM, §5) despite the scars of the past (AM, §9). As a result of her intellectual, cultural, and religious heritage, Africa is also a continent of hope (AM, §§9.11.13.) This is to be preserved, explored, and made known. It is a continent of immense wealth (AM, §§24.79) to be exploited for the good of all.

Africae Munus is a treatise on political theology because through this Exhortation "the Church asks herself what impact she can have, by virtue of her faith and the means of action she gives it, on the life of the city and its forms of organization, within the framework of a secularized society" (Gagey & Souletie, 2001: 68). Unlike the political theology of liberation in Latin America, which is based on a struggle line, the political theology of *Africae Munus* is based on a promotion or development line of homo africanus. This presentation highlights this orientation. It is divided into two sections: the obstacles to Africa's development, on the one hand, and the assets for Africa's development, on the other.

The Forgotten Africa

Benedict XVI's philosophy of hope is rooted in suffering: "*in every suffering there arises the star of hope*" (Spe Salvi). Thus, to identify the hope that is needed for Africa, there is need to analyze its anxieties and master its causes and questions. In short, it is necessary to be aware of the "*traumas and conflicts*" that Africa has experienced

(AM §11). According to Benedict XVI, the evils that undermine Africa are the *"local or regional wars, massacres, and genocides that take place on the continent"* (speech in Cameroon). He thinks that the violence visible in Africa is an eloquent testimony to the fact that the African way of living together is characterized by a background of ruptures, divisions, and the absence of "conviviality." It is, therefore, more appropriate to talk of living apart in Africa. To do this, we will expose belligerence, the anthropological crisis, and new forms of slavery, among others, as factors of the African decline.

Violent and Bloody Conflicts

In-depth studies have carefully documented the deconstruction of living together or *"local or regional wars"* in Africa. In a study about the factiousness of African local decline, Forbi Stephen Kizito records 267 coups or attempted coups in Africa between 1960–1990, several Constitutional coups—the forced changes that break the presidential term limit lock—as in Cameroon in October 2011, Senegal in 2012, etc. (Forbi, 2017: 232–43). In addition, Pascal Gauchon and Jean-Marc Huissoud make a conflictual African interpretation in their book entitled *Les 100 lieux de la géopolitique (The 100 geopolitical areas).* In this empirical study, the authors emphasize the 100 areas of armed conflict in Africa such as Sudan, Somalia, etc. (Gauchon & Huissoud, 2008: 7). According to them, *"political tribalism"* and ethnicity are responsible for *"the genesis and outbreak of conflicts in Africa"* (Gauchon & Huissoud, 2008: 57.) One reason for the above-mentioned conflicts is poor governance or political slavery. In post-independence Africa, some leaders made the leadership of their countries a means of enriching themselves and their families. The Arab Spring and other similar conflicts on the continent are consequences of the disastrous management of the *res publica*. Once elected to office, these leaders confiscate funds for their own interests and only remember the citizens they represent on the eve of the next election. Their re-election is obtained through bribing of voters— a morally unacceptable practice. This manipulation is a new form of slavery because what is rightfully the electorate's is now given to them as an incentive and a buying of their conscience, which they receive on their knees.

Talking of *"massacres and genocides"* that are spreading in Africa, the Pope is certainly referring to the Rwandan genocide. From 6 April to 4 July 1994, eight hundred thousand (800,000) Rwandans, mostly Tutsis, were massacred by Rwandans, mostly Hutus. The Rwandan genocide, which took place in 100 days, holds the sad record of the fastest genocide in history. Some explanations for the genocide can be traced back to colonial times with the educational bias in favour of the Tutsis at the expense of the Hutus who were forced to hard labor on the land. The animosity between these two ethnic groups never died down at independence in 1960. On the contrary, it kept on growing. Exiled citizens tried to return to the country several times, but the repression was bloody. A civil war broke out in 1990. The attack on the Rwandan president, Juvenal Habyarimana, on 6 April 1994, marked the beginning of the genocide.

The above is ample evidence of the relevance of the Pope's statement that Africa is experiencing trauma and conflict. Several initiatives have been taken by local governments and the international community to appease people, and reduce resentment and frustration in conflict areas. The Pope is part of this optimistic attitude that the negative situation in Africa does not have to be. According to him, these disastrous events *"must challenge us in a special manner,"* in other words, they must challenge Africans in the first place and others as well. The long and painful path of death must give a chance to peace, justice, and reconciliation.

The Anthropological Crisis

From the introduction of *Africae Munus*, Benedict XVI clearly identifies the problem of Africa: the African continent is facing an *"anthropological crisis"* (AM §11). Without developing a doctrinal exposition on the dignity of man, the Pope happily describes this meltdown as follows: *"Man is shaped by his past... Africa is experiencing a cultural shock that is undermining the age-old foundations of social life and sometimes makes it difficult to meet modernity"* (AM §11). In his speech at the Nsimalen airport in Yaoundé, he also underlined this plundering of the African as *"the situation of dehumanisation and oppression that plagues the African people"* (speech in Cameroon.) In concrete terms, what is this anthropological crisis that weighs on and threatens the life of the African? The anthropological crisis can be explained, among other things, through impoverishment, mediocrity, and globalization.

The challenges, which pose *"heavy threats"* (AM §72) to human life in Africa, can be summarized in a social fact that Engelbert Mveng calls *"anthropological impoverishment"* (Mveng, 1985: 203). Through this concept, he refers to the extraneous causes of the African misfortune, which are the crimes of the slave trade and the misdeeds of colonization. According to him, *"colonisation was a system of anthropological impoverishment, enslavement, and dependence"* (Mveng, 1985: 207). These two phenomena have impeded the human development of the African and hindered his impetus to live a full human life. They constituted *"the sheer negation of the humanity of the Negro-African"* (Mveng, 1985: 203). Anthropological annihilation is not seen from a quantitative point of view. It refers to a socio-economic reality of lack and deprivation that negatively affects human capacities. It *"is a precarious, fragile condition...This situation embraces man, every man, all men, at all levels"* (Mveng, 1985: 201). The African is, somehow, reduced to a state of "homelessness." *"Anthropological poverty"* therefore describes the condition of the African who is chronically and sustainably deprived of resources, means, choices, security, and the necessary power to enjoy a satisfactory living standard. The indicators of this human insecurity are traced in existential terms as follows: Africa's absence from global decision-making bodies, inferiority in bilateral discussions, spiritual emptiness, lack of educational infrastructure, moral decadence, indebtedness, cultural deprivation, dependence, corruption, etc. (Mveng, 1985: 211 & 213).

Engelbert Mveng's novelty lies in underlining the fact that in Africa poverty is not only a socio-economic issue, it is not only a question of "having," but above all a problem of "being." It is the indigence of being, the eminent and lasting vulnerability and fragility of the African being. *Anthropological poverty* is therefore not only a sociological observation of African misfortunes, but also questioning the conditions for sustainable human development in Africa.

Ebénézer Njoh-Mouelle describes the impoverishment of the African as *"mediocrity,"* in his book titled *De la médiocrité à l'excellence* (Njoh-Mouelle, 1998) (From Mediocrity to Excellence). Mediocrity brings together an assortment of obstacles intrinsic to Africa that hurt the African: misery, mediocrity, and Africanism. What is the nature, basis, and meaning of each of these impediments to African development? *Misery* is a state of extreme poverty, a situation where people are subjected to all sorts of ills such as disease, malnutrition, and undernourishment. This can be described as *physiological misery. Psychological misery* also exists, which is man's inability to exercise his higher mental functions.

Ebénézer Njoh-Mouelle meditates on African misery in two aspects, namely material, biophysical, or subjective misery, and spiritual, or objective misery. The material misery from which the African suffers:

> Has the effect not only of maintaining a physical debility favoring contamination but also of diminishing intellectual capacities and annihilating effort [...]. In other words, happiness is not when one has enough to eat daily, but perhaps because, by eating, one suppresses a certain number of handicaps to total self-fulfilment (Njoh-Mouelle, 1998: 27).

African misery is also spiritual and "is called ignorance, superstition, illiteracy. It is the real one, the one that maintains or reduces man to a state of sub-humanity through alienation and lack of freedom that it entails." (Njoh-Mouelle, 1998: 30) Ignorance and superstition as a mode of explanation are synonymous to abandonment to the forces of nature. This irrationality is dehumanizing because it demonstrates intellectual poverty and is a violation of the essential attributes of man, which are reason and freedom. To liberate the African from poverty, investment in the intellectual formation the human resources is a necessity. But the sad fact is the appalling development of human misery in Africa can be seen through wars, tribalism, genocide, and low wages.

Mediocrity is another impediment to African development. In the conventional sense, it is the state of being average. For example, mediocre wealth stands between opulence and poverty. By metonymy, mediocrity refers to competence or performance below what one would be entitled to expect. Ebénézer Njoh-Mouelle sees the African as the man in the middle, i.e., without personality. He is lost in the crowd. Secondly, African mediocrity reflects selfishness, greed, and the unbridled pursuit of illicit, insolent, and ostentatious wealth. These anti-social, anti-ethical, and anti-humanistic practices constitute serious impediments to African development.

> Today in Africa, the indiscriminate and indefinite accumulation of material wealth is done by certain categories of persons as if it were a question of doing everything possible to prevent others from accessing these same goods, out of meanness and not out of necessity. (Njoh-Mouelle, 2002a: 64)

Mediocrity is an anti-value and an impediment to the development of the African.

Africanism is another brake that dehumanizes the African. Ebénézer Njoh-Mouelle identifies two types of Africanisms. First, the Africanism of non-Africans (Europeans) which "is far from being a concern for the revaluation of African affairs... [but which wants] to take advantage of the unknown and unrecognized Africa" (Njoh-Mouelle, 2002b:11). A certain Africanism exists of Africans, i.e., thinking of Africans whose research focuses on African issues. This is the Africanism that hinders the African's achievement because this Africanism turns the African into a stranger to himself. According to our philosopher:

> It is a fact that most African researchers do not yet enjoy this independence of mind. It is as if they are only looking for what they have already found. And what they have found in the first place, in full subjectivity, is something very simple: everything that Africa has, everything that Africa has done is holy, just, and good, in the way of the commandments of the Lord. *(Njoh-Mouelle, 2002b: 16–17)*

The Africanism of Africans is static, uncritical, and narcissistic because it glorifies all African traditional practices and values. These African thinkers have forgotten that *"one does not return to one's roots to stay there indefinitely"* (Njoh-Mouelle, 2002b: 56). According to Njoh-Mouelle, the self-laudatory and narcissistic discourse of Africanists is counter-progressive. The author expresses the hindrance of this forward-looking discourse of Africans in the form of two questions: *"Where does our creativity lie today?"* (Njoh-Mouelle, 2002b : 23) and *"How can we indeed progress if, a priori, it is decreed that what was done yesterday, the previous situation, already represents the golden age and near perfection?"* (Njoh-Mouelle, 2002b: 30)

The African evil can be explained by internal and external factors. *Ad intra,* some philosophers believe that fetishism, superstition, mediocrity, Africanism, and other societal practices constitute obstacles to the fulfilment of the humanity of the African man. *Ad extra,* Engelbert Mveng attributes African immobility to neo-colonialism. The African who appeals to Africa and the Church in Africa, according to Benedict XVI, is the African who lives in a contrasting negative situation, a situation where what obtains is what should not be, the African in a situation of powerlessness of the being. It is in the face of this painful reality of the advent of a sustainable human development of the African that the pope's thoughtful approach is meant to challenge.

New Forms of Slavery

Another challenge for Africa is epistemological. It is a question of the memory of her wounded past. The Pontiff is not left indifferent to this wound, which today is taking on new forms. In remembering this past of Africa, the Pope notes that, "Africa keeps the painful memory of the scars left by fratricidal struggles between ethnic groups, by slavery and by colonization. Even today, the continent is confronted with rivalries, new forms of slavery, and colonization." (AM §9)

By referring to the *"painful memory"* of Africa, the Pope is fighting against the anesthesia of the memory of those who want to deny the sensitive issues of transatlantic slavery. In other words, he attests to the survival of the slavery issue, which cyclically comes up as an object of complaint at the local, national, and/or international level.

The new forms of slavery or modern slavery in Africa refer "to the mechanisms of slavery that are reproduced, in an altered form, despite the undeniable changes that abolition (at the beginning of the 20th century) and emancipation brought to the slave system." (Lecocq & Hahonou, 2015: 184) It is the exploitation of vulnerable persons. The Pontiff uses this expression to affirm that in Africa, slavery is not a thing of the past but is still practised today. Despite the independence of African countries, despite the liberation from previous slavery and colonial domination, Africa continues to experience new forms of slavery. It is new in the sense that these slaves are not registered in the stock exchange as was the case during the classical slavery period, but it is still slavery because it is the trade in humans. The visible and tangible forms of modern slavery are child labor and child soldiers, to mention only two.

"Forced" child labor. This category also includes child slavery. With the economic collapse and the high cost of living in Africa, a new phenomenon of "professional" recruitment of children as domestic servants is being experienced. We have "*shrewd businessmen [who] make a lucrative business out of recruiting people, especially*

140

women, for domestic work in cities and/or foreign countries." (Mucunguzi) The harmful consequences of domestic slavery are numerous. These include the risk of violence and abuse, the loss of schooling for these young people who have to give all their time to their exploiters, and the perpetuation of poverty because child labor is a brake or barrier to development. Among the reasons for child labor are: the precarious economic situation of parents who are obliged to send their children to work, parents who are poorly or badly informed about the risks of child labor or the benefits of education, the interests of employers who consider children to be easy and *"cheap"* labor, emergency situations such as natural disasters or conflicts which put families in a precarious situation and, as a result, increase the vulnerability of children.

Child soldiers. The involvement of children aged between fourteen and seventeen years in armed conflicts in Africa has increased within the last decade. According to Sabrina Myre (Myre, 2015) eight countries were accused of direct or indirect recruitment of child soldiers between 2014 and 2015. Five of these eight countries are in Africa. In Nigeria, besides the Boko Haram which forcibly recruits children into its ranks, the Civilian Joint Task Force, a government-backed self-defence militia, has one thousand nine hundred and forty-seven (1,947) child soldiers in its ranks. In the Democratic Republic of Congo, armed groups such as the *Mai Mai* and the *FDLR* have five thousand (5,000) recruited child soldiers. The Somali National Army and its allies, such as the *Ahlu Sunna Wal Jama'a*, use two thousand three hundred (2,300) child soldiers. In South Sudan, twelve thousand (12,000) child soldiers fight in the ranks of the South Sudan People's Liberation Army. In Sudan, children are recruited as support for the regular army (UN Secretary General, 2019). Among the causes of child soldier recruitment are the prolonged duration of conflicts, the blurring of lines between civilian and military targets, and the proliferation of weapons. Describing these child soldiers as "future barbarians" and "killing machines" only serves as a cautionary statement of Africa's bleak future (World Bank, 2002.)

Africa of Genuine Hope

The pope suggests that, for Africa to be a land of authentic hope, state authorities, traditional leaders, and all people of good will have to eliminate the causes of violent conflict by investing in "reconciliation, justice, and peace." (AM §§ 94.111) For Benedict XVI these three virtues are intimately intertwined and are part of the liberating prospect for Africa. His philosophy on these three concepts is not born of astonishment or admiration, as is commonly taught in philosophy, but of the experience of suffering and the "lack of reconciliation" that plague Africa.

The Concept and Basis of Hope:
The Concept of Hope

Benedict XVI does not directly define the concept of hope. However, from what has been said above, a comprehensive understanding of this concept can be identified. The act of hoping is related to, but distinct from, desire, expectation, and hope. Although these concepts have in common chronology of existence, they each have their specificity. Desire, in general, is the search for an object that one imagines, or knows, to be a source of satisfaction. Philosophy looks at desire in two ways: desire as lack, and desire as the power of affirmation and creation. Firstly, philosophers consider desire as a simple need accompanied by suffering and a feeling of lack. Another characteristic of desire is its insatiable nature. Desire always refuses to be satisfied, because as soon as it is satisfied it rushes back. It maintains an ambivalent relationship with its object; moving from object to object, desire is unlimited, condemned to radical dissatisfaction. Plato, in *The Banquet,* (199a-201d,) agrees with this approach to desire as lack and negativity. Thus, the first philosophical approach to desire inscribes human existence in a temporal manner, i.e., the opening up of consciousness to the dimension of time, to the transcendence that carries man towards a beyond, towards an elsewhere that is always brought back. Man is thus a being of appetite, i.e.,

142

a being in movement consisting in carrying himself towards something, in seeking to grasp it.

To define desire by negativity, lack, or privation does not exhaust the meaning of this ambivalent concept. Other philosophers, such as Spinoza, have emphasized the value and the positive nature of desire. Instead of thinking of desire as subordinate to the value of the desired object, it is instead thought of as a producer of value. Spinoza thinks that, instead of the pre-existing object determining the desire, it is rather the desire that precedes the object and produces it. He says *"we desire it not because we judge it to be good, but we judge it to be good because we desire it"* (Spinoza, *Ethics*, Book III.)

For Benedict XVI, hope at the anthropological level theorizes what it is to be human or to be man. The Pontiff believes that man is a being fundamentally open to transcendence, a being on the way to that which is beyond him, "the essential situation of man, the situation from which all his contradictions and hopes arise. Somehow, we desire life itself, true life, which does not end in death; but, at the same time, we do not know what it is towards which we are being driven." (Benedict XVI, 2007: 12) Hope pushes man towards a reality that is beyond him. It is man's *not-yet*.

Hope, according to Benedict XVI, is rooted in a temporal manner of existence of Africa and of the African. It is a plea to influence national policies and legislation to act on all fronts to "uplift" the African continent. Reliable and authentic hope is the "tool" that enables the African to face her present. Negatively, hope "is not the avoidance of suffering, the flight from pain, which heals man, but the capacity to accept tribulations and to mature through them, to find meaning in them." (Spe Salvi §37) It is the support of real life. Thus, the foundation and the challenge of the Pope's philosophy is not a sterile academic approach to hope, but a practical one that aims to "transform suffering through the strength of hope." (Spe Salvi §37) Hope is an opening of reason to the search for meaning that goes beyond the current negative hope.

The Basis of African Hope

Few thinkers exist who can truly be called philosophers of hope. Benedict XVI has made of it the driving principle of the entire African existence and the future of Africans. He approaches the theme in the light of an ontology of *not-yet*, or *not-yet-being*, as the implicit foundation of the act of hope. Africa's dehumanising situation is not the experience of a nihilistic despair but of a black experience. Thus, the dehumanising situation is for her, not a fatality but a "challenge." (AM§§5.21) In *Africae Munus* Benedict XVI proposes, among other justifications that legitimise African hope, "*the rich intellectual, cultural, and religious heritage of Africa,*" (AM §9), inclusive of dialogue as a socio-political foundation, (AM §11) spirituality, (AM §13) and education. (AM §74)

Despite the difficulties and the great pandemics that plague Africa, the Pope sees many reasons for hope and urges Africans to maintain their joy of living. "I also see a reason for hope in the rich intellectual, cultural, and religious heritage of Africa. She desires preserving, exploring it further and making it known to the world. This is an important and positive contribution." (AM §9) The Pope is not telling a success story through this statement. Rather, he is challenging Africans, expressing a wish and giving a prescription. For the Pope, African intelligence, culture, and religion must be considered as indispensable principles for the reconstruction of Africa.

The pontiff recognises that "the (African) man is shaped by his past" and that the cultural and social foundations of his life are shaken. However, he finds the "paths of hope by establishing a dialogue between members of the religious, social, political, economic, cultural, and scientific components." (AM §11) An inclusive intra-African dialogue or "African palaver" is, for the Pontiff, a foundation of hope. It is an indispensable instrument in the quest for peace in Africa and in a crisis-stricken world. A conversation that excludes no one and aims to include all sensitive issues, so as to include everyone. This inclusive dialogue centres around the service of peace, justice, and reconciliation. Without dialogue, lived in a climate of mutual listening and respect for the other, relations will remain tense and distorted. By choosing inclusive dialogue, the Pontiff hopes to contribute to improving relations between the different conflicting components in Africa.

Dialogue is, in essence, the rebuilding of trust, which the Pope calls the indicators of hope. For a dialogue to be successful it needs a reliable process consisting of specific preconditions: credible facilitation, sufficient commitment, adequate leadership, inclusiveness, etc., and strategies that will serve as leverage: building productive coalitions, setting up implementation infrastructures, guarantees, and follow-up mechanisms, etc. (cf. AM §§24.44) The African dialogue should not be seen as an isolated event, but as part of a long-term transition. The dialogue must consider memory work and transitional justice. The full inclusion of all concerned parties in the negotiation of agreements reduces the risk of sabotage during the implementation phase.

African hope also has a spiritual foundation. According to the Pope, spirituality is "the precious treasure ... the spiritual lung for a humanity that seems to be in a faith and hope crisis." (AM§13) Through this metaphor of the *lung*, the Pope expresses his optimism for Africa. God's springtime remains with her, if the continent continues to suffer. The reason for this optimism is that Africa is not yet affected by the great moral depravities, namely practical materialism and relativistic and nihilistic thinking, which have affected the West. Africa is still untouched by these two dangerous pathologies. The fact that it continues to defend family values and reject spiritual toxic waste such as the pressure to enact homosexuality laws or the politicisation of religious fundamentalism, for example, as a condition of financial aid to Africans, makes Africa a land of hope. Another reason why Africa is a "spiritual lung for humanity" is the demographic shift between the West and Africa: "While Africa, particularly, records an increasing number of Catholics, Europe sees its number decrease." It is incumbent on Africa to be aware of this fact and to be prepared to assume responsibility for the conduct of the Church affairs and African affairs.

Africae Munus recognises that "Africa, like the rest of the world, is experiencing an educational crisis" (AM §75). Illiteracy:

> is one of the major impediments to development. It is a plague equal to that of pandemics. Although it does not kill directly, it actively contributes to the marginalisation of the individual—which is a form of social death—and makes it impossible for him to access knowledge. Educating an individual is to make him a full member of the res publica, to the construction of which he can contribute. (AM §76)

To remedy this crisis, Africa needs a comprehensive and integrated programme that combines faith and reason. Education, which cannot be reduced to its sole academic dimension, must instill in citizens a sense of life. In short, this education must prepare them to better face life. Thus, the Pontiff insists on the priority of education and defends the rights of citizens to an educational project, which cannot be the responsibility of the State alone.

The Signs of Hope

What are the stars of the scoreboards or observable indicators of hope? What are the activities or states of life that assure us that the efforts and strategies of the workers of hope are operational? Among the indicators of hope proposed by the pope, we will focus on the three pillars of reconciliation, justice, and peace on the one hand, and the emergence of a *homo africanus novus* on the other.

The Three Pillars of Reconciliation, Justice, and Peace

According to Benedict XVI, the three pillars of reconciliation, justice, and peace are three fundamental signal concepts of the materialisation of hope. They intertwine and are a conceptual network of meaning. They can be distinguished intellectually in an abstract manner, but not dissociated. The pope expresses these ideas as follows: The Lord says, "Peace is what I leave with you, it is my own peace that I give you." He adds:

> "I do not do it as the world does." (Jn 14, 27) The peace of men that is obtained without justice is illusory and ephemeral. Human justice that does not stem from reconciliation through the "truth of love" (Eph 4:15) remains incomplete; it is not authentic justice. It is the love of truth—"the whole truth" to which only the Spirit can lead us (cf. Jn 16:13)—that traces the path that all human justice must follow in order to lead to the restoration of the bonds of brotherhood in the "human family, a community of peace," reconciled with God through Christ. Justice is not a matter of disembodiment. It is necessarily rooted in human coherence. Charity that does not respect justice and the rights of all is wrong. (AM §18)

However, precedence and unconditionality of reconciliation dominate other factors. Reconciliation is critical to achieving lasting peace, political stability, and a just society in Africa. Reconciliation is the *conditio sine qua non* for peace and justice. It is "the essential precondition for building justice and peace." (AM §19) "Genuine reconciliation brings about lasting peace in society." (AM §21) Further, he says, "Peace and justice are born from reconciliation." (AM §99)

Reconciliation

In what way is reconciliation a marker of hope? Reconciliation is an awareness that goes both upstream and downstream. Upstream, it is the return to the absence of hope in Africa's past. We did this earlier in the study of African fragility. Downstream, it is an awareness of the hope, through which the situation is reversible. In this section, this latter aspect of reconciliation will be our focus. Benedict XVI thinks, "Reconciliation is a pre-political concept and reality, which precisely for this reason is of the greatest importance for the political task itself." (AM §19)

Reconciliation as a Concept

A concept is a general idea that brings together the common characteristics of all elements belonging to the same category. Reconciliation is both an *a posteriori* concept and an *a priori* concept. Because it is derived from experience, it is an *a posteriori* concept. Reconciliation, as an empirical fact, is the effort to leave behind the weight of a tragic past through an overcoming energy. It is an *a priori* concept because it is the category of understanding or the condition for understanding the concepts of peace and justice.

Reconciliation is an equivocal concept. Reconciliation can be defined as the restoration of a relationship that engenders "enough trust" to stop dividing. (Rossoux, 2014: 6) In this regard, reconciliation brings divergent world views together and leads to an identical "universe of understanding." It can be seen as the antithesis of violence and its devastation (Rossoux, 2014: 23) as per revenge, which threatens all parties involved. Closeness and, ultimately, reconciliation are systematically preferred. In this light, the notion of reconciliation is often identified with that of peace. It is in this context that Benedict XVI should be understood, for whom reconciliation is not just a summary of visions for Africa, but also an ideal end of Africa's violently disrupted history.

Reconciliation is not just a post-conflict issue. It can occur at anytime and anywhere. Successful reconciliation can contribute to peace, prevent the recurrence of conflicts, and break the cycle of impunity. However, it is not a substitute for justice or amnesty. Experience shows that no panacea, no single model or practical roadmap for reconciliation exists. Given the complexity of different conflicts, reconciliation must be based on a local approach. This is why reconciliation in Africa is *a problem-solving tree*. The strength of the concept of the *problem-solving tree* is that it symbolises with simplicity a whole set of civic mechanisms that function as a political and social kaleidoscope. The objective of this institution is to create or maintain social links, to learn, to discuss important decisions to be made, or to settle disputes.

In a nutshell, reconciliation is a process and an outcome. It aims to improve relations between actors. The issues at stake in reconciliation are norms and values that are intertwined with an epistemological perspective.

Reconciliation as a Pre-political Reality

If we consider the "pre-political" concept in the context of the state of nature, it will mean the situation in which people found themselves before the institution of society and its laws. In other words, the situation in which people would have found themselves if society did not exist. Philosophers appraise this concept in different and contradictory ways. This is the case with Thomas Hobbes, for whom the pre-political state or state of nature is a state of war of each man against all. (Cf. Hobbes, 1962) Competition for scarce resources, selfish and conflicting tendencies, drive men to destroy and subjugate each other. Without a power capable of keeping them all in check, men remain in a state of permanent struggle for self-preservation, where fear and insecurity reign. In the real words of Thomas Hobbes, "continual fear and dread of violent death; the life which man lives is solitary, miserable, unpleasant, savage, and short." (Hobbes, 1962: 143) The counterpoint to Hobbes is taken by Rousseau, for whom the state of nature is a state of peace. "I see him satiating himself under an oak tree, quenching his thirst at the first stream, finding his bed at the foot of a tree which provides him rest, and there his needs are satisfied." (Rousseau, 1971: 162) It is in the likes of Rousseau's policies that the pope understands the concept of "pre-politics." The importance of reconciliation in Benedict XVI's political endeavour is obvious when he states that:

If the power of reconciliation is not created at heart, the inner presupposition for political commitment to peace will be missing. At the Synod, the Church pastors committed themselves to this inner purification of man, which is the essential precondition for building justice and peace. This purification and inner maturity towards true humanity cannot exist without God. (AM §19)

According to the pope, reconciliation is an inner drive that makes the new co-existence in Africa possible.

The Basis of Reconciliation

Love is the source, impulse, or origin of reconciliation. "Reconciliation, therefore, has its source in this love." (AM §20) Choosing love as the basis or explanatory reason for reconciliation, Benedict XVI attests that reconciliation is not a matter of law or morality. Reconciliation is not solitude but relationship. Reconciliation is based on otherness, not loneliness. Love, which is being-with and being-for, is intrinsic and even identical to reconciliation because reconciliation without love is not authentic; it is only an appearance. (Cf. Benedict XVI, 2005) It is this love that Benedict XVI refers to as a *"communion between God and man"* and *"a reconciled humanity."* (AM §20) According to Benedict XVI, then, reconciliation is not a passion but a desire, a love-search, a dynamism towards the other. The purpose of love-seeking is the much desired "community of love" for Africa. Love is a selfless gift of self, modelled on the sacrificial love of Christ. Love-reconciliation means overcoming the challenges of ethnicity, tribalism, regionalism, racial segregation, exclusion in all its forms, etc. (AM §39)

Reconciliation is not based on forgetting or erasing the "fault" but on accountability, i.e., the ability or capacity to blame the wrongdoer.

Reconciliation cannot take place without memorization: To be effective, this reconciliation will have to be accompanied by a courageous and honest act: the search for those responsible for these conflicts, those who ordered the crimes and who engage in all sorts of trafficking, and the establishment of their responsibility. Victims have a right to truth and justice. It is important now, and in the future, to purify the memory in order to build a better society where such tragedies are not repeated. (AM §21)

Desmond Tutu also referred to reconciliation as memory work, without which it would not be built on solid foundations. He writes, "True reconciliation exposes horrors, abuses, pain and the truth. It can sometimes even aggravate the situation. It is a risky venture, but one worth trying. For, in the end, it is the face-to-face encounter with reality that brings about true healing." (Tutu, 2000: 30)

Reconciliation, as the power to release the agent from his act, goes hand in hand with accountability. In a nutshell, reconciliation according to Benedict XVI refers to two different realities given its binomial constitution. On the one hand, it is the guilty party or the person who is at the origin of the wound in Africa, and the wounded party which is Africa. A constitutive element, and also the issue of reconciliation for Benedict XVI, is the causes of the action of the guilty party. Reconciliation highlights the existence of a dilemma between peace and justice: Should peace (impunity) prevail over justice in Africa? African states, as well as the agents of reconciliation mentioned by the Pope, face difficult choices in balancing the requirements of justice and reconciliation with the political realities of combating impunity.

African Beacons of Reconciliation

This call for reconciliation by the Pope did not fall on deaf ears in an Africa that was already on the way to reconciliation. In order to end Apartheid in South Africa, Nelson Mandela showed a lot of firmness and will to impose and make his still sceptical people accept wiping out all the atrocities committed during the Apartheid period in favour of peace. For his country to survive, it was necessary to forgive and reconcile. Thus, on 19 July 1995, he created the *Truth and Reconciliation Commission*, chaired by Desmond Tutu, Archbishop of Cape Town. In Rwanda, the government thought it necessary to create the GACACA (18 June 2002) alongside the TPI, which provides for dialogue and a meeting between the perpetrators and the victims, thus allowing for possible reconciliation in the future. For the Rwandans, it is not enough to judge and condemn, but also and above all to forgive and reconcile. In Côte d'Ivoire the National Commission was called the Dialogue, Truth, and Reconciliation Commission (2011–2014) and its mission was to initiate a collective and impartial reflection on a peaceful cohabitation. This shows that, for Africans, reconciliation is supra-moral and supra-legal and prevents the use of violence and confrontation.

If reconciliation does not consist in ignoring the evil deed or in denying its existence, but in untying the agent from his deed, the lights and shadows of the papal writing will become clear. *Africae Munus* is well loaded with African misfortune: local wars, genocides, slavery, the dehumanisation of the African, a crisis of values characterised by a domination of individualism, or the abandonment of the community logic based on solidarity and living together, etc. The wounded or traumatised being is well known: it is Africa. "However, the guilty being is silenced or assumed through expressions such as 'reconciled humanity.'" (AM §§ 20 & 30) Is this silence to be read as a dissociation "between fault and self, between guilt and ipseity?" (Ricœur, 2000: 604) Positively, the concept of reconciliation is articulated in a binomial structure of forgiveness and promise. "Reconciliation overcomes crises, restores the dignity of people, and paves the way for development and lasting peace between peoples at all levels." (AM §21) Hannah Arendt also agrees on the "receptive" nature when she remarks that if "we were [not] forgiven, delivered from the consequences of what we have done, our capacity to act would be as if locked in a single act from which we could never recover;

we would remain forever victims of its consequences." (Arendt, 1983: 302–03) While revenge confines the process of reconciliation to a natural, automatic, and negative reaction, reconciliation creates a space of unpredictable novelty. Reconciliation does not react to evil action, in the sense that it is not conditioned by it. It innovates because it "binds up and heals wounded hearts." (AM §155)

Peace and Justice

Benedict XVI does not clearly define justice. Rather, he is satisfied when he describes it as a lived experience in the African socio-political, socio-economic, and socio-cultural contexts. He does not fall into the narrow view that peace and justice are in competition either. According to this line of thought, peace and justice are two successive and autonomous events. The assumption is that peace is only about ending violent conflict in Africa, followed by a concern with prosecution or criminal accountability—punitive justice. This extreme view ignores the close link between peace and justice. Benedict takes an integrative approach and treats peace and justice as two fundamental and simultaneous elements in ending violence and preventing its recurrence in Africa.

Justice, in Benedict's view, goes beyond the minimum required by distributive justice, namely the demand for compensation for wrongs suffered and the demand for punishment for those who have perpetrated wrongs. Justice, which should be called loving justice, goes beyond legalism and gives human justice a new horizon.

> Divine justice offers human justice, which is always limited and imperfect, the horizon towards which it must aim in order to be accomplished. It also makes us aware of our own need for forgiveness and God's friendship. This is what we experience in the sacraments of Penance and the Eucharist, which flow from the action of Christ. This action introduces us into a

justice in which we receive much more than we had the right to expect, because in Christ, charity is the summary of the Law (Rm 13, 8–10). Through Christ, the only model, the just are invited to enter the order of love-agape. (AM 25).

In this quotation, Benedict XVI proposes a conceptual revolution of justice; not the *justice of equity* but the *justice of love*. The Greek model of justice in the 4th century BC advocated for the extreme of amnesty to avoid bringing evil. The other extreme, coming from the courts, called for an irrevocable punishment of crimes. The *justice of love*, which is unprecedented in the history of humanity, is a third way between the forgetfulness of the Greeks and the vengeance of the courts. This justice without a court, according to Paul Ricoeur, privileges neither the law, nor the victim, nor the accused person, but "*the organic link that holds a human community together.*" (Ricœur dans Cassin, 2004. 169–70) It is supported by solidarity in all areas, be they political, economic, social, etc. (AM §11)

The *Africae Munus concept of justice of love* is in line with the traditional African concept that Desmond Tutu calls "restorative justice," translated as *justice réparatrice, la justice restauratrice* or *la justice reconstructive.* Desmond Tutu said:

> I would maintain, that there is another form of justice, a reconstructive justice, which was the basis of traditional African jurisprudence. In this context, the goal is not retribution; in line with the concept of ubuntu, the primary concerns are to repair damage, restore balance, restore broken relationships, rehabilitate the victim, but also the perpetrator, who must be given the opportunity to reintegrate into the community that has suffered from his offence or crime. (Tutu, 2000: 51)

It is neither distributive nor punitive. Punitive justice focuses on punishment. Restorative justice, in traditional African jurisprudence, aims instead to heal violations, correct imbalances, and restore broken relationships; to rehabilitate both the victim and the perpetrator, thus reintegrating them into the community. Punitive justice ignores the victim and the system is generally cold and impersonal. Restorative justice is hopeful because it is based on the possibility of the conversion of the criminal. Far from being lax in the face of crime, this justice is pedagogical because it gives the criminal the opportunity to realise the seriousness of his act through the sanction handed down. *Africae Munus* would gain in practical orientation and importance if it had given a place to the analysis of African habits and customs in matters of justice with a view to associating it with the implementation of the process of reconciliation and peace.

Benedict XVI does not engage in a simplistic peace that is the reconstruction of Africa after its traumas. He takes a holistic approach of prevention, intervention, and reconstruction. These are the components of peace for Africa. True to his logic of transcendence, the Pope values this peace, which is the result of the human effort to open up and share one's being with the other, as important but uncertain. This peace, though necessary, needs a stable and lasting foundation which is found in Christ. It is in this light that we must understand the distinction between the peace of the world which is *"the fruit of negotiations and diplomatic agreements based on interests"* and the authentic peace which is Christlike. (AM §30)

The Emergence of a Homo Africanus Novus

As mentioned earlier, Benedict XVI is motivated by an anthropological Afro-optimism that runs counter to the proponents of Afro-pessimism. He constantly points to the path of the future and of hope, all throughout the Exhortation. The case of Africa is not a hopeless one. However, the Pope is also aware that the task is difficult and does not fall directly within the Church's sphere of action. But this does not mean that the Church should take refuge in a disembodied spirituality:

> The task we have to specify is not easy, because it lies between immediate engagement in politics—which does not fall within the direct competence of the Church—and the possible retreat or escape into theological and spiritual theories; this risk representing an escape from a concrete responsibility in human history. (AM §17)

This hope was announced in Yaoundé when the Pope said that the negative anthropological situation *"is not irreversible."* Benedict XVI finds the source of this hope in the new African anthropology *"in the rich intellectual, cultural, and religious patrimony of which Africa is the custodian."* (AM §9) As for the means to achieve this emergence, he suggests that:

> In this anthropological crisis with which the African continent is confronted, it will be able to find paths of hope by establishing a dialogue between the members of the religious, social, political, economic, cultural, and scientific components. It will then have to rediscover and promote a conception of the person and his or her relationship to reality based on a deep spiritual renewal. (AM §11)

This new "anthropology [would be] rooted in natural law, and clarified by the Word of God and the teaching of the Church." (AM §72) *Homo africanus novus* is expected to have a formed conscience. "One of the duties of the Church in Africa is to build upright and receptive consciences to the demands of justice, so as to breed men and women who are concerned about and capable of realising this just social order by their responsible conduct." (AM §22)

Africae Munus is a theological anthropology because it is an answer to the question: What does it mean to be a human being in Africa? As we have seen above, Benedict XVI elaborates the new understanding of the African in a theological perspective, that is, *"enlightened by the Word of God and the teaching of the Church"* (AM §72). To say that this anthropology is theological does not mean that it is discriminatory in the sense that it is concerned only with Christians. Its scope, on the other hand, is the whole of African humanity with its diversified culture, creed, colour, etc. This anthropology is not disembodied but developed in relation to "the rich intellectual, cultural, and religious heritage of which Africa is a custodian," (AM §9) in "relation [to] the African reality." (AM §22) It is contentious because it radically rejects all structures that degrade man. It is resolutely opposed to everything that degrades or destroys the African beings.

The preservation of human transcendence requires the broadening of the horizons of political practice so that "the love of justice" opens up to "the justice of love." (AM §25) Indeed, "Divine justice offers human justice, which is always limited and imperfect, the horizon towards which it must aim in order to be accomplished." (AM, §25) Here the Pope urges the Church and the whole world to safeguard this dimension of human transcendence by combating any immanentism anthropology that would seek to confine and reduce man to politics.

Conclusion

Africae Munus is a plan of action and a roadmap that unfolds as a strategy for action in view of the "being of the Church," and by extension, the development of the "African being." In the title of the Exhortation, this is obvious: "Africa's commitment." It is a Social Doctrine of the Catholic Church, hence the key concepts of reconciliation, justice, peace, and solidarity. It is a test and a challenge to the African in general and the Church in Africa in particular to hope for a better future. This hope is neither a-*topos* nor futuristic but a reality and a dream which taps today from Reconciliation, Peace, and Justice. Hope is a transcendental act from the justice of equity to the justice of love, from worldly peace to Christlike peace.

Today marks the 10th anniversary of *Africae Munus*. What changes has Africa witnessed? Has Africa resolutely set out on the road to hope? Despite the optimism of *Africae Munus*, its implementation within Africa encounters obstacles. How can the transformation experience in the Church requested by this Exhortation be lived in an Africa when the authoritarian structure of power and leadership does not encourage lay participation and sometimes is abusive? What reconciliation is possible in Africa when Pentecostal and Independence Christian churches are at loggerheads over the religious status of the African culture and the African traditional religion? *Africae Munus* is an African *kairos* provided it enters into dialogue with African pre-social and pre-cultural people.

However, it is its non-discriminatory character that is encouraging about the Exhortation. By calling on all religions in Africa, the Pope gives the impression that the Catholic Church in Africa is not a closed esoteric sect but a divine presence ready to collaborate with others, for the coming of the kingdom of God. Ecumenical collaboration conveys a vital message that the religions of Africa can live together in collaboration.

The Judicial Point of View

Although one might be tempted to make systemic and spiritual theology in Pope Benedict XVI's teaching more prominent, the significance of his contribution in the sphere of ethics should be noted as well. This is the objective of our research, which intends to focus on Benedict XVI's social teaching by examining some major texts addressed to the churches and peoples of Africa. Why must we not ask about the contribution of his social doctrine in the face of socio-political challenges such as the management of public assets in our "democracies in the making," the mastery of violence-producing mechanisms and the implementation of peace in an Africa torn by wars of interest and fratricidal conflicts? Why don't we take seriously the emergence of an African identity in this increasingly global culture? Can we remain indifferent to the ecological threats in an Africa devastated by the exploitation of multinational companies and subjected to the dictatorship of a liberal and essentially capitalist economy? These are all areas of interest that deserve our attention in dialogue with the social doctrine of Benedict XVI.

Benedict XVI and the Issue of Sexual Abuse of Minors by Clerics

Jean Marie Signie, SCJ[1]

Introduction

Benedict XVI's papacy goes down in history as the one during which the Church was strongly shaken by revelations of numerous cases of sexual abuse committed by clerics on minors, though most of these abuses were committed in the decades before his papacy. In our paper, we will look at Benedict XVI's attitude towards these scandals and what impact his action or attitude has had on the Church in Africa. Our paper will be divided into three parts: first, we will look at the work of Cardinal Joseph Ratzinger before his election to the throne of St. Peter; we will also look at his work as Pope in the face of the sexual abuse crisis; and finally, we will look at the impact of his work on the Church in Africa.

Before his Papal Ministry: Cardinal Josef Ratzinger: The Constitution *Crimen Sollicitationis*

On 16 March 1962, the Holy Office (now the Congregation for the Doctrine of the Faith) published the *Crimen Sollicitationis* document, approved by Pope John XIII. This document was sent to all bishops with the recommendation that it be kept strictly confidential in the secret archives of the Curia, and that no reproduction or commentary be allowed. The *Crimen sollicitationis* thus replaced another document of the same nature published in 1922 by the Holy Office and approved by Pius XI. These two documents indicated the procedures to be followed for the treatment of the solicitation offences as well as those provided for in canons 2359 §2 CIC / 17.[2]

> If they [the clerics] commit any offence against the sixth commandment with minors below sixteen years of age, or practise adultery, rape, "bestiality," sodomy, incitement to prostitution or incest with their blood relations or first-degree relatives, they are to be suspended, declared infamous, deprived of any function, benefit, title, or office they may have, and in the most severe cases they are to be dropped.

The *Crimen sollicitationis* was the procedural document of reference until its revision in 2001, with the publication of John Paul II's *motu proprio, Sacramentorum sanctitatis tutela*[3] on 30 April 2001, followed by the new procedural norms published by the Congregation for the Doctrine of the Faith[4] on 18 May 2001. Since 1981, Josef Ratzinger (the future Benedict XVI) became the one to oversee the application of the *Crimen sollicitationis*.

The First Revelations of Sexual Abuse in the Church

The first revelations of sexual abuse by priests and religious began to emerge in the 1990s in the USA, albeit in a timid manner. The Church was subject to accusations of doing nothing and protecting criminals. *Crimen sollicitationis*, which would have been revised with the publication of the new Code, was not revised, and so remains the current norm for dealing with these cases. Cardinal Ratzinger, prefect of the CDF, was to ensure its application.

However, the American episcopate soon realised that procedures that were appropriate to the context and that could respond to the current crisis had to be adopted. It took actions such as the establishment of the *ad hoc* commission on sexual abuse *Restoring Trust* in November 1994 and the publication of documents such as *Canonical Delicts Involving Sexual Misconduct and Dismissal from the Clerical State* in 1995, the Program of Priestly Formation in

1993, *Proposed Guidelines on the Transfer or Assignment of Clergy and Religious* in 1993, all with the approval of the Holy See.

The Sacramentorum Sanctitatis Tutela and the New Norms of 2001

The *motu proprio Sacramentorum sanctitatis tutela* (SST) apostolic letter, promulgated by John Paul II and the norms issued by the CDF for the application of the SST revised the *Crimen sollicitationis* in force since 1922 and taken up again in 1962. The SST deals with a number of crimes considered as the most serious crimes, the treatment of which is reserved to the CDF, among which is the crime of sexual abuse of minors by clerics. With the numerous cases coming to light and the accusations against the Church of protecting perpetrators becoming louder, it was time to prove the contrary. Joseph Cardinal Ratzinger was the one to do so, either directly or indirectly. Indeed, although both documents were signed by John Paul II to come into force, there is no doubt that drafting them was the work of the CDF headed by Cardinal Ratzinger who was responsible for dealing with the said cases.

We must point out that unlike Crimen, *Crimen sollicitationis*, SST was not sealed off. Unfortunately, it was not widely disseminated, especially in our countries. Yet, it was the publication of this that seemed to have provoked the avalanche of revelations and condemnations in North America and Europe.

The Charter Promulgated by the US Conference of Catholic Bishops and the Essential Norms for the USA

After the publication of the *SST*, one of Cardinal Ratzinger's first major actions was the approval of the charter of the US Bishops' Conference[5] barely six months after the promulgation of the new norms. It marked a revolution in handling cases, a revolution that stands in stark contrast to the *Crimen sollicitationis*. Indeed, this charter, which contains 17 articles, is also in some ways the first Church document (albeit a special one) in which the authorities acknowledged that the scourge has still not been properly addressed, and asks for the forgiveness of the victims, their families, and the society:

> The consequences of pedophile acts are disastrous and long lasting. We reach out to all who suffer, especially to victims of sexual abuse and their families. We ask for forgiveness for the pains they have suffered and offer them our assistance. In the face of so much suffering, healing and reconciliation require efforts that go beyond human capacity. Only God's grace, mercy and forgiveness can enable us to move forward, confident in the promise that Christ has made to us.

The 17 articles each indicate an action to be taken which can be as follows:

1) Helping victims to heal and to be reconciled with them: this involves setting up a process in each diocese for: psychological help to be given to the victims; spiritual assistance to be given to them; the setting up of support groups for the victims and their entourage both in the diocese and in the parish communities; the involvement of other social services decided upon by mutual agreement between the victim and the diocese; pastoral care which should enable the bishop "to meet the victims and their families, to listen with patience and compassion to the narrative of their experience and their concerns, and to share the deep sense of solidarity and concern." (art. 1)

2) The provision of mechanisms for dioceses to respond quickly to allegations of child abuse. This consists primarily of an office to coordinate pastoral action for those who allege sexual abuse by the clergy, to advise the bishop in the evaluation of such allegations, and to regularly review diocesan policies and procedures in this area. (art. 2)

3) Prohibition of confidentiality clauses in cases of sexual abuse,

except for serious and substantial reasons stated by the victim. (art. 3)

4) The obligation to inform administrations of allegations of sexual abuse of minors; the respect of civic law on reporting and cooperation with civil authorities; the obligation for dioceses not only to inform victims of their right to file complaints with administrations, but also to support them in this process. (art. 4)

5) The obligation to open an investigation in accordance with the Code of Canon Law whenever there is a complaint of sexual abuse of a minor, and to follow the canonical procedure in this matter. The Charter also added the obligation for the offender to undergo a psychological and medical examination provided that this does not interfere with the civil investigation. At the end of this preliminary investigation, every effort must be made to clear the clergyman if the accusations prove to be unfounded; otherwise, the appropriate measures must be undertaken and sanctions imposed, including dismissal from the clerical functions. (art. 5)

6) The promotion by dioceses of correct moral behavior and the obligation of dioceses to set limits for clergy and persons who work on behalf of the Church and are in regular contact with youths who have confidence in their care. (art. 6)

7) Transparency and openness with the community in dealing with cases of sexual abuse of minors, but with respect for the privacy and reputation of individuals. (art. 7)

8) The creation of a national office for the protection of children and adolescents, with the aim not only of applying the principles set out in the Charter consistently, but also of making the bishops responsible and helping them in their endeavors. (art. 8 and 9)

9) The creation of "safe environment" programmes for children in dioceses, in which "the guidelines to be followed by clerics and those in contact with children in relation to sexual abuse are made clear to clerics and the community at large." (art. 12)

10) Ad hoc committee on sexual abuse must include representatives of all ecclesiastical regions of the country. (art. 10 and 15)

11) The study by the dioceses of the background of all diocesan and parochial persons in regular contact with minors. (art. 13)

12) The transfer of a cleric who has committed a pedophile act to another diocese or religious province to take up a ministry there must be forbidden. For such a transfer to be possible, it is ordinary to first send a quem to the chaplain, in a confidential manner, all information concerning possible sexual abuse of minors, and indicate whether the person has been or could be a danger to minors. (art. 14)

13) The collaboration of bishops and major superiors of religious institutes in dealing with cases of alleged sexual abuse by a member of the institute who is a minister in the parish. (art. 15)

14) The readiness of the Bishops' Conference to cooperate with other Churches and religious communities, religious bodies, educational institutions, and other bodies in research in the domain of sexual abuse of minors. (art. 16)

15) The commitment to review the training of seminarians in order to provide the People of God with mature and holy priests, and to develop systematic programmes of ongoing formation in the dioceses with the aim to help priests live their vocation day by day. (art. 17)

After the publication of this charter, a group of American bishops, commissioned by the U.S. Bishops' Conference, developed the Essential Norms for the USA. Although these Norms received the *recognitio* of the Congregation of Bishops, the support of the Prefect of the CDF was of crucial importance for the approval of the document. Cardinal Levada, prefect of CDF, said in 2012:

> Under the careful stewardship of Cardinal Ratzinger, then Prefect of the CDF, the Holy See was able to ensure a coordinated response to the growing number of reports of sexual abuse, and to deal effectively with the

canonical issues surrounding them, including against the decisions of bishops and Major Superiors. As the media sex abuse storm began in late 2001 and 2002, leading the U.S. bishops to adopt their Charter for the Protection of Children and Young Adults, a committee of bishops was able to develop the Essential Norms, which, after receiving the recognitio of the Holy See, became an additional binding legislation for the U.S. bishops, and a great help in providing guidance in dealing with a large number of historical cases that surfaced as a result of media publicity. I would like to express my personal gratitude to Pope Benedict XVI, who, as prefect at the time, played such an important role in implementing these new norms for the good of the Church, and for his support in approving the Essential Norms for the United States.[6]

During Benedict XVI's Papacy

We will focus on other actions: the derogations from the 2001 norms, the pastoral letter to Catholics in Ireland, the modification of the 2001 norms and the letters from the CDF to help Bishops' Conferences draft recommendations.

Derogations from the SST: The Concession of Special Faculties to Some Deaneries of the Roman Curia: The Case of the Congregation for the Evangelisation of Peoples[7]

In the last years of his papacy, Pope Benedict XVI granted special faculties to some congregations of the Roman Curia in the area of dealing with cases of sexual abuse: these include the Congregation for the Doctrine of the Faith, the Congregation for the Evangelisation of Peoples, and the Congregation for the Clergy. We will focus here on those conceded to the Congregation for the

Evangelisation of Peoples, since the Churches of Africa, always considered as *ad gentes* mission territories, depend on this Dicastery.

According to the norms in force, cases of sexual abuse of minors must be dealt with through a rigorous judicial procedure, but can also, with the authorisation of the CDF, be dealt with through an extrajudicial penal procedure. But in most mission territories, including Africa, courts are non-existent or non-functional. It has always been almost impossible to use the judicial channel in our African countries to deal with cases of moral indiscipline of clerics, and even the administrative procedure provided for in the 1983 Code of Canon Law[8] was not always easy to apply in these territories, given the prohibition in canon 1342 §2 of that code against inflicting or declaring a perpetual sentence by decree.

Already, on the 30th of April 2005, Benedict XVI confirmed a faculty granted to the CEP on 3 March 1997, allowing this Dicastery to submit directly for resignation from the clerical state with dispensation from all the obligations deriving from sacred orders, including clerical celibacy, the cases of clerics incardinated in the ecclesiastical districts of the mission territories dependent on the CEP and having no judicial structure, recognised as being guilty of serious sin against the sixth commandment according to canon law number 1395 of CIC/83. By granting the new faculties to the CEP on 31 March 2009, Benedict XVI extended the 2005 faculties.

The reason for this faculty concession is clearly mentioned at the beginning of the letter: "to remedy certain situations of irregularity in the behaviour of the clergy in the mission territories concerning cases of scandalous conduct in the area of morals, obstinate disobedience to the legitimate superiors, and the disastrous management of ecclesiastical goods." In fact, this includes four special faculties:

The first extended to all mission territories, the faculties of 1997 and 2005 mentioned above, which could only be applied to territories without a judicial structure (ecclesiastical tribunal) and is applied under the precise conditions mentioned in the faculty.

The second faculty grants the CEP "the special faculty to examine, according to the procedure in force, and to bring directly to its sovereign decision the request for dispensation from clerical obligations presented by clerics of mission territories and those who are members of societies of apostolic life for the mission ad gentes dependent on the CEP, as well as those of institutions of consecrated life of diocesan right having their principal headquarters in missionary districts." It should be noted that as early as 1980, this competence was given to the CDF, and as early as 1989 it was granted to the Congregation for Divine Worship and the Discipline of the Sacraments, then transferred to the Congregation for the Clergy in 2005 through a decision by Benedict XVI. Today it can also be exercised as a special faculty by the CEP within the limits of the legislation.

With the third faculty Benedict XVI granted the CEP "the special faculty to intervene by virtue of canon 1399, either by acting directly or by confirming the decisions of the Bishop if the competent Bishops so request, in the case of a particularly serious violation of the laws, or because of the necessity and urgency of avoiding an objective scandal." Indeed, canon 1399, to which reference is made here, covers a very broad sphere, also that of sexual abuse of minors.

The fourth and last faculty is in fact a derogation. Benedict XVI, through this faculty, concedes to the CDF "the derogation from the prescriptions of canons 1317 and 1342 § 2 and 1349, concerning the application of permanent sentences, to be applied to deacons for serious cases and to priests for very serious cases, always submitting the relevant cases to the Supreme Pontiff for approval in specific form and decision."

These special faculties were accompanied by a description of the procedure to be followed in the application of faculties so granted.

The Pastoral Letter to Catholics in Ireland

Pope Benedict XVI on 19 March 2009 sent a letter to the Christians of Ireland, shaken by a chain of revelations of sexual abuse committed by priests and religious on vulnerable children and young people in their country. He opens his letter with: "I can only share the dismay and sense of betrayal that many of you have felt on learning of these scandalous and criminal acts and of the way in which the Church authorities in Ireland have dealt with them."[9] Benedict XVI explains the reason for his letter: to express his closeness to the Christians of Ireland and to offer them a path of healing, given the seriousness of the offences committed, and the often inadequate response to them by the church authorities in Ireland.[10]

Prior to this letter, Benedict XVI earlier summoned all the Irish bishops to Rome to report to him on how they dealt with issues of sexual abuse in the past and to present to him the steps they had taken to respond to this serious situation. They also presented him with an analysis of the mistakes made and the lessons learned, as well as a description of the programmes and procedures put in place.[11] Earlier during their *ad limina* visit in 2006, Benedict XVI asked the Irish bishops to "establish the truth about what happened in the past, to take all the necessary measures to prevent it occurring in the future, to ensure that the principles of justice are fully respected, and, above all, to support the victims and all those who are victims of these monstrous crimes."[12]

Benedict XVI indicates in this letter what he believes to be the way forward for the Church in Ireland to heal from this painful wound: To acknowledge first of all before the Lord and before the others, the serious sins committed against defenceless children. The Pope said, "such recognition, accompanied by sincere sorrow for the harm done to these victims and their families, must lead to a concerted effort to ensure the protection of children against such crimes in the future."[13]

In his letter, Benedict XVI recalls some of the causes of this crisis in Ireland, such as: inadequate procedures for determining the suitability of candidates for priesthood and religious life; insufficient human, moral, intellectual, and spiritual training in seminaries and novitiates; a tendency in society to favour the clergy and other public figures; and a misplaced concern for the reputation of the Church and to avoid scandal.[14]

He further addresses, in particular, each category of Christians directly concerned with the problems of sexual abuse of minors: victims of abuse and their families, priests and religious who have abused children, parents, children and youths in Ireland, priests and religious in Ireland, bishops, all the faithful in Ireland.

1.1. The Review of the SST

On 21 May 2010, Pope Benedict XVI approved and ordered the promulgation of the revised SST Norms. The changes focused on certain substantive and procedural norms in order to make the law more capable of dealing with the complexities of cases of sexual abuse of minors.[15] In addition, these changes mainly result in the granting of new competences to the CDF.[16] The new features are summarized below:

The Changes Introduced in the Text

Any person of full age who does not habitually enjoy a perfect use of reason is now equated with a minor under eighteen years of age; (art.6 §1 n.1)

- The acquisition, possession or disclosure, for a libidinous purpose by a cleric, of pornographic images of minors under 14 years of age, in any way and regardless of the instrument used, is added to offences; (art.6 §1 n.2)
- Also, from now on, the preliminary investigation can and must be carried out by the Congregation for the Doctrine of the Faith; (art. 17)
- The President of the Tribunal in office as of now has the power to take precautionary measures, mentioned in canon 1722 CIC and in canon 1473 CCEO, even during the preliminary investigation. (art. 19)

The New Powers Granted to the CDF

- The right, by mandate of the Supreme Pontiff, to judge the Cardinal Fathers, Patriarchs, Legates of the Apostolic See, Bishops and other natural persons mentioned in canons 1405 §3 CIC and 1061 CCEO; (art.1 §2)
- The end of the statute of limitations for criminal action to twenty years remains extended, except for the right of the Congregation for the Doctrine of the Faith to derogate from it; (art.7)
- The power to grant tribunal staff, lawyers, and procurators the dispensation from the obligation to be a priest, or to be a doctor of canon law; (art.15)
- The power to invalidate acts in the event of a violation of purely procedural rules by the lower courts, with the exception of the law of defence; (art.18)
- The power to dispense with the judicial process, proceeding *per decretum extraiudicium*: the Congregation for the Doctrine of the Faith, after evaluating the nature of each act, then decides on a case-by-case basis, *ex officio* or at the request of the Bishop or the Hierarchy, whether or not to authorise recourse to the extrajudicial procedure (in any case, perpetual expiatory punishments are inflicted only by mandate of the Congregation for the Doctrine of the Faith); (art.21 §2 n.1)
- The power to refer the case directly to the Holy Father for the *dimissio e statu clericali* or for the *depositio, una cum dispensatione a lege caelibatus*: in this instance, always without prejudice to the right of the accused to defend himself, in addition to the extreme gravity of the case, the offence being examined must be clearly ascertained; (art.21 §2 n.2)
- The power to have recourse to the higher level of judgement of the Ordinary Session of the Congregation for the Doctrine of the Faith, in the case of recourse against administrative acts issued or approved by the lower units of the same Congregation, in cases of reserved offences; (art.27)
- As pointed out by the CDF, these modifications are in fact a

consolidation of practices already recognised and approved by Benedict XVI coming after John Paul II.

The Circular to Assist Bishops' Conferences Draw up Guidelines to Deal with Cases of Sexual Abuse of Minors by Clerics[17]

The numerous revelations of sexual abuse scandals perpetrated by clergy and clerics in various countries made it clear that many Church authorities around the world were not ready to adequately respond to this crisis, except for a few Bishops' Conferences that had developed guidelines or norms to address the problem in their countries. Cardinal Levada, prefect of the CDF in 2012, listed the following countries as already having guidelines or norms: "Canada and the United States in North America, Brazil in South America, Great Britain and Ireland, Germany, Belgium and France in Europe, South Africa, Australia and New Zealand in the southern hemisphere."[18] Most of these conferences thus only reacted to media revelations of scandalous behaviour by clerics. What was needed was a proactive response from the conferences, which is what the CDF hoped to achieve in the future as it issued this Circular.

As the Cardinal Prefect of the CDF says, this letter, with the aim to help the Bishops' Conferences develop guidelines to deal with cases of sexual abuse of minors by clerics:

> invites the Bishops' Conferences of the world to address the various aspects of this issue: they should give due attention to the canonical discipline of clergy guilty of such crimes; they should have norms for evaluating the suitability of clergy and others who are ministers in Church institutions and agencies; they should oversee educational programmes for Church families and communities to ensure the protection of children and the youths from sexual abuse crimes in the future; and they must be pastors and fathers of all sexual abuse victims

among their flocks who may call upon them for redress or assistance.[19]

This important document, published during Benedict XVI's papacy, is divided into three sections, and repeats the various points that Benedict XVI dealt with in the past, whenever he has had the opportunity to speak on how to deal with cases or scandals of sexual abuse. In fact, the first section, which deals with the general aspects of the problem, deals first of all with the victims of sexual abuse and their families, whom the Church, through the Bishop or her delegate, must be ready to listen to, as well as to commit herself to providing them with spiritual and psychological assistance, as Pope Benedict XVI did during his apostolic journeys, showing a particularly important example of his willingness to meet with and listen to the victims of sexual abuse and to address them with words of compassion and comfort.[20] Further, the protection of minors, which sometimes involves the development of an educational programme of prevention to ensure a "safe environment" for minors. The third general consideration is the importance of ensuring adequate training for priests and clerics. The fourth consideration is that of the accompanying of clerics by the bishop; he should "keenly see to the constant training of the clergy, especially during the first years after sacred ordination, with particular emphasis on the importance of prayer and mutual support in a priestly fraternal manner," inform priests of the damage inflicted on the victim of sexual abuse by a cleric and of his responsibility on the canonical and civil levels, to teach him also to recognise what could be the signs of possible abuse of minors by anyone; and to deal with cases of abuse reported to him, according to the canonical and civil discipline, respecting the rights of all parties.

The last general consideration relates to cooperation with the civil authorities, because sexual abuse of minors is not only a canonical offence, but also a crime that is prosecuted in civil proceedings. It is therefore important to cooperate with the civil authorities within the framework of the respective competences, and, in particular, "always the prescriptions of the civil laws with regard to referring crimes to the competent authorities, without infringing the sacramental internal forum." The document reiterates that this cooperation "is not limited only to cases of abuse committed by clerics, but also concerns cases of abuse involving religious and lay personnel of church structures." After these considerations, the CDF briefly summarises the canonical legislation in force concerning the crime of sexual abuse of minors committed by a cleric, and finally gives guidelines on how to proceed.

How Does This Action by Benedict XVI Benefit Africa?

As Benedict XVI said in his letter to the Catholics of Ireland, "The problem of sexual abuse of minors is not unique to Ireland." So, Africa cannot wait for cascading revelations in the media before being concerned about this serious problem. Even if there are no documents by Benedict XVI or published under his papacy addressed directly to Africa, we must recognise that all the letters and speeches of this Pope, as well as the various documents published under his papacy each time with his specific approval or not, are also addressed to Africa and are, therefore, of great interest to her. Moreover, the reading of some of these documents sound as if they were addressed to Africa; the situations described in them are so similar to African situations. This is the case with the letter to the Catholics of Ireland, in which Benedict XVI points out the causes not only of the sexual abuse scandals, but also of the inappropriate treatment of the deeds by the Church in Ireland.

Indeed, like in Ireland, in almost every family in some African countries today there is someone—a son or daughter, an aunt or an uncle—who has given his/her life to serve the Church. And these families "rightly have great esteem and affection for their loved ones who have consecrated their lives to Christ, sharing the gift of faith with others and putting that faith into practice in generous service to God and neighbour."[21]

Furthermore, over the last decades, the Church in our African countries has been facing new and serious faith challenges, arising from the rapid transformation and secularization of our societies. There is also a very rapid social shift, often with counter effects to people's traditional adherence to Catholic teaching and values. While the sacramental and devotional practices that sustain faith and allow it to grow are not yet neglected, there is a tendency even on the part of priests and religious to adopt ways of thinking and to consider secular realities without sufficient reference to the Gospel. The tendency to avoid penal approaches to irregular canonical situations also exists. According to Benedict XVI, such a context is conducive for the emergence of the disconcerting problem of child sexual abuse, which contributes to weaken the faith and the loss of respect for the Church and her teachings.[22]

Other factors which, according to Benedict XVI, have contributed to the birth of the child sex abuse scandals are currently very much present in most of our African countries. As mentioned earlier, the Pope states that: "inadequate procedures for determining the suitability of candidates for priesthood and religious life; insufficient human, moral, intellectual and spiritual training in seminaries and novitiates; a tendency in society to favour the clergy and other public figures, as well as a misplaced preoccupation with the reputation of the Church and with avoiding scandals, which has resulted in the failure to apply canonical penalties in force and to protect the dignity of each person."[23] Even an uninformed person can say without fear of contradiction that these elements are present today in African countries.

Conclusion

Today in Africa, when the scandals of sexual abuse of minors by clerics are mentioned, the tendency is to underestimate the prevalence of this problem in the Churches of our continent. Some bishops do not even hesitate to assert that paedophilia is a Western trend and that even if there are cases of child abuse in the Churches of Africa, these are isolated cases, rare cases. If Africa wants to avoid being dragged through the mud in a few years' time, it would be in her interest to follow Benedict XVI's teachings and appeals which have now been taken up and are being reinforced by Francis. The Churches in Africa must have the courage to confront the above-mentioned risk factors, even if this means giving up some social privileges in order to avoid "such tragic consequences on the lives of the victims and their families," which have darkened the Gospel light which is already not very visible on this continent.[24] They should learn from the mistakes of others, and put in place mechanisms for the protection of children, revise training programmes for clerics and other consecrated persons, apply canonical discipline in this area, and finally take the lead in breaking the law of silence in our society and coming out of the "closed doors."

Preparation for the Priesthood in the Legislative Agenda of Benedict XVI

Pr. Jean Paul Betengne[1]

Introduction

Canon 213 of the Code of Canon Law states that "The faithful have the right to receive help from the spiritual products of the Church, especially the word of God and the sacraments, from the consecrated pastors." Such an expectation can only be fulfilled if the clerics who have the duty to ensure this right of the faithful are well prepared and willing to assume it. Pope Benedict, being particularly committed to the new evangelization, could not fail to underline the importance of the training of the clergy, to the Church especially in a secularized and ever-changing world. After underlining the commitment of Benedict XVI to the training of the priest in relation to his ontological status, we will see the place of the priest in the new evangelization according to this Pope's teachings, before drawing some guidelines for the training of diocesan clergy in Africa.

The Ontological Status of the Cleric and the Preparation for the Priesthood

In order to underline the interest of Pope Benedict XVI in the problem of clergy training, let us first stop at two legislative reforms that this Pope has encouraged, on the one hand, the attachment of seminaries to the Congregation for the Clergy, and on the other, the reform of ecclesiastical studies in philosophy.

The Affiliation of Seminaries
to the Congregation for the Clergy

Pope Benedict XVI, through the *Motu proprio Ministrorum institu-tio* of 16 January 2013, transferred competence over seminaries from the Congregation for Catholic Education to the Congregation for the Clergy. Such a decision is significant and reflects the Pope's idea of the adequacy of training for the future assumption of the offices inherent in the sacrament of Holy Orders. It is, moreover, on the occasion of the closing of the Synod of Bishops on the New Evangelization on 27 October 2012 that the Pope shared his legislative project. At the beginning of his speech on that day, he stated that: "In the context of the reflections of the Synod of Bishops, [...] and at the conclusion of a process of reflection on the themes of seminaries and the catechism, I am pleased to announce that I have decided, after prayer and further reflection, to transfer competence over seminaries from the Congregation for Education to the Congregation for the Clergy." Taking the opportunity of the *Motu Proprio* mentioned, the Pope made a point to clarify the difference between Catholic education in general on the one hand, and the education of young people for priesthood on the other. He did so by explaining the respective competences of the two congregations in charge of the two. The Congregation for Catholic Education is responsible for the promotion and organization of Catholic education. The aim of Catholic education is to prepare children and young people for the harmonious development of their physical, moral, and intellectual gifts, so that, by acquiring a more perfect sense of responsibility and a right use of freedom, they become capable of participating actively in social life. Thus perceived, Catholic education is for all men, regardless of status or class. It is different from priesthood training in the Major Seminaries which aims to prepare future soul pastors. Such an essential difference justifies the fact that the competence over seminaries belongs to the Congregation for the Clergy, which must see to it that the organization and "government of seminaries respond fully to the requirements of priestly education." There is, therefore, a priestly education that is distinct from, but not in opposition to, simple Catholic education. Indeed, part of priestly education, especially intellectual formation, can be provided by the church institutions of higher learning under the Congregation for Catholic Education; priesthood formation is of a different kind.

Drawing on the history of the institution of the permanent seminary as a place of formation for future clerics, Benedict XVI recalls, following his immediate predecessor, John Paul II, that the formation of future ordained ministers is specific and that the university, which promotes classical intellectual training, is not the appropriate environment for this training. Benedict XVI is far from being naive. He is not ignorant of the importance and usefulness of academic training for the efficient exercise of the priestly ministry. That is why he recalls the complementarity between the classical institutions of higher education and the major seminaries as the proper framework for preparation for the priesthood. In this regard, he specifies: "The Congregation for Catholic Education is competent in organizing academic studies in philosophy and theology, after having consulted the Congregation for the Clergy, with regard to their respective competence."

The Reform of Ecclesiastical Studies in Philosophy

How is the reform of ecclesiastical studies in philosophy desired by Benedict XVI and carried out by the Congregation for Catholic Education through the reform decree of 28 January 2011 relevant to the subject at hand? The answer to this question requires that we look first of all at the mission of ordained ministers in relation to the communities of the faithful entrusted to their care. Cannon1008 of CIC/83 in the former draft recalled that, "Sacred ministers are consecrated and elected to be pastors of God's people." Meanwhile, accompanying the faithful must take into account the circumstances of time and place. It is to respond to this fundamental concern that the philosophical course prior to theological studies for those preparing for the priesthood is instituted, as recalled in cannon 251, namely that "Philosophical training, which must be based on its still valid patrimony and take into account the progress of philosophical research, will be given in such a way as to improve the human training of seminarians, to sharpen their minds and to make them more suitable for the study of theology."

It is, therefore, with a view to preparing future priests to better respond to their mission that Pope Benedict XVI wanted the reform of ecclesiastical studies in philosophy. In the long preamble to the reform text, it is stated that "In a world rich in scientific and technical knowledge, but threatened by relativism, only the 'sapiential perspective' provides an integrating vision and confidence in the capacity of reason to serve the truth. This is why the Church strongly encourages a philosophical training of reason open to faith, without confusion or separation." Better still, "When the philosophical foundations are not clarified, the ground slips from under the feet of theology."

A solid philosophical training will, therefore, enable the future priest to be better prepared to respond to the incessant questioning that preoccupies the minds of the men and women of his time he will be responsible for pastoral care. And, in the context of the new evangelisation, in this period where many concepts and ideologies abound and circulate at great speed, some of which are anxiety-provoking and confusing, the priest must be capable of proposing a reasonable and relevant pastoral accompaniment, both on the spiritual and intellectual levels.

The Priest and the New Evangelisation

The election of Ratzinger to the See of St. Peter was not welcomed by those who constantly hope to see the Church adopt postures in favour of a certain liberalisation on various socio-anthropological issues as a response to the secularisation of the world and particularly of Europe. By choosing Benedict as his reigning name, the new Pope made it clear what he intended his papacy to be about as well as his understanding of the problem of secularization. Indeed, according to the French Catholic newspaper

Lacroix, Benedict XVI chose his reign name in reference to both Benedict XV, the Pope of Peace, and Benedict of Nursia, the patron saint of Europe. Beyond the anecdote, this choice explains the commitment of Benedict XVI to take up the challenge of secularization through the new evangelization.

The Challenge of Secularization and the Need for a New Evangelization

Pope Benedict XVI considers secularization to be one of the great challenges for the Church and that in the face of such a challenge, action is more than urgent. In his address of 10 March 2008 to the participants in the general assembly of the Pontifical Council for Culture, which had as its theme, *"The Church and the Challenge of Secularization,"* Benedict XVI stated that, "Secularization [...] puts the Christian life of the faithful and of pastors to the test. [...] It distorts the Christian faith from within and in depth and, as a consequence, the lifestyle and daily behavior of believers." Then the Pope concluded his speech by inviting the pastors of the People of God "to a tireless and generous mission to confront the disturbing phenomenon of secularisation." Two years earlier, receiving the German bishops on an *ad Limina* visit, Benedict XVI already recalled the need to face the challenge of secularisation with courage. He stressed that to do this adequately would require a new commitment that would make the Catholic faith visible again.

The new evangelisation is thus, for Benedict XVI, the most relevant way to face the challenge of secularisation. Although it is acknowledged that his interest in this question predates his accession to the See of Peter, Benedict XVI institutionalised it on 21 September 2010 with the Apostolic Letter given in the form of a *Motu proprio Ubicumque et semper* by which he institutes the Pontifical Council for the Promotion of the New Evangelisation. The new Dicastery has been assigned the mission not only to promote a renewed evangelisation in countries where the first proclamation of the faith already resounded, but which are experiencing a progressive secularization of society and a kind of eclipse of the sense of

God, but also to guarantee the growth of a clear and profound faith in contexts where piety and Christian feeling are still alive.

Thus, the new evangelization requires the commitment of the whole ecclesial body, in all parts of the world. It is a permanent "demand for a renewed proclamation method. [It] means intensifying missionary action in order to fully respond to the Lord's mandate." In order to encourage this overall movement within the Church, Benedict XVI convened a General Assembly of the Synod of Bishops in October 2012 with *The New Evangelisation for the Transmission of the Christian Faith* as its theme. Concluding this synodal assembly, the Pope recalled that the new evangelisation concerns the whole life of the Church and that it applies in particular to ordinary pastoral work, which is called to constantly invent new methods capable of maintaining the missionary flame of Christians.

The New Evangelisation Priest

The new evangelisation process does not change the traditional actors of evangelisation, which itself retains the same ambition, which is to lead humanity to fully adhere to Christ. Clerics, consecrated persons, and the laity all have a particular role to play in this work. In this light, the priest, without changing his nature or status, is also called to renew himself in order to face these current concerns. It is, therefore, possible to think of a kind of priest of the new evangelisation.

Taking into account his main mission of being a pastor to the People of God, the priest of the new evangelisation is first of all called to renew himself. In daily life, the priest, especially the parish priest, is the hierarchical contact from whom the Christians expect teaching, guidance, and exhortation. Cannon 757 reminds us of this as it states that "the priests, as co-workers with the bishops, are assigned the task to proclaim the Gospel of God; parish priests and other priests who have been entrusted with the care of souls are principally bound by this duty towards the people entrusted to them." Since the new evangelisation calls for new and relevant pastoral methods for the context and the time, the person in charge of souls is expected to be prepared for the up-heaval imposed by the renovation. In fact, it is a question of al-lowing oneself to be carried along by this drive which allows pastoral questions to be revitalised by always seeking in the rich and secular tradition of the Gospel, the updated answers to the concerns of the men and women of this era.

In 1999, during John Paul II's papacy, the Congregation for the Clergy addressed a Circular Letter to the Bishops and through them to the priests, recalling that, "The need for a new evangeli-sation urgently requires finding an approach to the exercise of the priestly ministry which corresponds to the present situation, which imbues it with vitality and makes it capable of responding adequately to the circumstances in which it is to be carried out." Aware that such an approach requires diverse and variable meth-ods and practices according to the milieu, the Roman Congrega-tion interspersed the Circular Letter with a questionnaire inviting each priest to a personal work of discernment in order to help him find the best way to renew himself.

It is in the same line of thought, that Pope Benedict XVI ded-icated a Year for Priests to mark the 150th anniversary of the death of the holy Curate of Ars. In the Indiction Letter, the Pope speci-fies the purpose of his pastoral and spiritual project for priests, namely "to help promote a commitment to interior renewal in all priests in order to make their evangelical witness more incisive and vigorous in today's world." In this context, the Pope later specified, with the new Directory for the Ministry and Life of Priests promulgated during his papacy, that "the priest must above all revive his faith, his hope, and his sincere love for the Lord, in order to be able to offer Him to the contemplation of Christians and of all men as He truly is."

What Guidelines for the Training
of Diocesan Priests in Africa?

Secularization challenges identified by Benedict XVI as today's major apostolic concern also challenges Africa, which for a long time was considered religious by nature. How must it be tackled? In any undertaking that calls for action, good preparation ensures success. It is in this sense that the issue of the training of diocesan priests in Africa takes place here.

Initial Training

Canons 233 §2 and 235 require that the diocesan bishops prepare in an appropriate way those who are called to the priesthood. In reality, the content of the training of future priests is universally determined, with the opportunity left to the particular Churches to make the necessary additions so that this training meets the real needs of the Christians of the area concerned. This is the purpose of the *Ratio fundamentalis.*

This said, the perspective outlined by Pope Benedict XVI on "the type of the priesthood" invites us to go further. The Archbishop Ricardo Tobón Restrepo of Medellín reminded us that, "Profound is the cultural change we are experiencing. We cannot make marginal adaptations to what we have always done. [...] We are working, but we are not able to influence enough to build a new world; often, on the contrary, it is the world that gains ground on us. The challenge of responding to the newness of God also begins with the training of future priests. The training and life of seminaries must be renewed." Benedict XVI's magisterium in this perspective remains relevant.

Benedict XVI proposes the new evangelisation as the main action to be undertaken by the Church to respond to the challenge of secularisation. For a long time, however, it has been ignored that this problem also affects Africa, and in no small measure. Prominent African theologians had nevertheless worked to draw our attention to the need to treat the problem of secularisation as an important pastoral issue in Africa. In particular, our late Father and Professor Eloi Messi Metogo, in his memorable essay on religious indifference and unbelief in Black Africa, very clearly posed the problem of the death of God in Africa, as had already been proclaimed in the other continents: Can God be dead in

Africa? Without giving a definite answer to the question, the theologian affirmed that "we think that religious indifference, secularisation, and atheism are not African problems." This statement, which is as pithy as it is eloquent, invites us to take into account the problem of secularisation in the training process of diocesan priests in Africa. This is exactly what Benedict XVI is calling for.

In his *Letter to Seminarians* published on 18 October 2010, Benedict XVI goes back to the path to the ministerial priesthood that seminary training offers. While acknowledging that "seminary time is also and above all a time of study," he chooses to speak to the recipients of his Letter more about the non-intellectual aspects of training that are important to him. This is because these aspects are important in giving the future priest the spiritual training and pastoral reference points he will need to lead the men and women of his time to God. For this, seminarians must, above all, work to become and remain true men of God. "The priest is not an administrator of some association whose membership he seeks to maintain and increase. He is God's messenger among men. He aims to lead to God and thus also to increase the true communion of people among themselves. That is why, dear friends, it is so important that you learn to live in constant contact with God."

The second thing that seminary life should help to incarnate in the lives of future priests is intimate union with Christ through the sacraments of the Eucharist and Penance. Thus, the Pope reminds us that, "The Eucharist is the centre of our relationship with God and of the pattern of our life. Celebrating it by participating in it inwardly and thus encountering Christ in person must be the centre of all our days." As for the sacrament of Penance, Benedict XVI says, "It teaches me to look at myself from God's point of view, and obliges me to be honest with myself. It leads me to humility." Finally, Benedict XVI invites the seminarians not to let die in them the feeling of popular piety which, certainly, can appear irrational and must therefore always be purified, but which "deserves our love and [...] makes us complete People of God."

These three of Pope Benedict XVI's instructions on seminary training also indirectly addressed trainers. They call for training through practice and example, which cannot be achieved by simply communicating the knowledge that the intellectual dimension promoted by the sacred sciences, supplemented by the secular sciences, is responsible for. Regarding this intellectual training, Benedict XVI invites seminarians to give it their full attention, through this wise warning: "It is completely erroneous to always immediately ask the pragmatic question: Will this be of use to me later? Will it be of practical, pastoral use?" According to Benedict XVI, a good and solid intellectual training is actually the best way to be able to respond to the concerns of the contemporary world.

Constant Training of Diocesan Clergy

The need for constant training of the diocesan clergy is no longer doubtful; no one doubts its value as an aid and encouragement to those who dedicate themselves to the priesthood ministry on a daily basis. In this regard, the new Directory for the Ministry and Life of Priests, promulgated under Benedict XVI's papacy, states that: "It is clear that the most detrimental effect of [the] surging secularisation is the priestly ministry crisis. This is expressed, on the one hand, by a marked decrease in vocations and, on the other, by the spread of both a loss of the sense of the supernatural character of the priestly mission and the propagation of inauthentic forms which often, in their extreme forms, have created situations of great suffering."

In view of the interest expressed by Benedict XVI in the problem of secularisation, the constant training of the clergy, already affirmed by other Church documents, is given renewed interest. It is in this context that the Pope indicates the meaning of constant training in *Africae Munus*. Addressing priests, he writes, "In view of the complexity of the situations with which you are confronted, I invite you to deepen your prayer life and your ongoing training; let this be both spiritual and intellectual."

Following the guidelines of this contribution and without

neglecting the other dimensions of continuous training, all of which are equally important, let us emphasise in particular intellectual training, in which, according to the new Directory for the Ministry and Life of Priests, "... particular importance should be given to the most important themes for cultural debate and pastoral practice, such as, for example, those concerning social ethics and bioethics.

Special attention should be given to the problems posed by scientific progress, which so profoundly influence the mentality and life of our contemporaries. The priest must ensure that he remains adequately informed in order to give reason for hope (cf. 1 Pet 3:15) by answering the questions of his Christians. He is obliged to keep abreast of scientific progress, carefully consulting competent experts and sound doctrine. [For] when presenting the word of God, he must take into account the evolution, growth, and intellectual training of those with whom he is speaking and know how to adapt to their level."

It is a matter of ensuring a permanent renewal of the knowledge acquired, not in an academic form, but rather through spiritual exercises, workshops for exchange and sharing of experiences, where pastors in the field confront the realities lived in their apostolic fields with those of others, with the aim of finding solutions to go further. As the new Directory on the life and ministry of priests reiterates, "All this process must converge towards conversion to Christ, so that the truths of the faith, the spiritual life and ministerial activity contribute to the progressive growth of the whole presbyterate."

Conclusion

In reflecting on how to tackle this contribution on the training of diocesan priests, it seemed obvious to us, in order to underline Benedict XVI's particular contribution, to address it in connection to the problem of secularisation. We agree that he is not the first Pope to highlight this issue. However, his unceasing commitment to rekindle the enthusiasm of Christians to be salt and light in the world has convinced us to pursue his call to constantly seek adequate responses to the challenge of the secularisation of our societies. Commenting on the work of the Synod on the New Evangelisation, convened by Benedict XVI from 7 to 28 October 2012, one author wrote: "At the end of the synod, it must be said, on the contrary, that the Church as a whole is called to live a true internal revival. An expression, such as renewed evangelisation, would correspond well to this process." The author specifies that, "The starting point is the novelty of the contexts: it is this that calls for a new evangelisation. That this implies an interior renewal of each person and each community is obvious; but the call to creativity is also very important." I find this a fine tribute to Pope Benedict XVI and an invitation to continually seek the best way to ensure the efficient training of diocesan priests by following his intuitions.

Africa, Witness to Pope Benedict XVI's Resignation

Rev. Fr. Dr. Engelbert Meyongo Nama[1]

Introduction

Beyond its physical, spiritual, or social causes, to resign from power, which often constitutes a willful act in the political or religious sphere, is an event of unusual character. For some it is a bolt from the blue, the sky falling to earth, for others a bold act, an institutional innovation, a dramatic move. While the act may have something intrinsically Stoic about it, it nevertheless places its authors in the anthology of great historical figures who have stunned the world. In fact, "the gesture does not correspond to what seems generally expected of social actors, to act as best they can for themselves, to rise in hierarchy, to rise or remain in power."[2]

When Diocletian, the bloodthirsty emperor of the third and fourth centuries and predecessor of Emperor Constantine, decided to relinquish his power, the Roman Empire lived in relative political stability for almost twenty years. External threats diminished considerably. Contemporaries were, therefore, struck by Diocletian's decision in 305 to voluntarily relinquish power and leave it to his successors who had already been enthroned. Diocletian's abdication is held to be a bold institutional innovation, for from Augustus to Diocletian no emperor had abdicated. Imperial power had a life-long duration and ceased only with death. Death, be it natural or violent, was what ended a reign, when it was necessary to change the prince.[3]

Recognised as the most powerful monarch of the first half of the sixteenth century, Charles V inherited various powers from

Spain, his colonial empire and the seventeen provinces of the Netherlands. At the end of a life of struggle, undermined and disillusioned by his failures, weakened by old age and disease, he progressively stripped himself of his power in 1558, ceded all his powers to his son Philip, and retired to the Hieronymite monastery of Yuste, in a small house built for him.[4]

Not far from us, on 4 November 1982, the then Cameroonian President Ahmadou Ahidjo announced in a radio address that he was resigning from office. The resignation came as a complete surprise. President Ahidjo had held undivided power for nearly 22 years and had been re-elected as head of state in early 1980. His term of office was due to end in 1985.[5] When asked about the reasons for his resignation, the former president said, "I took the decision to resign on my own because I believe that power is not a personal privilege, but a service of the State and that one should not cling to it against all odds, even if one is experiencing health challenges, even if these are curable and temporary."

Going back in history, we can examine the thirteenth-century abdication of Francis of Assisi who, in 1220, renounced the leadership of the Order he had founded. On the day of his abdication, he said, "From now on, consider me dead but here is Brother Peter of Catania, whom you and I will all obey." Seeing the brothers weeping and affected by the pain caused by their groans, St. Francis prayed saying:

> Lord, not being able to take care of this family that you
> have entrusted to me until now. Now, because of the
> weaknesses that you know, sweet Lord, since I can no
> longer look after this family, I recommend it to our min-
> isters. Let them be bound on the day of judgment to
> give an account before you, if any of their brethren have
> perished through their negligence, their example, or
> also through their harsh correction.[6]

History records that Francis remained a subject until his death, acting more humbly than any of the others.

When Benedict XVI relinquished his papacy in 2013, the controversy centered on this sovereign and free decision to leave a power that was not given to oneself and that one must keep until the end, following the example of John Paul II. Questions arise about the vocabulary used to express the mourning of power: is it a resignation, a term refused by the Vatican press director, who understood the term in the sense of abandoning one's post, a non-canonical vision close to "I wash my hands of it," a bit like cowardice or throwing in the towel.[7] It is therefore imperative to shed more light on the terms used in order to properly address this question on this attempt at a canonical reading of Pope Benedict XVI's renunciation, and then, beyond questions of terminology, to address the aspect of the impact exercised by Pope Celestine V on Benedict XVI's renunciation. Returning to the canonical background on questions of causes and motives for the pope's renunciation, we shall mention very briefly the question of emeritus in general.

Terminology

Renounce is a thirteenth-century word, borrowed from the Latin *renuntiatio*. This noun is equivalent to the Latin verb *renuntio, avi, atum, are*, which means to renounce, to give up the use or enjoyment of something, to denounce a contract. The verb *renuntiare* is formed from *re* marking the movement backwards, in return, and from *nuntiare*, to announce in return, to announce publicly, to report or to give a counter-order. The word abdicate is close to it. Indeed, borrowing from the Latin *abdicare*, from ab (to) and *dicere* (to say) means "not to grant," "to refuse to award." In a political sense it means to give up (power), to give up (possession), rights, to resign from office, to give up power, etc. Also borrowed from Latin in the 14th century, the word resignation derives from the supin *demissum* from *demittere* "to let fall," from demarking the movement up and down and from *mittere* "to send." The word refers to the action of renouncing one's functions, an office or an official dignity.[8] It is at the moment when the pope strips himself of his supreme power that some of these words take on greater prominence.[9]

Benedict XVI and Celestin V

Historically, the name Benedict is a name that reflects God's plan. On the one hand is Benedict XV, the prophet of peace during and after the First World War and author of the encyclical letter *Maximum illud*, and on the other is Benedict, the father of the monks and of the new beginning of Christianity in the barbaric times after the collapse of Roman society. On Wednesday 27 April, at his first audience in St Peter's Square, Benedict XVI said:

> St. Benedict is a fundamental point of reference for the unity of Europe, and a powerful reminder of the unavoidable Christian roots of its culture and civilization. From this father of Western monasticism, we know the instruction given to monks in his Rule: "put nothing absolutely above Christ." At the beginning of my service as successor to St. Peter, I pray St, Benedict helps us keep Christ firmly at the center of our lives. May he always be in the first place in our thoughts and in our every activity.[10]

While the two Benedicts guided the action plans of Benedict XVI's papacy, other less visible but equally present factors accompanied his decision to step down.

Following the Aquila earthquake in April 2009, Pope Benedict XVI travelled to northern Italy to pray for the victims of the earthquake. On the same occasion, he visited the Basilica of Our Lady of Collemaggio, where the relics of the holy Pope Celestine V (1294–1296) were rescued from the rubble. On that occasion, he placed his enthronement pallium there. The pallium has always been both the sign of the pope's high rank and the symbol of apostolic succession and the fullness of his episcopal function *(plenitude pontificalis officii)*, so that the removal of the pallium from the pope clearly signifies his deposition, for by stripping him of the pallium he is stripped of his function, his power.[11] In the homily inaugurating his papacy on 24 April 2005, Pope Benedict XVI explained his meaning of the pallium in evocative terms:

> The pallium, a pure woolen cloth which is placed on my shoulders, is a very ancient sign, which the Bishops of Rome have worn since the end of the fourth century, it can be considered an image of the yoke of Christ, which the Bishop of this city, the Servant of the Servants of God, takes upon his shoulders. The yoke of God is the will of God, which we accept. And this will is not for me an external weight, which oppresses us and takes away our freedom... The will of God does not alienate us, it purifies us—sometimes even in a painful way—and leads us to ourselves.[12]

While welcoming the pallium as the investiture of his dignity and *potestas*, the Roman pontiff privileges in the juridical act of renunciation more the dichotomy of God's will—human freedom. God's will is manifested ostensibly by a yoke received and joyfully accepted from God. This divine will is not binding or alienating; it is an inner awareness that favors a reflection and a free and responsible decision.[13] Thus, the Pope's decision to renounce his Papal ministry appears as the consequence of an act born of a double movement of divine will and human freedom. Through the symbolic gesture of placing the pallium on the relics of Celestine V, Benedict XVI symbolically renewed the extraordinary act of his predecessor, a gesture that he made few centuries later after having previously explained its cogency and the conditions of its legitimisation during his enthronement.

This almost obvious proximity between the two pontiffs is also evident in other areas. On the one hand, from the point of view of the voluntary abandonment of the mission, followed by a choice of life, that of integration or return to the monastic life. Whereas the first was already a monk before and after his resignation, the second made this choice after his renunciation. This decision is explained by the search for space of silence, a unique way of permanent dialogue with God on the modern questions facing the Church and the world. On the other hand, from the point of view of legitimising his resignation from the pontifical office, it is based on the *justa causa*, namely age, physical unfitness, and the prevalence of the common good of the Church. Thus, although several centuries separate these two popes, their destinies and a common mission vision undeniably bring them together. However, both in the Middle Ages and today, the double resignation of Pope Celestine V and Benedict XVI has raised and continues to raise many questions, particularly about the modalities of abandoning the office.

Reasons for the Resignation

Three issues determine the resignation. First, the failure to apply the oath sworn before God and the people. The question on the spiritual level is: Does he who has not given himself power have the power to renounce it? Can I renounce what I do not have the power to acquire? There is therefore a willingness to let go of the ordinary laws and rules of society. Then there is a Weberian drive to question or even threaten the established order. The prophet, in the name of his charisma, changes the order of things, i.e., the status quo, to the point that the world is never again as it was before—that is the driving force of history. Finally, we have the subjective and personal determination to leave power, often under the beneficial or calculated instigation of a doctor. While some leaders have left power through bodily weakness, illness, or old age, others have been the victims of a spurious medical diagnosis cleverly put together by an outside opposition. Afterwards, they tried to re- turn to power by other less legal means. Determinants are therefore both private (subjective) and public (objective).

Between the two lies a relationship between power and substance. Between the natural and the supernatural aspects. From the beginning, at St. Peter's Square in Rome, Benedict XVI already said that he had no programme, because the only programme of a pope is to listen to God. "My true programme of government is not to do my own will, not to pursue my own ideas, but, together with the whole Church, to listen to the word and the will of God, and to allow myself to be guided by Him, so that he himself may guide the Church in this period of our history."

It is easy to understand why in this context Pope Francis favours the model of Christ, that of a God abdicating his immortality, the king refusing earthly power, rejecting the power that defiles and corrupts.[14] He who abdicates does not simply give up power, it is in fact an act of power where the individual, imposing his choice, withdraws, as a mixed person, to his natural body and abandons the political body;[15] this is according to Ernest Kantorowicz's vision. As naturally a mortal man, the pope can be subject to illness, physical deterioration, and death. But in this mortal body of the pope lies an immortal body. When a pope dies or abdicates, the pontifical power is not dead but is passed on to the next pope, without any change in him. The king has two united, indivisible bodies, each of which is entirely contained in the other: the political body and the natural body. To say that the Pope is withdrawing into his private body does not mean that he is giving up active ministry. He does not return to a life of travel, meetings, receptions, conferences, etc.

> I do not abandon the cross, but I remain in a new way close to the crucified One. I do no longer bear the power of office for the Church government, but in the service of prayer I remain alone, as it were, in the precincts of St. Peter. St. Benedict, whose name I bear as Pope, is a great example to me in this. He showed us the way to a life which, whether active or passive, belongs to the work of God.

A Pope Emeritus

Beyond the canonical debates on the real status of a pope emeritus, there is also the clear question of the relationship between two popes, the one in office and the pope emeritus. Pope Francis frequently receives the Pope Emeritus, whom he considers the Grandfather of the house. He pays tribute to the work of Joseph Ratzinger who, after his historic renunciation, promised allegiance to the Pope. If he is Pope Emeritus, it therefore means he is also Bishop Emeritus. He therefore values the fraternal relationship that should unite the bishop in office and the bishop emeritus. In this regard, the prescriptions of the Directory for the Pastoral Ministry of Bishops, Apostolorum Successores retains a current and prophetic meaning:

> The Bishop Emeritus will endeavour not to interfere in any way, either directly or indirectly, in the conduct of the diocese and will avoid any attitude and relationship which could even give the impression that he constitutes almost a parallel authority to that of the diocesan Bishop, with detrimental consequences for the life and the pastoral unity of the diocesan community. In this light, the Bishop Emeritus will always exercise his activity in full agreement with and dependent on the diocesan Bishop, so that everyone understands clearly that the latter is the only one at the head of the diocese and that he is the one primarily responsible for the government of the diocese.

As such, Pope Benedict consecrates the spiritual link to be maintained with the office and with the powers that be.

To the best of our knowledge, Pope Emeritus Benedict XVI did not propose to the African people, and very specifically to African leaders, any text on the modalities of governance. He did not make any moralising speech reminding the bishops emeritus of the virtue of "quitting." However, his renunciation in itself constitutes a didactic-pedagogical field for all those who have received the mission of governing a people but consider themselves to be indispensable or even irreplaceable.

Conclusion

Canon 332:22 states: If it happens that the Roman Pontiff renounces his office, it is required for validity that the renunciation be made freely and that it be duly manifested, but not that it be accepted by anyone. These conditions were undoubtedly met in Pope Benedict XVI's renunciation. Given the human temptation to cling to power despite human warnings, Joseph Ratzinger did not shy away from the wolves, but, after discernment, returned to his monastic vocation to maintain the spiritual bond that binds him to the Church in obedience to the Church's Magisterium. For all this, the issue remains as to the application to the Roman Pontiff of the rule laid down by Paul VI in *Ingravescentem Aetatem* on resignation at the age of 75.

The Area of Social Sciences

Benedict's attention focused on several major themes and teachings. In the areas of "faith and politics" he addresses the theme of the granting of freedom and the risk of the "colonization" of consciences through an ideology that denies the fundamental certainty about man.[1] In the area of education he emphasizes the transcendent dimension of education and teaching. He thus denounces a purely utilitarian conception of education which would forget its "high aspirations."[2] Concerning science he speaks of a modern "shift" in epistemology which is in fact the disconnection between science and ethics. Technical activity carries its own justification, assuming the elimination of ethics as a standard source regulating this technical activity itself. He then leads a fight against technicality which denies the ethical responsibility of science. Despite the rigid doctrine, he also discussed with other world religions and faiths. This panel then presented a range of themes that are dear to Benedict XVI.

Benedict XVI's Concept of Opening a Loophole on What Blocks an African Concept

Dr. Anata Mawata Augusta[1]

Introduction

The ideology of development is the belief in a march towards a better economic, political, social, and cultural situation after a break with tradition. This situation can only come about as a result of a transformation of Man in all his dimensions. The term development is equivalent to the term progress, which was in use before the 1960s. (Francois Alain) It is the most present ideology in Africa today. In this paper, we will first see how this ideology constitutes a heavy burden on the African. Later, we will discuss Benedict XVI's view in relation to this ideology. Finally, in the third part, we will see how this thought opens a clue to the *heavy load*.

The Burden of the Ideology of Development

In Africa, development ideology legitimizes and leads to attacks on human life because, like its twentieth-century counterparts, it seeks to reform history on the basis of concepts that abolish the reality of human nature and sacrifice the immediate need for human beings to the future and ultimate goal.

This is how the following acts of violence have become so dismayingly commonplace in the daily lives of Africans. In several countries, people's homes are razed to the ground in order to hand over land to multinationals for the direct investments needed for development (...). On the Nguéli highway, a Chadian council area bordering the town of Kousseri in Cameroon, old women are raped and their meagre provisions, the only guarantee of their survival, are confiscated because they are accused of smuggling goods that are harmful to Chad's public finances (a policy of fraud repression.) In the streets of Bangui, Ndjamena, Yaoundé, etc., small hawkers in city centres are brutalized and their only livelihood destroyed to make the city more beautiful, as provided for in the urban development policy. People are forced to live in the swamps, on slippery or swampy ground, because the land is the property of the state and the elites who are the mainstay of development. Local languages are discarded in favour of French, English, and even Chinese to allow for a better assimilation of development tools and concepts by the populations (education policies.) Human lives are suppressed to facilitate the urban movement of key actors in the development of the state, as was the case in November 2019 in N'Djamena as the convoy of the President of the National Assembly passed by. As for those of the weakest, they are legally suppressed through policies of *voluntary interruption of pregnancy or reproductive health* on the grounds that they constitute an obstacle to the freedom of individuals, which is worse than a bottleneck to economic growth.

Faced with such a juggernaut, the African populations, besieged, stripped, deprived, and expropriated, adopt the tactic of *poaching*, i.e., "those calculated actions determined by the absence of a proper person." (Certeau Michel) As for the intellectuals, their relationship with this ideology is similar to that of their Parisian counterparts in the 1970s vis-à-vis the structuro-Marxist, i.e., a religious belief. (Serge Proulx, p171) Thus, all the difficulties, successes, stalemates, and plots of the African's existence do not escape the prism of development analysis. The relationship of these African intellectuals can nevertheless be broken down into three categories that can guide their practices and their conception of development policy.

The first category is that which advocates a total adherence to development ideology. Following the example of the philosopher Marcien Towa, it advocates a material and cultural domestication of science and technology on the one hand, and a change of mentality on the other, including the rejection of all transcendence. (Towa, P54) This position seems to be the most popular in Africa, in view of the development mechanisms[2] that are deployed there and the fortune of the *Technoscience concept.* It is flawed in that it considers the ideology of development "as a general model of the process of social evolution, indifferent to the spatio-temporal framework to which it applies," according to Habermas. (Berten, 85)

The second category favours a development that combines African culture and Western technology. This is because it is especially sensitive to the erosion of cultural elements generated by the deployment of ideology of development. We can place the philosopher Hebga and his disciples in this category. This philosophy is present as well in the political and spiritual movements. Its functioning, not just entails a high risk of slipping into irrationality and obscurantism, it comes up against cultural diversity and the current globalised experiences of populations. The last category is the one that approaches development from the daily life of the people; this is the sociology of the bottom. It militates, for example, for a kind of recognition of the informal economy, of grassroots associations, those actors largely forgotten by the deployment of the development enterprise from the state. Nevertheless, its founder:

> Jean Marc Ela admits that beyond the informal economy, Africa needs stable enterprises, i.e., a substantial economy of production, trade, and services (...) and he wonders whether African culture is capable of producing the necessary commitment for a renewal of the economy, and whether the African heritage of family solidarity constitutes an obstacle to the personal independence which the entrepreneur needs for the success of his projects. (P31, Yao Assogba)

It also constitutes an admission of faith in the development ideology and its blindness to its violent nature.

Despite the diversity of their approach to development, these thoughts have in common their avoidance of the denial of the ontological human nature of any development enterprise. The hypothesis that explains this evasion is that the technical benefits of development are so effective that they are best kept despite their disadvantages. Nevertheless, this silence seems to implicitly endorse the violence that accompanies the deployment of the development enterprise in Africa and constitutes a great inconsistency for those thoughts that seek to free the African from all forms of violence.

This is where the philosophy of Benedict XVI is of great help. Indeed, it allows us to confront the question of the denial of human nature intrinsic to any development economy while maintaining its technical benefits.

Benedict XVI's Development Ideology

The work of Benedict XVI, Ratzinger the theologian, is extremely composite in the variety of topics it addresses. It deals with the problems of human rights, the economy, freedom, and truth. (Aidens Nichols)

Before entering into the heart of Benedict XVI's philosophy, it is appropriate to make a few clarifications. Benedict XVI is not a reformer, nor a conservative. (Hans Kung) Nor does he come from such a milieu as his detractors like to say. Very often, his thoughts and actions are hastily read and even opposed, and reduced to his activity as head of the Congregation for the Doctrine of the Faith. Benedict XVI advocates for the recognition of women's right to work and education, (13 February 2007, 2009) for democracy, and for science and technology. Also, as his biographies indicate, (Millestone) his father, Joseph Ratzinger, was an outspoken opponent of Nazism and his mother, Maria Paintner, a former worker. He is also a strong advocate of the equality of peoples. Indeed, in his address to the Latin American Bishops' Conference on 13 May 2007, he said that "without knowing it, the Indians were looking for Christ in their rich religious traditions.

Benedict XVI's on Opening a Loophole on What Blocks an African Concept

Christ was the saviour for whom they silently longed. With the water of baptism (...), the Holy Spirit came to fertilise their crops, purifying them and developing the many seeds that the Incarnate Word had placed in them." He wanted to show that Christ is in no way a contribution of Western culture to other peoples but a universal reality and a presence to all peoples. This fact establishes their equality and dignity. Nor is Benedict XVI insensitive to human misery and ignorant of extra-European realities, as the indictments of his approach to liberation theology (of his work) would have us believe. As proof, in 2006, in the Encyclical *Caritas in veritate*, he proposed an approach to poverty that takes into account the dignity of the person and does not reduce it to his propensity to consume. He is not against relativism either, but rather "against the one-sided absolutism of relativism or freedom." (*Credo today*, p. 229) Is he post-modern? If postmodernism is understood as any position of distancing oneself from the unheard-of faith in modernism, from any kind of globalisation mechanism, yes. If, on the other hand, post-modernism is this evacuation of God, this rejection of the possibility of meaning and of the distinction of values, or even "a vector for the enlargement of individualism," (Berten) then, no. Finally, Benedict XVI fits much more into the *Neoconservative* category of Habermas' typology of critics of modernism. (Berten A) Neoconservatives are those:

> ...who ultimately adopt the most positive attitude towards the achievements of modernism. They welcome the development of modern science, as long as it only leaves its domain to advance technical progress, capitalist growth, and streamlined administration. For the rest, they advocate a policy of defusing the explosive forces of cultural modernity (...). They only accept the rational instrumental developments of science and technology and leave ethics to the state or religion (Berten, p. 94).

Benedict XVI's philosophy on progress is transversal to several of his writings. But it is in *Spe Salvi, Sauvé dans l'espérance,*

(Spe Salvi, Saved in Hope,) that this issue is attacked head-on. The Encyclical *Spe Salvi* was published on 30 November 2007, the second year of Benedict XVI's pontificate, in the context of the great political and media offensive of the ideologies of moral relativism in preparation for their political deployment. In fact, in the West, 2006 and 2007 were the years of *discussion for the revision of the bioethics laws,* of bills opening the legal recognition of homosexual practices and unions, of strong media coverage of bioethical experiments and other research on human cells, etc. What links these dispersed initiatives is a belief in scientific progress combined with a vision of freedom as the overcoming of human limits, as autonomy. Benedict XVI decided to take up the challenge that these ideologies pose to the Christian faith. According to him, "the Christian must not shut himself up in the ghetto of an idealistic backwardness or a literal respect for tradition.[3] He must seek dialogue with his time and meet the challenges of the modern world." (*Creed Today,* p.228)

Spe Salvi thus exposes the illusions, impostures, and dangers of the ideology of progress, which consists in making people believe that human freedom can in no way come about through transcendence, but rather through technology, politics, science, and in our time, through the market. In order to achieve such an error, these ideologies simply consider freedom and reason to be self-sufficient. But reason and freedom need a guide; left to their own devices, they breed many misfortunes, including the totalitarianisms that have marked the history of humanity.

Currently, this ideology of progress is at the origin of the paralysis of Western societies in the face of death on the one hand, and on the other, of policies with a deadly logic. On the contrary, Christian hope, the presence of God in the historical horizon of man, which is both "informative" and "performative," is a source of freedom. This is because it allows him to bear his finiteness and provides him with the moral resources necessary to make everyday life better. It is this hope that enables man to use science and technology for humanity's freedom. Benedict XVI cites Bakhita, the African slave woman who was liberated materially but also in her conscience through her encounter with Christ, among the people transformed by Christian hope.

Benedict XVI addresses the theme of development in the conceptual part of the search for the origin of spiritual individualism as a result of the contamination of Christianity by the ideology of progress. True to the tradition of the German Enlightenment, he "emphasises the historical character of Man. It follows that all theological claims about man must root their transcendental claims in the context of human history." (Aidens, pg. 394) Thus he unfolds the cause of the ideology of progress in three historical periods. The first is that of Bacon, the second that of the French Enlightenment, and finally that of Positivism and Marxism.

Concerning Bacon, Benedict XVI says, "It is the new correlation between experience and method that puts man in a position to arrive at an interpretation of nature in conformity with its laws and thus to arrive, ultimately, at 'the victory of art over nature.'" (SS,14)

In *De dignitate et augmentis scientiarum*, Bacon, in reaction to the prevailing Scholastic rationalism, states that knowledge comes from experience and not from human reason. The latter is limited in its ability to understand nature because it anticipates and projects onto things, what is not. He therefore advocates the creation of a device for exploring nature that will help reason to better understand what its senses reflect back to it. This device is designed to be performed by several people in order to confirm the results. Bacon is thus the father of experiment and science as a community activity. (Jaquet Chantal) In the same light Bacon criticises the purely speculative dimension of Greek science which is irrelevant to the real world, which "wisdom is all in words and sterile in writings." (Jaquet Chantal) He substitutes a knowledge of nature that is complementary to its mastery. Indeed, knowledge of nature allows one to imitate it by creating objects. These objects in turn help to better explore nature. The relationship between nature and technology is a cumulative process and constitutes a kind of virtuous spiral.

Thus, as time goes by, man has a greater knowledge of nature, and therefore has more and more possibilities to master it. It is this propensity, over time, for greater knowledge of nature, and therefore greater control over it, that Bacon calls progress. Bacon thinks that man will reach a stage where his knowledge of nature will enable him to have total control over it. This reasoning "is then also applied to theology: this new correlation between science and practice would mean that the dominion over creation, given to man by God and lost through original sin, would be restored." (SS, 15) Applied to morality, this reasoning leads to the deduction that the act does not consist in evaluating good and evil, but is reduced to evaluating advantages and disadvantages, because the good itself does not exist. According to Aidan Nichols, a commentator on Benedict XVI, "this tendency to render the moral dimension superfluous by recourse to a quasi- mechanical guarantee of social justice is very much in the register of the emasculated concept of reason that Bacon and Comte bequeathed to European civilisation." (p. 314)

As an Englishman and politician, Bacon calls on the state, the nation, not the Church, to create institutions and other conditions for the deployment of science. He thus replaces Divine Providence with the state. At the same time, freedom is reduced to its natural dimension as a possibility offered to human bodies, without any link to transcendence. Science, through its discoveries, thus allows man to go beyond the limits of his human nature. Bacon can thus be ranked among the forefathers of transhumanism and of this "art or technique of extra-medical transformation of the human being by performing on his body," what Jérôme Goffette called anthropotechnics. Reason, on the other hand, is limited to creating the conditions that allow this freedom to reign. In Bacon's context, where the conditions of freedom are guaranteed by the Church and the States, "the two concepts thus carry within them a revolutionary potential of enormous explosive force." (SS, 18)

It is this revolution that the notoriously "anti-clerical *French Enlightenment Proponents*" adopted. (Viot) They materially and symbolically uninstalled the religious cult and the *order of God* and replaced it with that of the *Goddess Reason and the established order of political decisions*. For the revolutionaries of 1789, the Church and the monarchy were the main obstacles to freedom. They should therefore be abolished to allow the reign of reason to guarantee Liberty. The French Revolution has as an episode of Terror whose atrocity in terms of human toll remains emblematic. According to a certain historiography (François Furet, Patrick Buisson,) terror is the first form of totalitarianism, preceding those of the twentieth century which are Nazism, Fascism, and Stalinism. *Terror* is one of those moments that led Benedict XVI to conclude that "ignorance of his existence, atheism, is expressed concretely as the absence of respect of human beings for one another and to know God means to have a new vision of man." (SS, p. 25)

The third historical period is nineteenth-century positivism and Marxism.

> The nineteenth century did not deny its faith in progress as a form of human hope, and it continued to regard reason and freedom as guiding stars to be followed on the path of hope." Count Augustus, the father of Positivism, takes up Bacon in his writings with the same naive confidence in progress. He rejects the principle of a political organisation based on morality and replaces it with one based on science. Benedict XVI notes that this "liberation, based on the marginalisation of morality and consequently of responsibility and conscience, implies a search for perfection of an intrinsically immoral kind. (SS18)

The nineteenth century was also the century of technical discoveries and creations that produced a new social situation with the industrial proletariat class. Faced with their miserable condition of life, Karl Marx proposed to the proletarians a freedom no longer by technical means, but of politics:

> A revolutionary leap was needed. Karl Marx took up this aspiration of the moment and, with vigorous language and thought, sought to launch this great new

and, as he considered it, definitive step of history towards salvation—(...) Once the truth of the beyond had been dispelled, the truth of the hereafter had to be established. The criticism of heaven becomes a criticism of earth, the criticism of theology becomes a criticism of politics. Progress towards the better, towards the definitively good world, does not simply come from science, but from politics—from a scientifically thoughtout politics, which knows how to recognise the structure of history and society, and which thus points the way to revolution, to the change of all things. (SS)

The implementation of Marx's theses by Lenin, Trotsky, and Stalin resulted in over 20 million deaths in the former USSR alone.

Other emblematic illustrations of the propensity of the ideology of development to produce cruelty are the First World War and the Second World War. The First World War, with its millions of deaths and all the horrors that technology in the service of war enabled, was experienced as a collapse of the liberal dogma of progress and, therefore, of the liberal conception. (Millestone, p. 64) The Second World War, with its Nazi and Fascist totalitarianism, is the height of this cruelty. The current phase of development is one of ultra-liberalism. Faith is placed in market mechanisms despite the cruel nature of their imperfections. According to Benedict XVI, it leads to a fear of suffering, including death, and to economic and social policies with a deadly logic.

Ultraliberalism is also at the root of the failure of Western pluralist democracy. Indeed,

> Crises bring it close to the precipice; shifts in the life of the spirit threaten to steal the ground from under its feet. Joseph Ratzinger judges that the main threat to democracy lies in its unwillingness to accept the intrinsic imperfection of human things. Foremost among the enemies (perhaps unwittingly) of democracy are those who believe that in a liberated society, the good will be

irrevocably maintained through structures. (Aidan Nichols, p. 314)

Ultraliberalism is politically materialised outside the Western world through development aid, which has the effect of driving men away from God through the pride of their supposed knowledge. It has made the Third World the Third World in the modern sense. Such aid has discarded the existing moral, religious, and social structures and has introduced its technocratic mentality into the vacuum thus created. (*Jesus of Nazareth*, p. 53)

Of the various issues raised by Benedict XVI in his critique of development ideology, we will pick out three in an attempt to break the secrecy that it holds over the African. These points are as follows:

1) An assessment of the violent footprints of development;
2) The teaching of a beneficent science;
3) A political contract based on trust in people and not in the mechanisms of institutions.

What does Benedict XVI's Philosophy Offer Us to Face the Onslaught of Development Ideology?

Benedict XVI is not the first critic of development ideology. In the social sciences, Max Weber, father of the term *modernity*, by prophesying its uncertain future because of the distance from the Christian faith, opened the way. He was followed by a plethora of authors including Polanyi and iconoclastic anthropologists such as Sahlins and Baudrillard. Nevertheless, these critics come up against the question of the technical benefits of the ideology of development. Sahlins' description of the self-sufficiency and abundance of so-called primitive economies[4] leads to the conclusion that scientific discoveries, such as those of Pasteur and Fleming in the field of medicine, transport, and ICT revolutions, are futile. Benedict XVI nevertheless manages to overcome this

211

obstacle by showing that it is the vision of a freedom and a reason that poses itself as self-sufficient that produces the violent character of the ideology of development noted by these authors, and not the techniques themselves. It is, therefore, possible to benefit from technical achievements without falling into violence.

An Assessment of the Violent Footprints of Development

Benedict XVI lifts the veil on the myth that development is neutral and shows how it is ontologically violent. He thus calls on us to assess any violent footprints of development policies in Africa. Given the intensity of development injunctions in Africa, Africa cannot be immune to such violence. In terms of research, one could ask what part ontological development violence played in the great massacres and other genocides that took place in Africa at the end of the 20th century. How did reason and freedom, seen as self-sufficiency and blind trust in the institutions, lead to the events in Rwanda (1994) or to the crimes committed under the Habré regime (1982–1990) in Chad? Such a theory has rarely been explored; culturalist, historical, or even demographic perspectives were preferred. Another interesting avenue of research is that of the seeds of totalitarianism in Africa. Particularly, it is necessary to see how certain current groups, in this case the black supremacists who are very present on the web, in their posture of explaining everything about the domination of Africa, by racism, by a pseudo black essentialist identity, are likely to degenerate into totalitarianism in the long term.

A Beneficent Science

Benedict XVI shows that the self-sufficient logic of reason underlying the ideology of progress is at the root of its violence and failure. Such a logic is the underbelly of science as currently taught in our educational institutions. The following avenues can be suggested to curb this situation towards less ideological, pedagogical, and training logics: to propose in the content of teaching the grop-ing, hazardous, and limited character of knowledge; to replace the presentation of knowledge from authors or chronologically by thematic perspectives; to privilege epistemological postures which allow us to answer social malaises without bringing in the *Great Solution* and to show that the *Great Solution* to solve all the ills of the society is non-existent; developing models that allow for the analysis of regressions and progressions, or even stagna-tions of knowledge; mitigating the long term and universal scope of the teachings to emphasise the immediacy and proximity of knowledge and problems.

Furthermore, these teachings present science as antithetical to faith. This is the result of those philosophies that blame attach-ment to faith as the cause of Africa's backwardness in science. Benedict XVI shows that only faith can make science a means of human liberation. Without faith, science becomes a monster.

A Political Contract Based on Trust and Not on Institutions

The theses defended by Benedict XVI also invite us to distance ourselves from those in time, which give central place to institu-tion games. Indeed, *the consolidation of democratic institutions in Africa* is the main axis of the intervention strategies of African states, the European Union, the World Bank, the UNDP, etc. Through these strategies, these organisations are admitting their inability to respond to the current needs of the population, are lending themselves to the prevailing political irresponsibility, and are blurring ethical consciences in terms of political responsibility. Two recurrent cases illustrate this trend. The first is the fact that in terms of the ethical assessment of financial crimes, the judge-ment emphasis is no longer placed on the immoral character of the act itself, but rather on the fact that the person has been ap-prehended by the judicial institution. The second is the tendency of African leaders to amend constitutions to stand for re-election without regard to their word and their responsibility to the moral content of the constitution. For this reason, we propose a political contract based on trust in the present moment and in the individual responsibility of Man. Trust in the present moment is "simply the response to what, in a given situation, constitutes immediate necessity: the hungry must be fed, the unclothed must be clothed, the sick must be cared for, the imprisoned must be visited," (The Essence of Faith, p. 25) and the uneducated must be educated. "This policy must be independent of party and ideology. It is not a means to change the world ideologically and it is not at the service of worldly strategies, but it is the implementation here and now of the love that man constantly needs." (The Essence of Faith, p.25) As for the trust in man's responsibility, it consists in placing him before the consequences of his political acts as a respondent to a higher moral authority.

In view of the current situation, such a proposal is naïve, and could even be considered a joke. But we respond that it is serious, because the proposal is so relevant that Habermas the atheist, aware of the inability of reason and freedom to help themselves and therefore aware of the need for a guiding authority, is paired *with* Joseph Ratzinger, the Catholic theologian, and Prefect of the Congregation for the Doctrine of the Faith, in the fight against the defeatism of modern reason, and proposed a reconciliation between Greek reason and the Judeo-Christian faith. (Sandro Magister)

African traditions seemed to have understood this need for a contract based on the moral responsibility of man since time immemorial. Indeed, the idea of the person's responsibility to a higher rational being is present in all African languages: "*mianye dji noubate,*" for the Sars of Chad, "*tchape djinou*" according to the Banem of Cameroon, "*Zapa bamon*" according to the Sango of the CAR, "*Ma djogwa amome Zamba*" according to the Etons of Cameroon and many others.

The Impact of Justice and Peace Commissions in the Civic Engagement of Catholic Christians in Cameroon

Dr. Martial Aimé Wakeu

Introduction

An observation of the reality of most African societies reveals that evils such as violations of fundamental human rights, tribalism, ethnocentrism, violence and wars, embezzlement of public funds, and foreign partisan interventions afflict Africa. The result is a situation of gross injustice, social inequality, and suffering that calls for justice, peace, and reconciliation for unity among the people of a country. At the dawn of the third millennium, Pope Benedict XVI, in his post-synodal exhortation *Africae Munus*, entrusted the commitment of Africa to the Lord Jesus Christ to the episcopate, the clergy, consecrated persons, and the lay faithful. This mission invited Africa to deepen its Christian vocation by inviting it to *"live, in the name of Jesus, reconciliation between persons and communities, and to promote peace and justice in truth for all."*[1] In other words, he invited every African Christian to commit himself or herself to the construction of a reconciled Africa, through the ways of truth and justice, love and peace. (AM, 3) This invitation is clearly relevant for African Christians in general and Cameroonian Christians in particular, in view of the many conflicts and tensions that are breaking the social fabric on both sides.

While recognising that the "construction of a just social order is a matter of the political sphere" and that "the Church has no technical solutions to offer and does not claim to interfere in the

State politics," (AM, 22) Benedict XVI nevertheless stresses that the Church has a mission of truth to fullfil and that she cannot remain outside the problems of men; it may be seen as an accomplice. (AM, 22) He entrusts this mission of sanctifying the temporal order to the lay Christians in particular: "Through her lay members, the Church makes herself present and active in the life of the world. The laity have a great role to play in the Church and in society."[2] (AM, 128)

In order to carry out this training mission, the Church was already involved in the civic education of citizens and in accompanying the electoral process in various countries through the Justice and Peace Commissions. In this way, the Church intended to contribute to the education of the people and to the awakening of their conscience and civic responsibilities. (AM, 23) Indeed, these commissions had been set up in many particular churches in Africa in response to the recommendations of Pope John Paul II's post-synodal Apostolic Exhortation *Ecclesia in Africa*. They were presented as true instruments of evangelisation through the awakening of Christian consciences to the defence of human rights, good governance, etc.; to the civic training of Christians and non-Christians to promote justice, peace, and reconciliation.[3] (IL, 19) The Justice and Peace Commissions of the Archdiocese of Yaoundé was created in 1969 by Bishop Jean Zoa with the mission of promoting justice, peace, and the integral development of the population through the defence of the dignity and fundamental rights of the human person.

Since the creation of the Yaoundé Diocesan Commission for Justice and Peace (CDJP-Y) and in the light of the Encyclical of Benedict XVI committing the Church of Africa to the service of reconciliation, justice, and peace, is it appropriate to ask about its impact in the emergence of an active and committed citizenship of Catholic Christians in the city of Yaoundé? This paper aims to answer this concern while highlighting the perception of Christians with regard to civic engagement and the role that this commission plays for them.

Benedict XVI and the Commitment of the Church in Africa to Reconciliation, Peace, and Justice

At the dawn of the third millennium, Pope Benedict XVI, through his post-synodal apostolic exhortation *Africae Munus*, invited the episcopate, the clergy, consecrated persons, and the lay faithful of the Church in Africa to place themselves at the service of reconciliation, justice, and peace in order to be the "salt of the earth" and the "light of the world." It is this invitation that we wish to revisit here.

Building a Reconciled, Just, and Peaceful Society: An Emergency for African Societies

In his message to the bishops of Mali on their ad limina visit on 18 May 2007, Pope Benedict XVI recalled that "the commitment of the Christians to the service of reconciliation, justice, and peace is an urgent imperative."[4] This invitation remains a major concern today in view of the multiple tensions, unease, and conflicts that the African continent is experiencing on both sides. Indeed, Pope John Paul II's first Synod for Africa[5] and the subsequent post-synodal Apostolic Exhortation *Ecclesia in Africa*[6] already emphasised that, in order to be relevant, the Church in Africa must not only be directed towards reconciliation, justice, and peace, but should also proceed to the formation of Christians for justice and peace; the strengthening of the prophetic role of the Church; the appropriate remuneration of workers; and the setting up of the Justice and Peace Commission to achieve this credible witness. (IL, 17)

Following on from *Ecclesia in Africa* and in keeping with the proposals of the synod fathers for the second special assembly for Africa, Benedict XVI in his post-synodal apostolic exhortation, *Africae Munus,* deepens the process of reconciliation, justice, and peace. He reminds the laity that they must be involved in the future of Africa, both socially and politically. The social doctrine of the Church should help them in this sense through its knowledge and experience. This can promote the development of the continent and the advent of a future that respects man. Therefore, initial and constant training, and pastoral accompaniment should serve this purpose.

The Urgency of Reconciliation

For Benedict XVI, Africa needs reconciliation not only because its mind keeps the painful scars left by fratricidal conflicts between ethnic groups, by slavery, and by colonisation, but also because today it is confronted with new rivalries, forms of slavery, and colonisation. (AM, 9) As Pope John Paul II already pointed out in the exhortation, *Ecclesia in Africa*, "in spite of the contemporary civilisation of the 'global village,' in Africa as elsewhere in the world, the spirit of dialogue, peace, and reconciliation is far from being in the hearts of all people. Wars, conflicts, racist and xeno-phobic attitudes still dominate the world of human relations." This is why the Church must commit itself and work for recon-ciliation. Moreover, social and ecclesial experiences call upon the Church to seek ways and means to rebuild communion, unity, episcopal or priestly fraternity, to clothe herself with prophetic courage, to commit herself to the training of lay leaders strength-ened in their faith to act in politics, so that they work to make dif-ferences live together in society. (IL, 54)

Although reconciliation is "a pre-political concept and reality" and for this reason "of the greatest importance for the political task itself," (AM, 19) Benedict XVI argues that it has its source in the love of Christ who restored humanity to the love of the Father. Thus:

> The experience of reconciliation establishes communion on two levels: on the one hand, communion between God and people, and on the other, because the experience of reconciliation also makes us (the reconciled humanity) "ambassadors of reconciliation," it also re-establishes communion among people... Thus, reconciliation is not only God's plan to bring back to himself in Christ the hu-manity separated and stained by sin, through forgiveness of sins and love. It is also the restoration of relationships

between people through the resolution of differences and the removal of obstacles to their relationships through their experience of God's love. (AM,20)

To achieve this reconciliation, one needs an inner purification, i.e., conversion. Without it, there would be no political commitment to building justice and peace. And if the power of reconciliation is lacking, there can be no real commitment to peace. This in turn requires God's grace.

> Indeed, it is God's grace that gives us a new heart and reconciles us to him and to others. Humanity was only restored to the love of the Father by Christ. Reconciliation, therefore, has its source in this love; it is born of the Father's initiative to renew the relationship with humanity that was broken by man's sin. (AM, 20)

Reconciliation restores peace, harmony, union of hearts, and serene coexistence between people or communities. It helps overcomes crises, restores people's dignity, and paves the way for development and lasting peace among people at all levels. (AM, 21) Its main actors are government officials, traditional rulers, and ordinary citizens. Benedict XVI reminds us that in order for reconciliation to become effective, it must be accompanied by a courageous and honest act as well as the search for those responsible and the determination of their responsibility. For the victims of the various abuses have a right to truth and justice. Hence the need to purify the memory in order to build a better society where the various tragedies are no longer repeated.

The Urgency of Justice

The human conscience is challenged to face the many injustices that exist in our world in general and within Africa in particular. The Church is called to hear the cry of the poor, of minorities, of women whose dignity is violated, of the marginalised, of poorly paid workers, of refugees and migrants, and of prisoners. (IL, 62) Thus, Benedict XVI reminds us that justice obliges us to "give each person his or her own personal belonging" and that in order to be lived in all dimensions of life, private and public, economic and social, it needs to be supported by subsidiarity and solidarity, and even more so to be animated by charity. For "according to the principle of subsidiarity, neither the state nor any larger society should substitute itself for the initiative and responsibility of individuals and intermediate bodies." Solidarity is the guarantor of justice and peace, of unity, so that "the abundance of some makes up for the lack of others." And charity, which ensures the link with God, goes further than distributive justice. For if "justice is the virtue that distributes personal goods to each [...] it is not the justice of man that pulls man from the true God." (AM, 24) This is why he maintains that justice must have its roots in reconciliation through the "truth of love." In the absence of this, it remains incomplete and is not authentic justice. It is the love of truth, (to which only the Spirit can lead us,) that traces the path that all justice must follow in order to lead to the restoration of the bonds of brotherhood in the "human family, a community of peace," reconciled with God through Christ. Indeed, justice is not disembodied and is necessarily anchored in human coherence. (AM, 18)[7] Even if the construction of a just social order falls within the competence of politics, it nevertheless calls for the responsibility of each citizen and the action of the Church. For the creation of this just social order should be done according to the logic of the beatitudes, which invite us to give preferential attention to the poor, the hungry, the sick, the foreigner, the humiliated, the prisoner, the despised migrant, the refugee, or the displaced person, etc. (AM, 27)

The Urgency for Peace

For Benedict XVI, reconciliation and justice are the two essential presuppositions of peace and to some extent define its nature. (AM, 17) In fact, the peace of men that is obtained without justice is illusory and ephemeral. Peace, therefore, has as its source "love in truth." (AM, 28) Thus, the Church is called to continue to reflect on how to build a society of peace through mutual aid, readiness to welcome the other, fraternal service of the weak (children, the sick, the elderly), justice and love among brothers and sisters, and the restoration of parental authority in families. (IL, 68)

Political Commitment:
A Path to a Society of Reconciliation, Justice, and Peace

For Benedict XVI, the establishment of a reconciled, just, and peaceful society requires a political institution which has the duty to establish a just social order. For this reason, the Church in Africa must contribute to the building of society in collaboration with government authorities and public and private institutions committed to the construction of the common good. (AM, 81) In other words, for the construction of a just social order, "one of the tasks of the Church in Africa is to breed upright and receptive consciences to the demands of justice, so that men and women may grow capable of achieving this just social order by their responsible conduct." (AM, 22) Although it is not the public role of the Church to involve herself in politics, it should be stressed that she has a say in it at the risk of escaping from concrete responsibility in human history into theological and spiritual theories. (AM, 17) In fact, its involvement in this field can be seen in two ways, "an indirect mode for pastors and a direct mode for the laity."[8] Consequently, the task of participating actively and directly in political life falls mainly to the laity, hence the need to train them well in the spiritual life and social doctrine of the Church, so that Christian virtues inform their social and political actions. This training mission is entrusted to the Justice and Peace Commissions of every diocese.

The Justice and Peace Commissions
and Civic Training of Christians

Continuing from his predecessors, Pope Benedict XVI reiterates that the local Church is committed to the civic training of the people, to the awakening of their conscience and their civic responsibilities through the Justice and Peace Commissions. Indeed, through them, the Church has been involved in the civic education of citizens and in accompanying the electoral process in various countries. It is through this educational role that the Church is recognised in many countries as a peacemaker, an agent of reconciliation, and a justice crusader. (AM, 23) In fact, these commissions have been real instruments of evangelisation through the awakening of Christian consciences to the defence of human rights, good governance, etc.; they have greatly contributed to the civic training of Christians and non-Christians to promote justice, peace, and reconciliation. This enables it to fulfill its mission of truth at all times and in all circumstances, in favour of a society that is commensurate with man, his dignity, and his vocation. (IL, 19) In view of the role that these commissions play in the Church and society, what evaluation can we make of the activities of the Yaoundé Diocesan Commission for Justice and Peace (CDJP-Y) with regard to the civic involvement of Christians in this city? Before looking specifically at this question, let us first look at the level of civic involvement in Cameroon.

The State of Citizen Engagement in Cameroon

According to the Auzou dictionary (2012), citizenship refers to the quality of a citizen or one who exercises that quality. It also refers to the participation in the life of the city. It "presupposes a conscious subject who, in his daily relations with other members of his community, is capable of making choices and acting responsibly on the basis of laws, rules, regulations and key principles that codify his or her rights and duties."[9] (Essi, 2017, p.67) It is in this light that Yankep (2017) defines active or committed citizenship as the implementation in everyday life of one's role as a citizen. She thus distinguishes between two types of citizens: the passive citizen, who chooses not to participate, and the active citizen, who participates. For her, active citizenship involves, among other things, associations, the exercise of the rights of association, free expression, strike, and demonstration.[10] Considering the conception of the sociologist T. H. Marshall, cited by Isabelle Ngo Nyouma, Kapchie (2017) recalls that the concept of citizenship includes the civil element, the social element, and the political element. The civil element refers to the rights necessary for individual freedom, namely freedom of expression and worship, the right to property, the right to enter into contracts, and the right to justice. The social element encompasses all rights ranging from the minimum right to economic well-being and security, to the right to fully participate in the social heritage, and to live a civilised life according to the prevailing norms of a given society. The political element refers to the right to participate in political power, as a member of a body vested with political authority, or as a voter of the members of that body.[11] What about civic involvement in Cameroon?

Despite the willingness of a large part of the population to come together and discuss societal issues, civic engagement remains problematic, if not an illusion in the Cameroonian context. (Kapchie, 2017) Not only do many social obstacles hinder its effectiveness and slow down its efficiency, (Nankep, 2017) but also its effectiveness remains conditioned by certain historical, political, social, and cultural constraints, as well as a clear knowledge of rights and duties, institutions, and the relationships that are supposed to govern relations between leaders and the governed. (Essi, 2017) Moreover, the notion of citizenship is struggling to enter the mainstream, not only because of a lack of interest and understanding of the issues and importance of citizenship, but also because of many factors that, over time, create a gradual rupture between the people and the state. (Ngwé and Kramme-Stermose, 2017) This lack of civic involvement has created several problems in Cameroonian society: the insufficiency, or even the absence or loss of civic and citizen values; the weak consideration of individual rights and freedoms; the lack of a sense of the state and republican institutions among a good number of citizens; a loss of patriotic commitment; the loss of a sense of positive traditional values; the degradation of the environment, particularly in the cities, due to widespread indiscipline; the lack of a sense of family responsibility; the lack of professional awareness, laxity and recklessness; the growth of corruption; moral decadence; the persistent political, ethnic, and religious intolerance; the growth of banditry and delinquency, etc. In view of the above problems, it is appropriate to question the impact of the activities of the CDJP-Y in Cameroon in general and in Yaoundé in particular.

The Yaoundé Justice and Peace Commission (CDJP-Y) and Christian Civic Engagement: Impact Assessment Methodology of Data Collection and Results Obtained

In order to analyse the impact of the Yaoundé Justice and Peace Commission on the civic commitment of the Christians in the city of Yaoundé, we conducted a survey of this structure and of Christians during the second half of October 2019, that is, from 15 to 30.

At the Yaoundé Justice and Peace Commission (CDJP-Y)

As a result of an interview with the leaders of this structure and the analysis of its documents, we gathered information on its background and objectives, its main activities relating to civic commitment, its methodology, and its means of action. This approach also enabled us to highlight the difficulties that the CDJP-Y encounters in promoting active citizenship among Christians.

Background and Objectives

The Yaoundé Diocesan Justice and Peace Commission was created on 12 January 1969 by Bishop Jean Zoa in accordance with one of the wishes of the Second Vatican Council to create a Pontifical Commission for Justice and Peace and the publication of a *Motu Propio* by Pope Paul VI on 6 January 1967 creating this commission. This commission seeks to promote justice, peace, and the integral development of the population through the defence of the dignity and fundamental rights of the human person. This general objective is achieved through several strategic objectives, namely:

- Strengthening the capacities of the population and grass-root organisations with a view to their self-promotion and full participation in national public debate by contributing to the creation of functional parish Justice and Peace Committees (PJPCs) involved in the search for peace and justice
- Strengthening the capacities of the members of the PJPCs
- Strengthening partnerships between all development actors for equitable public policies that are in line with the general interest by improving capacities for context analysis and advocacy to influence public policies in the direction of respect for rights and the general interest, and by improving integration into networks and the visibility of the actions of the DCJC and PJPC
- The reinforcement of actions to fight against major scourges and the promotion of the culture of peace through the promotion of the dignity of the human person in the Archdiocese of Yaoundé; the contribution to humanising prisons and protecting prisoners

The Yaoundé Archdiocese today has 180 parishes and Eucharistic Centres. Where there is no (functional) PJPC, the parish priest organises the PJPC. Membership varies (3 to 15 people per PJPC). However, it can be noted that there are about 50 functional PJPCs in the 180 parishes and Eucharistic Centres in the Yaoundé Archdiocese. Their activities are coordinated by the YDJPC.

The YDJPC Activities in General and Those Related to the Promotion of a Committed Citizenship

In order to achieve the various objectives mentioned above, the YDJPC organises several activities, including:

- The creation, animation and training of Parish Committees for Justice and Peace
- The training on consciousness to justice by passing on the evangelical principles of social life
- The setting up of a legal council for pastors, the Christians, the voiceless, and the disenfranchised
- Reconciliation in various conflict situations
- Scientific and technical studies on all aspects of development (educational, cultural, economic, social, etc.) as well as on the problems of peace itself, which go beyond development
- Denouncing and repairing injustices through legal assistance
- Multifaceted assistance and legal support

Within the framework of its mission to promote justice, peace, and integral human development, the Yaoundé DJPC organised several activities to enable Christians and all men of good will to participate in the life of the nation. To this end, several training workshops, educational talks, and radio broadcasts to train and raise awareness of members of the Parish Justice and Peace Committees and the population on democratic culture, knowledge of their rights and duties, participation and electoral observation, citizen participation, commitment, and behaviour to be adopted within society and in political life, were organised.

In the same light, it also develops a culture of accountability among citizens, establishes a civic dialogue between the population and the nation's elected representatives (MPs, mayors, municipal councillors) which not only makes it possible to raise awareness of the rights and duties of citizens, but also to encourage them to participate in the political process. In other words, this civic dialogue between the nation's elected representatives and the population invites the population to learn about the role and responsibilities of elected representatives; to take an interest in public affairs; to become involved in the choice of leaders on the basis of democratic principles and social projects that guarantee the development and well-being of all; and to be involved in monitoring the activities of elected representatives in the exercise of their duties. As far as national and local elected representatives are concerned, the main concern is getting them closer to the populations; to listen to the needs and expectations of the populations and to report on the actions and projects carried out, etc.

Methods and Means of Action

As a method of action, the YDJPC associates as far as possible the separated Christian brothers, believers, and all men of good will in its activities. It also relies on the commitment and concrete witness of its members through their work for peace and justice. This is how it works in the Archdiocese of Yaoundé through:

- Permanent offices at its headquarters every working day. This allows it to receive beneficiaries and the voiceless
- Radio broadcasts to raise awareness on the duty of social justice
- Children's and pupils' competitions for peace organised on the occasion of the World Day of Peace on 1 January, broadcasting selected works
- The dissemination of the Holy Father's messages on peace
- The production of leaflets, brochures, and circulars
- The effective setting up of parish committees at the base (action plan, activities, relations with the YDPJC)
- Training sessions for all members of the Parish Justice and Peace Commissions, Catholic Action Groups, Marian associations, catechists, charismatic groups, etc.
- Occasional presentations to public authorities to demand the respect of human rights (rates, difficulties, nature of the commitment)
- Collaboration with other Diocesan Justice and Peace Commissions and networking
- Collaboration with ecumenical associations and other believers, for common actions to promote human dignity, justice, and peace

Difficulties Encountered in Promoting Active Citizenship Among Christians

The YDJPC encounters many difficulties in carrying out activities to promote active citizenship among Christians. These include:

- The lack of interest in the management of public affairs and the common good
- The reticence of most Christians towards politics due to: the frustrations and apathy of those in power, defeatism towards any possible change, the non-respect of the rules of the game of the participatory process, a biased electoral system at the base
- Reluctance of some national elected representatives towards the DJPC and the PJPC initiatives
- Lack of enforcement: we work with the good faith of the parties and advocate amicable settlement rather than going to court
- A kind of double life for the Christian: the one he lives in the Church is different from the one he lives outside. In short, there is a lack of unity of faith and human life
- The blatant lack of knowledge of the Church social doctrine, which is still hidden in the documents
- The lack of knowledge of the role of the JPCs within the Church at the level of some clergy and laity: this Church institution is confused with a Catholic action movement, whereas it is a reflection group
- The representation that we have of the Church because of our history and culture: the lack of participation in the life of the Church; the history of colonisation
- Selfishness or even egocentricity and the prevailing poverty which makes it difficult to satisfy one's own needs
- The lack of regular feedback on the activities of the PJPC to the DJPC
- The limited means available to the CJPC and the DJPC to accomplish their various missions. It should be noted that these

institutions work with volunteers and the goodwill of their
members, who make their own resources available for action

- The almost insignificant number of members and the distance
of the parishes from the centre of the DJPC

Among Christians in the City of Yaoundé

Within the framework of this study, we carried out a survey
among a sample of 100 Christians in the city of Yaoundé, which
we obtained using the simple random method. The objective was
to collect their perception of the PJCs and how they affect them.
We went particularly to chapels and Christian places of worship
to hand out our questionnaire. After presenting the purpose of
our research, we obtained the following information from those
who agreed to participate in our project.

Socio-Demographic Data

Our sample consists of 60 women and 40 men. The mean age is
29 years. Their professional status is varied: most are students;
others are civil servants, workers in the formal and informal private sector, as well as unemployed and retired persons. Many respondents are not active in any Catholic Action group. Those who
are, participate in CLC, choir, readers' group, and protocol. Most
of them have been in the church since childhood and only a few
for only three years. The majority of the respondents were single,
the others married and a few in common-law relationships. All
have at least the GCE A levels and most are in higher education.

Knowledge of the Justice and Peace Commission (JPC) and its Role Among Christians

As far as knowledge of the JPCs is concerned, half of our respondents, i.e., 50 out of the 100 have already heard of them and the
others have never heard of them. Of those who have heard of

JPCs, only 15 respondents really know what role they play in the Church and among Christians. The rest have a vague knowledge of their activities and missions: "challenging people to be Christians," "supervising Catholic couples and associations," "helping Christians with their legal problems," "promoting living together," "helping to live in society," etc. He considers it to be a Catholic action movement just like the others, whereas it is in essence a group for reflection, training, and action to consolidate the culture of peace and social justice. For example, the goal assigned to the one in the Archdiocese of Yaoundé which interests us here, is "to reflect on human promotion and to mobilise the people to provide more concrete solutions to the problems of justice and peace that immediately affect citizens."

It should also be noted that of the 50 respondents who had heard of the JPCs, few had ever benefited from the services they offer: 8 respondents out of the 50. This represents a very low percentage. Training and/or awareness-raising is the main service they have received. The themes, in order of occurrence, concern the fight against major social evils (tribalism, corruption, bad governance), knowledge of the rights and duties of the citizen, the defence of the dignity and fundamental rights of the human person, the preservation of cultural values and respect for the emblems of the nation, the practice and promotion of peace around oneself, the safeguarding of common goods and the search for general interest, the practice and promotion of justice around oneself, entrepreneurship, and the responsible practice of one's daily work.

Even if the rate of use of the services remains low for those who have already benefited from them, they have done so once or three times at most, they appreciate the quality and relevance of the service provided and their level of satisfaction is very high. They feel that they have had a positive impact on their lives and in the adoption of new behaviours. For example, some say that the training and/or awareness-raising received has enabled them to become aware of their role in society, to avoid bad company and bad environments, to lead a simple and fairer life, to learn to solve problems by turning to Christ, to have a taste for community service, to live better in the community or to respect the values of others, etc.

Finally, it should be noted that the quality and relevance of the services provided by these commissions predispose the beneficiaries to recommend them to their entourage. Therefore, they are ready to advise and encourage other Christians and any person of good will to participate in the activities organised by the JPCs. They believe that they can not only help Christians to solve the various problems they encounter in the Church and society, but also that they can arouse in them the desire and enthusiasm to become actively involved in the life of the nation by serving as a framework for structuring their action, as a place for information, awareness and training. Moreover, they believe that these commissions can be the ideal framework to help them become authentic Christians who unite their Christian faith and their human life in all its dimensions.

What are the Interpretations of the Results Obtained?

The commitment of the Church in Africa to reconciliation, justice, and peace is still a real challenge in view of the multiple social and political conflicts and injustices that plague Africa, in general, and Cameroon, in particular. One may wonder eight years after the proclamation of Pope Benedict XVI's encyclical inviting the church on the continent to engage in this path while showing its urgency if it has really been received. Even if there are timid changes observed on both sides, there is still a long way to go; moreover, a transformation should start within the Church itself to extend to the whole society. This is still not the case, insofar as several evils and divisions still shake the Church: we can still remember in Cameroon the case of the assassination of Monsignor Balla, bishop of Bafia, or even the position of the Episcopal Conference during the presidential elections which is not always unanimous. Genuine conversion, hypocrisy in relationships, tribalism, xenophobia, manipulation, lack of interest in preserving the common good, timidity or lack of enthusiasm for genuine political commitment, etc. remain a reality in our various societies.

Nevertheless, it should be noted that the JPCs play a very important role in the Church, among Christians, and in society as a whole. They are an effective instrument that can not only help to establish reconciliation, justice, and peace in the society, but also a powerful tool for civic commitment of Christians and people of good will. In spite of the many difficulties they encounter on their way, they are resolutely moving towards the fulfillment of their mission. However, they are still largely unknown in the Church and in society. Few Christians really know the function and the different missions. Consequently, they do not approach them to benefit from their various offers.

One of the great challenges facing the PJCs is not only to allocate the necessary funds for their proper functioning, but above all to raise awareness and popularise their missions among both clergy and Christians. To achieve this, they can play on the multiplier effect by relying on the follow-up of the beneficiaries who can testify around them to the benefits of the services received, and above all lead them to commit themselves to these commissions to enable their entourage to know them better.

Conclusion

This reflection aimed to evaluate the impact of the Justice and Peace Commissions in the civic commitment of Catholic Christians in Cameroon by relying on the ideas of Pope Benedict XVI who, through his post-synodal exhortation *Africae Munus*, invited not only the Church in Africa to commit itself to the service of reconciliation, justice, and love, but also to invest each particular Church in the civic training of the population, in the awakening of their conscience and their civic responsibilities through the Justice and Peace Commission. In view of the multiple tensions and conflicts that are tearing the social fabric, the numerous obstacles, and historical, political, social and cultural burdens, as well as, a lack of knowledge of rights and duties, institutions and the relationships that are supposed to govern the relations between leaders and the governed, which slow down the effectiveness of an active or committed citizenship in Cameroon, we started from the premise that the Justice and Peace Commissions have a minimal impact on the development of such citizenship among Christians because of ignorance of their role and the methods they use to achieve this end.

At the end of our reflection, we confirm this hypothesis insofar as citizen commitment in Cameroon remains a real challenge for the Cameroonian people. Not only are there many obstacles to the effectiveness and efficiency of such an initiative, but also the specific role of these commissions remains largely unknown to most Christians. Nevertheless, the positive impact it has in changing the behaviour of Christians can be highlighted. In a nutshell, it can be said that the advent of a reconciled Africa, through the paths of truth and justice, love and peace, remains not only a topical issue in most African countries in general and in Cameroon in particular, but also that it is struggling to become embedded in the customs of the people. Pope Benedict XVI's invitation therefore remains topical and urgent for Africa if Africa intends to experience real development. In spite of the timid change that can be observed here and there, the road ahead remains very long and requires that the Church and these commissions rely on paradigms such as those of the psychology of commitment in order to further encourage Christians to commit themselves to this path, but also that these commissions find ways to finance themselves.

The African Reception of Benedict XVI's Social Philosophy:
Between Commitment and Apoliticism, What Is to Be Said?
Enama Saint Daniel Marcel

Introduction

History reveals that the Catholic religion is one of the major instruments that was used for the penetration of African societies by colonial ideology. It is therefore in its co-existence with the colonial political project that the Christian religion has become impregnated with African realities. To quote Jean Godefroy Bidima, it participated in the "cultural vandalism" by which colonisation stripped African societies of their identities. In such a context, the construction of the political order was sufficiently rooted in religious discourse. This representation, over time, has discredited religion to the extent that the political project for which it has been the platform has proven to be enslaving. However, Pope Benedict XVI, aware that "today the continent is still confronted with new forms of slavery and colonisation," (A.M., no. 16) stipulates that "the Church respects and loves Africa." (A.M., no. 13) This respect and love reaffirmed by Benedict XVI for Africa is reflected in the attention he paid to the continent either through official visits to Cameroon, Angola, Benin, etc., or through open letters, *Africae Munus*. Was this enough to repair the damage?

The question remains unanswered, but it should be noted that African current events do deserve some attention. It is constantly dominated by questions relating to political power, to the extent that we have been able to speak of the "need for the state" (SALL (dir.); 1996:5) or even its reconstruction with the aim of "putting an end to the long wandering." (same) More concretely, Benedict XVI thinks that it is more a question of building social order in conditions of peace, justice, and reconciliation, which is exclusively a matter of politics. (A.M., no. 28) However, years earlier, Achille MBEMBE, noting the impact of religious references on contemporary African societies, stated that because "the future of Christianity in Africa is played out in reference to the future of indigenous societies, (...) it will be difficult to avoid pronouncing on the nature of the oppositions and conflicts that structure domestic power relations." (MBEMBE, 1988: 188) This is what Benedict XVI calls "theological and social responsibility"; (A.M., no. 24) the difficulty of which is to situate oneself between two extremes, namely "immediate involvement in politics—not a direct competence of the Church" and the "withdrawal or possible escape into theological and spiritual theories." (same) The risk of the first extreme for the Church is to substitute itself for the State and the second is "constituting an escape from a concrete responsibility in human history." (same) Being neither, the Church must "liberate the truth" if faith is to be authentic, that is, lived. By contrasting this posture of the Church with the context in which it is inscribed, it is appropriate to question the conditions of possibility of the double movement of social commitment and religious apoliticism.

Therefore, how can the Church in Africa invest so much in the quest for truth without stripping it of all its dimensions, especially political? In other words, is the socially committed and apolitical posture of the Church in Africa still sustainable? What are its impulses, its ambiguities, and its reception for Africa? Answering this question is attempting to summarise Benedict XVI's social philosophy in relation to Africa; thought that we will try as much as possible to put into context considering the socio-political realities of Africa in order to deduce the difficulties of impregnation and the teaching that can result from it.

Benedict XVI's Social Philosophy

Faced with the pronounced atheism that has animated the West since its break with Judeo-Christian thought of Platonic inspiration, we are today witnessing what should be called "spiritualities for a world without God" (Verlinde; 2011: 681) where "atheism is necessarily, irrevocably imposed." (same) Based on Luc Ferry and Marcel Gauchet, Verlinde believes that never before have the West and God been separated. (same) This Western religious retreat gives us a glimpse of Africa as a land that should preside over the future of Christianity, insofar as the number of Christians keeps growing more and more. According to Anne-Marie Goguel, "one of the features of the African situation is the importance of Christian references (...), the common attachment to the Christian faith to the point of being able to form the basis of a possible consensus on common values acceptable to all." (Goguel; 1988: 681) The commitment of Africa to the Church is, therefore, justified as much as that of the Church in Africa as the post-synodal Apostolic Exhortation *Africae Munus* attests. Benedict XVI thus contrasts "the commitment of Africa to the Lord Jesus Christ" (A.M., no. 1) and "exhorts the whole Church to look at Africa with faith and hope." (A.M., no. 1) This commitment or outlook is translated at the social level by the main apostolate domains, namely education, health, and the world of communication. Only the last two fields will be considered, given the functional similarity that the Pope grants to educational and health institutions.

The Apostolate in the Domain of Health

Benedict XVI shows his attachment to human beings by inviting respect for their dignity in the world of health, a dignity that comes from their status as members of the Body of Christ. It is Christ who calls for our presence and assistance in a sick person. This is why the Pope insists that all those involved in the domain of health care must "see in every patient a suffering part of the Body of Christ." (A.M. no. 140) Despite the difficulties of their professional field, they must above all think of the humanity in each patient. And the Pope exhorts and encourages, "Dear health care workers, be bearers of Jesus' compassionate love to the suffering masses! Be patient, be strong and keep courage! In the case of pandemics, financial and material means are indispensable, but you must also tirelessly inform and train the population, especially the young." (A.M. no. 140) The pedagogic dimension in health care remains a key priority of the Pope. The African population has a great need to be trained in health issues, because the context requires this. In some regions, customs and traditions, cultural traditions, and the negligence of communities sometimes lead to resistance to vaccines, in particular, and to a lack of access to the modern health structures available to them.

This being the case, the Pope Emeritus does not fail to recommend to the managers of health institutions to put Christian ethics at the centre of their activities, without becoming mercenaries for their brothers and sisters. Speaking of these institutions, he enjoins them saying: "Let them not become a source of enrichment for individuals. The management of the funds granted must aim at transparency and serve above all the good of the patient." (A.M. no. 141) Finally, Benedict XVI suggests that a chapel should always be built in health facilities, which reminds everyone that God is the Master of life and death, as well as multiplying the number of small dispensaries to provide local care and first aid. Hence the importance of raising awareness through communication.

The Apostolate in the World of Information and Communication

With regard to the world of information and communication, Benedict XVI once again follows in the footsteps of his predecessor John Paul II. The latter had already drawn the attention of the media to the central role they have to play in promoting the communion of the human family and the *ethos* of societies (cf. E.I.A.). But for the Pope Emeritus, it is necessary to be lucid about the ambivalent character of the media today, "We all know that the new information technologies can become powerful instruments of cohesion and peace or effective promoters of destruction and division. They can be morally helpful or harmful, propagate truth as well as falsehood, offer the ugly as well as the beautiful." (A.M. no. 143) With the media, one can form and distort, inform and misinform, humanise and dehumanise. This is the reality of our technological era.

To avoid this pitfall, the German Pontiff invites us to reconsider the foundations of media activity: to put respect for universal human values in the foreground, which requires an integral image of the human person and the common good. Enlightened by this image, the media must have "as their principal aim the promotion of the dignity of persons and peoples," and be "expressly animated by charity and placed at the service of truth, goodness, and a natural and supernatural brotherhood." (A.M. no. 144) This is why, according to the Pope Emeritus, "the Church must be more present in the media in order to make them not only an instrument for spreading the Gospel but also a tool for the training of African peoples to reconciliation in truth, to the promotion of justice, and to peace." (A.M. no. 145) For this to be effective, it is necessary to train journalists in ethics and respect for the truth, to encourage those who are Christians not to be afraid to manifest their faith, and to integrate the public and private media. In short, according to Benedict XVI, following the recommendations of the Synod, it is a question of ensuring that the organs of communication place themselves resolutely at the service of "peace, justice, and reconciliation in Africa," in order to allow "this continent to participate in the current development of the world." (A.M. no. 146)

The Meaning of Apoliticism According to Benedict XVI

The Church's increasingly obvious involvement in contemporary African societies is evident in its relationship with power, the state, and societies (Mbembe; 1988: 205). For Pope Benedict XVI, it is time to "question the public role of the Church and its place in the African space today." (A.M. no. 17) To commit oneself to the field of action, disregarding the specificities that are deployed there in order to seek popular support for non-political ends, is the meaning that Benedict XVI gives to religious apoliticism. For, he says, commitment to the construction of the social order does not mean interference in politics for the Church. By showing the two extremes in which the Church's action is situated, the Pope distinguishes between the political and religious spheres and also clarifies the Church's role.

For him, it is not an issue of the Church building any social order; she participates in this construction and her task "consists in forming consciences that are upright and receptive to the demands of justice, so as to raise men and women may who are concerned about and capable of realising this just social order for their responsible conduct." (A.M no. 22) According to Ludovic Lado, training citizens to behave responsibly means disseminating the Church's social doctrine through education. The Church plays its role as a "watchdog" which is nothing less than its prophetic role in favour of suffering humanity. (Lado; 2012:166) Moreover, Lado believes that it is this function that further strengthens the Church's distance from the political order, insofar as "the recurrence of the term immediate signals the search for this distance (...) but a distance that does not mean indifference." In fact, the prophetic function requires the Church to denounce the unjust order. Based on the movements of secularisation and secularism that require autonomy of the bodies, the two forces present here, that are the Church and the State, "must therefore complement each other and not compete." (Ntep; 2006:53) By being the "watchdog," the Church sharpens reason, if not prepares reason for right action. This is why Bishop Ntep, going in the same direction, affirms that "the Church does not therefore build social structures for reasons of ideology." (same: 54) If there is any ideology, it is underpinned by and always tensed with Love; what the author calls "the Church's charitable activity" defined by three essential chracteristics:

- The response to an immediate need
- The break with any ideological tendency
- Disinterestedness in the sense of breaking with the instrumental or utilitarian reason, which is limited to the simple and only profitability of the action (same: 54)

At this stage and as explained, we can conclude with A. Mbembe to an "incredible secularisation." (Mbembe; 1988:206) More illustrative is the case of Cameroon which, since 2014 has signed the Framework Agreement with the Holy See on the legal status of the Catholic Church in Cameroon. Article 1 of the agreement stipulates the separation of the two orders, each autonomous and independent of the other. It stipulates that, "The Republic of Cameroon and the Holy See reaffirm that the State and the Church are each in its own order independent and self-nominated." (Cf. Framework Agreement, 2014) Thus, recognising the exclusive competence of the Holy See in the administration of its entities, the Church only has the right to inform the State on any decision resulting from the exercise of this exclusive competence. Furthermore, the Agreement specifies in its article 4 that "the Republic of Cameroon recognises the right of the Church to engage in the service of human, social, cultural, moral, spiritual, and material development (…)." However, Lao points out that "although enshrined in most constitutions, the outlines of state secularism in Africa are difficult to determine." (Lado; op. cit.) This is why it is necessary to go beyond institutional debates and declared practices and to question the "popular methods of Christianity" (Mbembe; op.cit.) by resorting to a "bottom-up" approach.

Benedict XVI's Social Philosophy Tested against the Socio-Political Realities of Africa

The political situation in Africa as it appears today reflects the deep crisis affecting its system of political organisation and the nature of the means that contribute to this organisation. Although global, this stalemate is due more to the crisis of power, which itself stems from the failure of grafting the state in Africa. Its importation into Africa (B. Badie) was accompanied by a reroute of its structure and of the instruments relating to the smoothing of this same structure. More concretely, in order to account for this situation, we do not pretend to explain all African politics. We will mention a few elements of the context, including the system of governance and the nature of the electoral model, insofar as these two elements question the legitimacy of the power of leaders and the freedom of societies.

Elements of the Context
The System of Governance in African States

The system of governance in most African states is considered opaque, centralised, and prosaic. Its various names testify to this; whether it is underdeveloped, neo-patrimonial, in the bush, elsewhere, authoritarian, witchcraft, and recently stationary (Eboko and Awondo; 2018:6), the state in Africa, and hence its system of governance, is characterised by a neutralising mechanism whose technology of power consists in annihilating any innovation or change. The aim is, as Eric Owona Nguini and Hélène Laure Menthong point out, "to make central state power eternal." (Owona and Menthong; 2018:97)

Such a system of governance is not the result of chance. It emanates from historical overtones, the contours of which must be identified by resorting to socio-history. As a result of the encounter between traditional African societies and Western societies in a context driven by colonial logic, the system of governance as a managerial model of societies floats between these two cultural spheres. Noting this, Jean-François Bayart thinks that, "the failure of the graft (...) does not refer to a traditional culture, the definition of which is impossible, but rather to the colonial period and its legacy of independence." (Bayart; 1990:6) In order to better understand this state of affairs, three factors according to Bayart are to be considered: the historical lines of social inequality, the indigenous cultural repertoires of the political, and the post-colonial political economy. (same: 15)

The first factor, which is historical, tends to reproduce the colonial pattern of domination with an administration marked by the constraint of forced labour and the exclusivity or centrality of power. This explains, according to Bayart, the constant opposition between "social elders" (dominant class) and "social younger" (subjugated class).

- The second is directly linked to the administrative model, whose power is exclusive and determined by:
- The heritage of an oral civilisation
- The sacredness of authority
- The inventory of the invisible occurrences
- The lineage egalitarian ethos which paralyses the efficiency of the administration through the interference of friendship ties and kinship

The last point, namely political economy, just wants to tie the post- colonial states to the Western-inspired liberal requirement. Still to be seen is whether African economies, given their low purchasing power, could cope with the invasion of rampant capitalism.

It is this kind of structuring, which articulates both internal and external logics, that has given rise to, or reinforced, the patronising and client-based practices that can be observed today on both sides of the continent. The "need for statehood," formulated above, means the denial of statehood to African political areas in view of the permanent predation that is observed there. For example, Dominique Darbon thinks that in Africa, in view of all that has just been said, there is no state; what exists is only a structure of exploitation at different levels. To this end, he states, "In short, the state is constituted, but neither in the place nor in the way it is constituted (...), there has been no state in Africa but a simple bureaucratic structure of exploitation." (Darbon; 1990:45) To maintain themselves as such, it should be said that the structures of political organisation in Africa, insofar as they are identified with places of accumulation and redistribution of wealth (Mbembe), they manage by the same logic to straighten out the political space by trying as much as possible to manage in a more or less long time the split between the state and society. By what mechanism is such a scenario possible if society, through elections, presides over its destiny?

Electoral Model in Africa

Analysing the electoral process in the African context leads to the general question of the validity or otherwise of democracy in Africa. This has been the subject of an abundant literature to which we prefer not to return. In short, just like the administration model, the electoral model has also been re-employed by the logic of the dominant actors. In the light of Pascal Mukonde Musalay, we can say that the electoral process as it takes place in Africa is more of an "electoral democracy." (Musulay; 2009:21) This differs from true democracy only in terms of quality, hence of its content. The author states on this issue that "all regimes that perform poorly in terms of the quality of democracy (...) but happen to manage conflicts related to the struggle for power through elections can be qualified as electoral democracy." (same) In other words, elections without choices are comparable to political rituals whose function is to consolidate if not legitimise illegitimate power. The temptation is great to say that the elections and the disputes to which they give rise, given the irregularities of which they are infatuated, are a "pure masquerade." (Bayart; 1978: 187) In order to better understand what voting means in African societies, it is necessary to examine the social contexts, not in order to compare them with those of the Metropolis, but in order to decipher the perceptions, symbolic repertoires, and their influence on the electoral process. Without being pessimistic, let alone optimistic, we must admit that socio-political dynamics in Africa are maturing and that resistance to their emergence is growing. How long will this last? History and current events will tell us more.

From Utopia to Crisis Thinking

Confronting Ratzinger's philosophy with the socio-political realities of Africa which are so dense and diverse, means going back to note the difficulty of imbuing such a vision in an African context. How can we deal with "a bribe-taking and kleptocratic political elite that is rather resistant to the elementary requirements of social justice and electoral transparency?" (Lado; op.cit.: 163) Can the Catholic Church truly assume its prophetic function? Between refraining from positioning itself in relation to African politics as required by its apolitical nature and playing its full role in "liberating the truth," the Church's action seems at first sight limited. The Church, according to Lado, has to choose between "reasonable realism to safeguard the institutional interests of the Church or betrayal of its prophetic mission" (same: 169) because, he continues, "the concern not to embarrass the authorities of the host country may lead to evangelical reservations." (same) It is clear, then, that the Church's intention in practice can clash with the intention of the political class. Also, it is the political class that "delimits the regulation of the other spheres, which give it the right to interfere in the name of maintaining the political order." (same: 168) Through this right of interference, the Church's action can be captured and even directed by the state. In this context, the difficulty for the Church to ensure its task can *a priori* lead to the conclusion that Ratzinger's philosophy is utopian. However, this utopianism seems necessary and can be seen as a thought that settles in the reflection on the crisis in order to considerably reduce its impact.

To say that Ratzinger's philosophy is a thought on the African crisis means for us braving all the challenges for this thought to be effective. Contrary to a commonly accepted idea that makes the crisis the state of a situation that must be abandoned, let us say that the crisis is more a key moment of the decision because it is located between the perilous state and the future state that must be determined. The challenge of any crisis is therefore to make sustainable decisions. Attaining these sustainable decisions becomes a challenge in the face of difficulties that must be transcended. Benedict XVI's call for peace, reconciliation, and love in Christ is, in our view, this sustainable decision and the complexity of the political field in Africa, the difficulty. Speaking the "languages of crisis," will be a question of overcoming the language of non-involvement and the weight of the challenges. (Ela; 1998:11) Nicolas Berdiaeff put it so well, "we are living in the era of civilized barbarism (...) The materialistic character of civilization and the increasingly threatening power of technology require particularly a more intense spirituality than was required in past centuries." (Berdiaeff quoted by Njoh Mouelle; 2011:128) This is the meaning to be given to the hope that Benedict XVI places on Africa; an Africa that he entrusts to Christ because he says "if the Lord does not build the house, in vain do the builders labour." (A.M. no. 2)

Conclusion

In the end, thinking about the relationship between the Church, society, and the State in Africa, starting particularly from Benedict XVI's social philosophy, led us to make a brief review of this social philosophy in order to put it in a context with the socio-political situation of Africa. As vast as this situation may be, we have only noted the system of governance and the electoral model. The latter, considered opaque and framed with many pitfalls, at first sight poses the difficult task of imbuing Benedict XVI's social philosophy, which is intertwined between social commitment and the apolitical. This difficult immersion may reflect either utopian thinking, or thinking that is complicit with the political system. Analysed with a great deal of hindsight, Benedict XVI's social philosophy, beyond this hasty understanding, is an invitation to Africa, a challenge, and particularly that of the development of a just social order.

Endnotes

Presentation of the Colloquium

1   Benedict XVI, Address to Participants in a Congress Held on the Occasion of the 10th Anniversary of the Publication of Pope John Paul II's Encyclical, *Fides et Ratio*, 16 October 2008: "…[T]he Encyclical is characterized by its great openness to reason, especially in a period in which its weakness was theorized."
2   Joseph Ratzinger, *Faith and Politics*, Ignatius Press, 2018.
3   Benedict XVI, Address to Participants in a Congress Held on the Occasion of the 10th Anniversary of the Publication of Pope John Paul II's Encyclical, *Fides et Ratio*, 16 October 2008.
4   *Africae Munus*, nn. 81 and 108.
5   Benedict XVI, Address to Participants in a Congress Held on the Occasion of the 10th Anniversary of the Publication of Pope John Paul II's Encyclical, *Fides et Ratio*, 16 October 2008.

Keynote Address: Charles Moukala

1   E. Guerriero, *Serviteur de Dieu et de l'humanité. La biographie de Benedict XVI*, Paris, Mame, 2017, p. 516.
2   Benedict XVI, Homily at the Eucharistic Celebration on the occasion of the publication of the *Instrumentum Laboris* at Amadou Ahidjo Stadium (Yaoundé), 19 March 2009.
3   Benedict XVI, Homily at the Eucharaistic Celebration at São Paolo Church in Luanda, 21 March 2009.
4   Benedict XVI, Eucharistic Celebration for the closing of the second special assembly for Africa of the Synod of Bishops, 4 October 2009.
5   Cf. Benedict XVI, Meeting with government members, representatives of the Institutions of the Republic, Diplomatic Corps and representatives of the major religions gathered in the Presidential Palace of Cotonou, 19 November 2011.
6   Benedict XVI, Homily at the "Stade de l'amitié" of Cotonou, 20 November 2011.
7   Benedict XVI, Meeting with government members, representatives

of the Institutions of the Republic, Diplomatic Corps and representatives of the major religions gathered in the Presidential Palace of
Cotonou, 19 November 2011.

8   Ibid.
9   Benedict XVI, Encyclical, *Spe salvi,* 30 November 2007.
10   Cf. R. Garaudy, *La reconquête de l'espoir,* Paris, 1971.
11   Cf. Benedict XVI, *Spe salvi,* n. 1, 2s.
12   Ibid., n.2.
13   Benedict XVI, Homily at Eucharistic Celebration with the Bishops
     of I.M.B.I.S.A. at Cimangola Square in Luanda, 22 March 2009.
14   Cf. Benedict XVI, Homily at the Eucharistic Celebration on the Oc-
     casion of the publication of the Instrumentum Laboris at Amadou
     Ahidjo Stadium (Yaoundé), 19 March 2009.
15   *Spe salvi,* n.4.
16   Benedict XVI, Meeting with government members, representatives
     of the Institutions of the Republic, Diplomatic Corps and represen-
     tatives of the major religions gathered in the Presidential Palace of
     Cotonou, 19 November 2011.
17   *Spe salvi,* n. 21.
18   Ibid., n. 26.
19   Ibid., n. 28.
20   Augustine, *Confessions* X, 43, 70: CSEL 33, 279: Œuvres, Paris (1998),
     p. 1028.
21   *Spe salvi,* n.39.
22   Benedict XVI, Meeting with government members, representatives
     of the Institutions of the Republic, Diplomatic Corps and represen-
     tatives of the major religions gathered in the Presidential Palace of
     Cotonou, 19 November 2011.
23   Ibid.
24   *Spe salvi,* n.12.
25   F. Louzeau, "La théologie chrétienne du politique de Joseph
     Ratzinger," in *Recueillir l'héritage théologique de Benedict XVI. Centre
     de recherche et de spiritualité Notre Dame de l'inculturation à Cotonou en
     collaboration avec le Ratzinger Schülerkreis et la Fondazione vaticana
     Joseph Ratzinger—Bendetto XVI,* Paris, Éditions Parole et Silence,
     2016, p. 143.
26   Cf. E. Bloch, *Le Principe Espérance,* Paris, Gallimard, 1976.
27   J. Moltmann, *La théologie de l'espérance,* Paris, Les Éditions du Cerf,
     1970.
28   J. B. Metz, *La foi dans l'histoire et dans la société. Essai de théologie fon-
     damentale pratique,* Paris, Cerf (Cogitatio fidei), 1979; *Memoria passio
     nis. Un souvenir provocant dans une société pluraliste,* Paris, Cerf, 2009.

29 J. M. Ela, *Repenser la théologie africaine. Le Dieu qui libère*, Paris, Karthala, 2003, p. 13–14.

God's Word and Exegesis in Benedict XVI:
What Heritage for Africa?

1   Patrice MEKANA, SAC, is a Pallottine priest, PhD in Theology, specializing in Sacred Scripture, from the Institut Catholique de Paris. He is the Director of the Institute of Theology and Religious Studies (ITPR) in Yaoundé and teaches Scripture at the Catholic University of Central Africa and in other theological schools in Cameroon. His pastoral ministry focuses, among other things, on the formation of the laity and initiation into the Holy Scriptures.

2   Joseph Ratzinger-Benedict XVI, *Jesus of Nazareth: From the Baptism in the Jordan to the Transfiguration*, Doubleday, 2007; *From the Entry into Jerusalem to the Resurrection*, Ignatius Press, 2011; *The Infancy Narratives*, Image, Paris, 2012.

3   Joseph Ratzinger, "Preface" to *The Interpretation of the Bible in the Church*; Dean P. Bechard, ed. *The Scripture Documents: An Anthology of Official Catholic Teachings*, trans. Dean P. Bechard (Collegeville, MN: Liturgical Press, 2002); Benedict XVI, Apostolic Exhortation *Africae Munus*.

4   *Verbum Domini*, n. 22.

5   Joseph Ratzinger – Benedict XVI, *Jesus of Nazareth* Vol. 1, p. 16.

6   *Verbum Domini*, nn. 3 and 5.

7   Ibid., n. 7.

8   Ibid., n. 10.

9   Ibid., n. 23.

10 Joseph Ratzinger-Benedict XVI, *Jesus of Nazareth* Vol. 1, p. 11.

11 Ibid., p. 12.

12 Ibid.

13 Joseph Ratzinger, "Preface," op. cit., p. 19.

14 Ibid., p. 21

15 Cf. Joseph Ratzinger – Benedict XVI, *Jesus of Nazareth* Vol. 1, p. 12.

16 Cf. Joseph Ratzinger – Benedict XVI, *Jesus of Nazareth* Vol. 2, p, 10.

17 Cf. *Verbum Domini*, n. 30.

18 Cf. Sandra Schneiders, *The Text of the Encounter. L'interprétation du Nouveau Testament comme écriture sainte*, (The interpretation of the New Testament as Holy Scripture) Cerf/Fides, Paris, 1995, p. 111.

19 Cf. Joseph Ratzinger – Benedict XVI, *Jesus of Nazareth* Vol. 1, p. 18.

20 Cf. Ibid., p. 10.

21 Cf. p. 9.
22 Ibid., p. 14.
23 Cf. Ibid.
24 Cf. Ibid., p. 15.
25 Cf. Ibid., p. 20.
26 Joseph Ratzinger – Benedict XVI, *Jesus of Nazareth* Vol. 2, p. 8.
27 Joseph Ratzinger – Benedict XVI, *The Childhood of Jesus*, p. 7–8.
28 Addressing the members of the Special Council for Africa of the Synod of Bishops, Yaoundé, 19 March 2009, in *Africae Munus* n. 6.
29 Cf. E. Mveng, *Africa in the Church: Paroles d'un croyant*, L'Harmattan, Paris, 1985, p. 66.
30 E. Mveng – Werblowsky (eds.), *Black Africa and the Bible. L'Afrique Noire et la Bible*, 1972, p. 11.
31 Cf. *Verbum Domini*, n. 6.
32 Joseph Ratzinger – Benedict XVI, *Jesus of Nazareth*. Vol. 1, p. 63–64.
33 Cf. *Verbum Domini*, n. 2.
34 *Africae Munus*, n. 13.
35 Cf. Ibid., n. 150.
36 As in., n. 151.
37 Cf. E. Messi Metogo, *Dieu peut-il mourir en Afrique ? Essai sur l'indif-férence religieuse et l'incroyance en Afrique noire* (Essay on religious apathy and unbelief in Black Africa), Karthala-Ucac, Paris-Yaoundé, 1997, p. 205–206.
38 Francis, Encyclical *Lumen Fidei*, n. 24.
39 Cf. Camille Focant, *L'évangile selon Marc* (The Gospel according to Mark), Cerf, Paris, 2010, p. 405.
40 John Paul II, Apostolic Exhortation *Ecclesia in Africa*, 1995, n. 41.
41 Cf. Camille Focant, op. cit., p. 405.
42 Ibid., p. 406.
43 Cf. Ibid, p. 407.
44 *Verbum Domini*, n. 173.
45 Cf. *Verbum Domini*, n. 176.
46 Cf. Jean Zumstein, L'évangile selon saint Jean (The Gospel according to John) (1–12), Labor et Fides, Genève, 2014, p. 181.
47 Cf. Ibid.
48 Cf. Xavier Léon-Dufour, Lecture de l'Evangile selon Jean, Tome II, (Reading from the Gospel of John, Vol. II), p. 28.
49 Cf. Ibid., p. 23.
50 *Verbum Domini*, n. 149.
51 Cf. Pierre Prigent, *L'Apocalypse de Saint Jean*, (The Revelation of John) Labor and Fides, Genève, 2014, p. 449.
52 Cf. Ibid., p. 454.

53 Ibid., p. 455.
54 Cf. *Africae Munus*, n. 20.
55 Ibid., n. 21.
56 Ibid., n. 29.
57 Ibid., n. 32.
58 Ibid., n. 56.
59 Ibid., n. 57.
60 Ibid., n. 72.
61 Ibid, n. 30.

Pope Benedict XVI's View on the Liturgical Reform in the Face of the Challenge of Inculturation in the Churches of Africa

1 A priest of the Diocese of Mbalmayo, he holds a doctorate degree in liturgy, obtained at the Pontificium Institutum Liturgicum in Rome in 1996. He is a lecturer in several universities and theological training institutes. He has been Rector of St Paul's Seminary in Mbalmayo (1998), the Major Philosophical and Propaedeutic Seminary of the Ecclesiastical Province of Yaoundé (2002) and Dean of the Faculty of Theology of the Catholic University of Central Africa/Catholic Institute of Yaoundé (UCAC/ICY) (2005–2012). Father was awarded the rank of Professor 3rd grade in 2012. He is currently a permanent professor at the Faculty of Theology and director of the Interdisciplinary Research Group on African Theology (GRITA). Also, he is the Secretary of the Episcopal Commission for Liturgy and Inculturation as well as the Ceremonial Secretary of the National Episcopal Conference of Cameroon.
2 *Sacramentum Caritatis*, n.38.
3 John Paul II, Post-synodal Apostolic Exhortation *Ecclesia in Africa*, 1995, n. 59.
4 Cf. Christophe Geffroy, *Benedict XVI and "Liturgical peace,"* Editions du Cerf, Paris, 2008, pp. 28–29.
5 John Paul II, Post-synodal Apostolic Exhortation, *Ecclesia in Africa*.
6 Benedict XVI, Post-synodal Apostolic Exhortation *Africae Munus*, 2012.
7 Vatican II, Constitution *Sacrosanctum Concilium*, in *Acta Apostolicae Sedis* 56 (1964): 97–138.
8 Pius XII, Encyclical *Mediator Dei*.
9 Ibid.

10 Chapter I gives the general principles for the restoration and progress of the liturgy, found in nn. 5–46. Chapter II deals with the mystery of the Eucharist in nn.47–58. Chapter III handles the other sacraments and the sacramentals in nn. 59–82. Chapter IV deals with the Divine Office in nn. 83–101. Chapter V focuses on the theme of the liturgical year in nn. 102–111. Chapter VI handles religious music, found in nn. 112–121. Chapter VII deals with the theme of sacred art and worship materials in the liturgy, nn. 122–130.

11 The preface and the first chapter, particularly nn. 5–13, are a true summary of liturgical theology, which also relates the journey of the liturgical movement.

12 SC, n. 5.

13 Cf. SC, n. 6.

14 Ibid., n.7.

15 Ibid.

16 Benedict XVI, Cardinal Kurt Koch, Student Forum on Vatican II; *The Hermeneutics of Reform, Word and Silence*, Libreria Editrice Vaticana, Vatican City 2013, p. 103.

17 SC, n. 2.

18 Ibid., n. 10.

19 Ibid., n. 21.

20 Ibid., n. 14.

21 J. Ratzinger, Preface, in A. Reid, *Organic Development of the Liturgy: The Principles of Liturgical Reform and Their Relation to the Twentieth Centry Liturgical Movement Prior to the Second Vatican Council*, Ignatius Press, San Francisco, 2005, p. 9–13.

22 Benedict XVI, *Sacramentum caritatis*, 2005, n. 3.

23 Ibid., n. 2.

24 Cf. Ibid., n. 1.

25 J. Ratzinger, *Der Geist der Liturgie. Eine Einfuhrung*, Fribourg i. Br. 2000, p. 142.

26 J. Ratzinger, "Zur Frage nach der Struktur der liturgischen Feir," in Id., *Das Fest des Glaubens, Versuche zur Theologie des Gottesdienstes*, Einsiedeln, 1981, p. 55–67, cit. p. 65.

27 *Sacramentum caritatis*, n. 34.

28 Cf. J. Ratzinger, *Ein neus Lied fur den Herrn. Christusglaube und Liturgie in der Gegenwar*, Fribourg i. Br. 2000, p. 142.

29 John Paul II, Encyclical *Ecclesia de Eucharistia*, 2003, n. 34.

30 Cf. SC, n. 7.

31 John Paul II, *Ecclesia*, op. cit. n. 10.

32 Cf. Benedict XVI, *Verbum Domini*, 2010, nn. 56–58.

33 Ibid., n. 59.
34 Francis, *Evangelii Gaudium*, 2013, n. 137.
35 Cf. Instruction, "On some questions concerning the collaboration of the lay Christians in the ministry of priests," p. 22.
36 Instruction, "On some questions concerning the collaboration of the lay faithful in the ministry of priests," 1997, see article 3.
37 Cf. Instruction Inter Oecumenici, 26 September 1964, n. 53: *AAS* 56 (1964): 890.
38 SC, n. 8.
39 SC, n. 7.
40 Pope Benedict XVI, *Verbum Domini*, n. 66.
41 John Paul II, Encyclical *Slavorum Apostolis*, in *AAS* 77 (1985): 802–803; cf. Address to the Plenary Assembly of the Pontifical Council for Culture, 17 January 1987, n. 5, in *AAS* 79 (1987): 1204–1205.
42 John Paul II, Encyclical *Redemptoris missio*, 7 December 1990, n. 52, in *AAS* 83 (1991): 300.
43 John Paul II, Addressing the University of Coimbra, 15 May 1982: *L'Osservatore Romano*, 16 May 1982, p. 4.
44 John Paul II, *Ecclesia in Africa*, n. 59.
45 In the same manner, he cites Proposal 30 of the 1994 Synod, which led to the Apostolic Exhortation *Ecclesia in Africa*.
46 Likewise he cites Proposal 32.
47 Ibid., and Proposal 33 is repeated.
48 For more information, see Antoine Essomba Fouda, *Le mariage chrétien au Cameroun* (Christian marriage in Cameroon), Edition l'Harmattan, 2010, pp. 100–105.
49 John Paul II, Lettre de Fondation du Conseil Pontifical pour la Culture (John Paul II, Letter for the Foundation of the Pontifical Council for Culture), 20 May 1982.
50 SC, n. 14.
51 *Verbum Domini*, n. 66.
52 Cf. Saint Augustine, Sermo 288, 5: PL 38, 1307; Sermo 120, 2: PL 38, 677.
53 SC, n. 34; Cf. n. 50.
54 *Verbum Domini*, n. 67.
55 Benedict XVI, *Africae munus*, n. 32.
56 Ibid., n.22.
57 Cf. Ibid., n. 21.
58 Ibid., n. 157
59 Ibid.
60 Cf. Ibid., n.23.

Africa's Place in Benedict XVI's Social Teachings

1   Dr. Thomas Bienvenu Tchoungui is stable professor of theology at UCAC and currently serves as Vice Dean of this same Faculty.

2   Cf. Joseph, *Aus meinem Leben. Erinnerungen (1927–1977)*, Deutsche Verlag Anstalt, Stuttgart, 1998. See especially chapter 10, which recounts his memories of the Second Vatican Council and his transfer from Bonn to Munster [Der Konzilsbeginn und der Übergang nach Münster], p. 100–133.

3   Barthélémy Adoukounou, "African theology and culture at the service of the Church": interview published in L'Osservatore Romano on 26 February 2010.

4   Ibid.

5   Joseph Ratzinger, Opening Address of the Meeting with the Doctrinal Commissions in Africa, Kinshasa, 21 July 1987.

6   Ibid.

7   Ibid.

8   Ibid.

9   Barthélémy Adoukounou, "African theology and culture at the service of the Church," op. cit.

10 Joseph Ratzinger, Opening Address of the Meeting with the Doctrinal Commissions in Africa, Kinshasa, 21 July 1987.

11 Benedict XVI, Homily at the Ahmadou Ahidjo Stadium on the 19 March 2009.

12 Ibid.

13 Benedict XVI, Homily at the Church of Sao Paolo in Luanda on 21 March 2009.

14 In his commentary on the Annunciation according to Matthew, Benedict XVI states that "in the explanation of the name of Jesus given to Joseph in a dream, there is already a fundamental clarification of the way in which man's salvation is conceived and, consequently, what the essential task of the bearer of salvation consists of." *The Infancy Narratives*, 2012.

15 *Evangelii Nuntiandi*, n. 16

16 *Deus caritas est*, n. 20.

17 Ibid.

18 Ibid.

19 Ibid., n. 28.

20 Ibid., n. 28.

21 Ibid., n. 6.

22 Ibid., n. 6.
23 Ibid.
24 Ibid., n. 26.
25 Ibid., n. 45.
26 Ibid., n. 45.
27 Ibid., n. 6.
28 Ibid., n. 7.
29 Ibid., n. 7.
30 Ibid., n. 51.
31 Ibid., n. 51.
32 Ibid., n. 51.
33 Ibid, n. 43, note 105.
34 Ibid., n. 43.
35 Ibid., n. 44.
36 Ibid., n. 44.
37 Ibid., n. 44.
38 Ibid., n. 51.
39 Ibid., n. 51.
40 Benedict XVI, Homily in Luanda, 22 March 2009.
41 Ibid.
42 Ibid.
43 Cf. *Ecclesia in Africa*.
44 Benedict XVI, Homily in Luanda, 22 March 2009.
45 B. Adoukounou, op. cit.
46 Ibid.
47 *Kreuzweg mit Benedikt XVI am Kolosseum. Beten mit dem Heiligen Vater Karfreitag 2006*, Herder, Basel/Wien, 2006, p. 26–27:

> "Simon von Zyrene, du bist ein kleiner, ein armer, ein unbekannter Bauer, von dem die Geschichtsbücher nicht sprechen. Und doch machst du Geschichte! Du hast eines der schönsten Kapitel der Geschichte der Menscheit geschrieben. Du trägst das Kreuz eines anderen, du hebst den schweren Balken auf und verhinderst, dass er das Opfer erdrückt. Du gibst jedem von uns die Würde zurük, indem du uns daran erinnerst, dass wir nur dann wir selbst sind, wenn wir nicht mehr an uns selber denken (lk 9,24). Du erinnerst uns daran, dass Christus auf uns wartet auf der Strasse, auf dem Treppensabsatz, im Krankenhaus, im Gefängnis…in der Randzone unserer Städte. Christus wartet auf uns… (Mt 25,40) ."

Joseph Ratzinger and the Universality of Logos in Cultures: The Preference for Interculturality over Inculturation

1   Benedict XVI, *The Regensburg Lecture* (South Bend, IN: St. Augustine's Press, 2007), n. 12.
2   Ibid., n. 13.
3   Ibid., n. 14.
4   Ibid., n. 18.
5   Maurice Ashley Agbaw-Ebai, *The Aufklarung as the Hermeneutical Framework of the Christo-Ecclesiology of Joseph Ratzinger/ Benedict XVI* (Unpublished, 2019).
6   Eva Brann, *The Logos of Heraclitus* (Philadelphia, PA: Paul Dry Books Inc. 2011), 10.
7   Joel Wilcox, *The Origins of Epistemology in Early Greek Philosophy: A Study of Psyche and Logos in Heraclitus* (New York: Edwin Mellen Press, 1994), p. 50.
8   Ibid., p. 53.
9   Johannes Quasten, Patrology Vol. I. Westminster, MD: Christian Classics Inc. 1993., p. 209.
10 Irenaeus of Lyons, *Against Heresies* (Washington, DC: Ex Fontibus Co., 2016), III: XVIII, I.
11 Ibid., IV: XX, VII.
12 Pope Benedict XVI, *Church Fathers: From Clement of Rome to Augustine* (San Francisco: Ignatius Press, 2008), p. 32.
13 Ibid., p. 34.
14 Origen of Alexandria, *Against Celsus*, 6, 48 ANF, in *Patrology* Vol. II, by Johannes Quasten (Westminster, MD: Christian Classics Inc. 1993), p. 82.
15 Hans urs Von Balthasar and Joseph Cardinal Ratzinger, *Mary: The Church at the Source*, trans. Adrian Walker, San Francisco: Ignatius Press, 2005, p. 90.
16 Benedict XVI, *The Regensburg Lecture*, op. cit., n. 19.
17 Ibid., nn. 32, 36, and 51.
18 Ibid., nn. 52–53.
19 Emery de Gaál, "Ratzinger on Inculturation and his Preference for the Term 'Interculturality,'" (Unpublished Lecture, 2019), p. 6.
20 Marcello de Carvalho Azevedo, SJ, "Inculturation and the Challenges of Modernity," in *Inculturation Working Papers on Living Faith and Culture*, Rome: Pontifical Gregorian University, 1982, p. 16.
21 Joseph Ratzinger, *Truth and Tolerance: Christian Belief and World Religions*, trans. Henry Taylor, San Francisco: Ignatius Press, 2004, 63.

22 Ibid., 62.
23 John Paul II, Encyclical Letter *Fides et Ratio* to the Bishops of the Catholic Church on the Relationship Between Faith and Reason, Accessed November 20 2019, at http://www.vatican.va/content/john-paul ii/en/encyclicals/documents/hfjpiienc14091998 fidesetratiohtml.
24 Ratzinger, *Truth and Tolerance*, op. cit., p. 72.
25 The title "Christ, Faith and the Challenge of Cultures" is followed by the information: "Joseph Card. Ratzinger, Prefect, Meeting with the Doctrinal Commissions in Asia." Cf. Andrew Beards, "Christianity, 'interculturality,' and salvation," in *The Thomist* 64/2 (2000): 161–210.
26 Emery De Gaál, "Ratzinger on Inculturation," op. cit., p. 14.
27 Ratzinger, *Truth and Tolerance*, op. cit., p. 60.
28 Joseph Ratzinger, "Christ, Faith and the Challenge of Cultures," 2. Accessed November 20, 2019 at http://www.vatican.va/roman_curia/congregations/cfaith/incontri/rc_con_cfaith_199303 03_hongkong-ratzinger_en.html
29 Ratzinger, "Christ, Faith and the Challenge of Cultures," op. cit., p.1.
30 Emery de Gaál, "Ratzinger on Inculturation," op. cit., p. 27.
31 Benedict XVI, *Verbum Domini*, n. 12, accessed November 20, 2019, at: http://w2.vatican.va/content/benedict-xvi/en/apost_exhortations/documents/hf_benxviexh20100930verbumdomini.html. 2010.
32 Benedict XVI, Solemnity of the Nativity of the Lord: Homily of His Holiness Benedict XVI, St. Peter's Basilica, December 24, 2006.
33 Ibid., 64.
34 Ibid.
35 Ibid., 70.
36 Ibid., 71.
37 Ibid.
38 Ibid.
39 Benedict XVI, Address to Members of the Special Council for Africa of the Synod of Bishops, Yaoundé, 19 March 2009.

Love" and "Truth" in the Thought of Joseph Ratzinger/Benedict XVI

1 Father Fabrice N'SEMI is a doctoral student and associate researcher with the Groupe Interdisciplinaire de Recherches sur l'Église et la Société (GIRES).

2   A. Nichols, *The Thought of Pope Benedict XVI*, Burnes & Oates, 2007, p. 43.
3   Ibid.
4   See A. Solignac's introduction and notes to *Les Confessions*, Bibliothelque. Augustinienne series, nn. 13 and 14, Paris, 1962, p. 618
5   Ibid.
6   Ibid., XIII, 9 (p. 441).
7   Ibid., p. 621.
8   Ibid., p. 622.
9   A. Nygren (1944).
10 Benedict XVI, *Deus caritas est*, 2006: n. 2.
11 Ibid, n.3.
12 Ibid, n.4.
13 Ibid.
14 Ibid.
15 Ibid., n. 5.
16 Ibid., n. 4.
17 Ibid., n. 6
18 Ibid., n. 9.
19 Cantalamessa (2012).
20 Benedict XVI, DCE, n. 10.
21 Ibid., n. 12.
22 J. Ratzinger (1996),p. 103.
23 Ibid., p. 101.
24 Ibid., p. 105.
25 Ibid.
26 Ibid., p. 103.
27 Guerriero (2017), p. 284.
28 J. Ratzinger (2005).
29 Ibid., p. 162.
30 J. Ratzinger (1986), p. 24.
31 J. Ratzinger (2005), p. 207.
32 Ibid., p. 163.
33 Benedict XVI (2010), n. 1.
34 J. Ratzinger (1969) p. 158.
35 Benedict XVI (2009), n. 1.
36 Ibid.
37 Ibid., n. 3.
38 Ibid., n. 2.
39 Ibid., n. 2.
40 Lebrun-Keris (1963), p. 36.
41 Adoukounou (2001), p. 758.

42 John Paul II (1995), n. 63.
43 N'semi (2013), p. 19.
44 Bruckner (2019), p. 127.
45 Benedict XVI (2011), n. 1.
46 J. Ratzinger (1969), p. 172
47 N'semi (2016) p. 90.
48 Ela (1985), p. 27.
49 Benedict XVI, DCE, n. 1.
50 Ratzinger, Delhaye (1979), pp. 116–120.
51 Ibid., p. 119.
52 Tertullien, *Apologeticum*, III, 5.
53 Ratzinger, Delhaye (1979), p. 119.
54 Liturgy of the Hours, XV Sunday in Ordinary Time, 1980, p. 564.

Benedict XVI and the Issue of Sexual Abuse of Minors by Clerics

1   Père Jean Marie Signie, SCJ is ordinary professor at Ecole théologique Saint Cyprien de Ngoya (2005–2015); Stable professor and Director of the department of canon law at Université Catholique d'Afrique Centrale/Institut catholique de Yaoundé (2006–2015); Member of the Scientific Council of UCAC/ICY and member of Canadian Canon Law Society since 2006; member of the Canon Law Society of America since 2014; Member of *Consortium droit canonique et culture*; and canonical consultant to the *Conférence Episcopale Nationale du Cameroun* as well as the *Conférence des Supérieurs majeurs du Cameroun*.

2   Prof. Forbi Stephen Kizito, SJ, is a Cameroonian Jesuit priest, permanent lecturer at the Faculty of Philosophy, CATUC, and Dean Emeritus. He is a member of the Scientific Council of Kanien, a magazine published in Abidjan, Côte d'Ivoire, and of IBOGA REVIEW published in Spain. He is a Member of the UCAC/ICY Scientific Council. He is one of the group members of CERCAPHI (Cercle Camerounais de Philosophie), a research group headed by Pr. Ebénézer Njoh-Mouelle. He is the founder of the CINTREPED (Center for Interdisciplinary Research in Philosophy and Education) research group in Yaoundé.

3   Terms of Reference of "Lands of Mission and Evangelisation in Africa and Europe: Cross-reviews and Canonical Approaches," 16

January 2019, Colloquium held at the Catholic University of Central Africa (UCAC).

4   The 1917 Code of Canon Law.

5   John Paul II, Apostolic Letter given by Motu proprio "Sacramentorum sanctitatis tutela," by which the norms concerning the most serious offences reserved for the Congregation for the Doctrine of the Faith were promulgated, 30 April 2001. Henceforth referred to as STT.

6   The Congregation for the Doctrine of the Faith. Henceforth referred to as CDF.

7   U.S. Conference of Catholic Bishops, Charter for the Protection of Children and Young People, 13 November 2002.

8   Cardinal William Levada "The Sexual Abuse of Minors: A Multifaceted Response to the Challenge," paper at the Symposium at the Pontifical Gregorian University, 6 February 2012, p. 1.

9   See *Ius missionale*, 2007, pp. 257–260.

10 Benedict XVI, Pastoral Letter to the Christians of Ireland, 19 March 2010, n. 1a.

11 Ibid., n. 2a.

12 Ibid., n. 1b.

13 Ibid., "Address to the Bishops of Ireland on the *ad limina apostolorum*," 28 October 2006, reproduced in the Letter.

14 Ibid., n. 2c.

15 Cf. Ibid. n. 4b.

16 Ibid., n. 2.

17 See Congregation for the Doctrine of the Faith, Brief report on the modifications introduced in the *Normae de gravioribus delictis* reserved to the Congregation for the Doctrine of the Faith, 21 May 2010.

18 Congregation for the Doctrine of the Faith, Circular Letter to Assist Bishops' Conferences Establish Guidelines to Deal with Cases of Sexual Abuse of Minors by Clerics, 3 May 2011.

19 Levada, The sexual Abuse of Minors, p. 2.

20 Ibid., p. 3.

21 Here the text quotes Benedict XVI's letter to the Catholics of Ireland at n. 6 : "You have suffered terribly and I am deeply sorry. I know that nothing can wipe out the pains you have suffered. Your trust has been betrayed and your dignity violated."

22 Benedict XVI, Pastoral letter, n. 3c.

23 Ibid., n. 4a.

24 Ibid., n. 4b.

Preparation for the Priesthood
in the Legislative Agenda of Benedict XVI

1   Jean Paul Betengne is the Dean of the Canon Law Department of the Catholic University of Central Africa, Yaounde, Cameroon.

Witness to Pope Benedict XVI's Resignation.

1   Rev. Dr. Engelbert Meyongo Nama is a priest of the Diocese of Mbalmayo and a permanent lecturer in the Department of Canon Law at CATUC/YCI.

2   A. Boureau (ed.) Le deuil du pouvoir, *Essais dur l'abdication*, Paris, Les Belles Lettres, 2013, p. 12.

3   J. GAUDEMET, *Les Institutions de l'antiquité*, Paris, Montchrestien, 1994, p. 476; see also by the same author: *Eglise et Cité Histoire du droit canonique*, Paris, Cerf Montchrestien, 1994, p. 22; A. Bérenger, *Le métier de gouverneur dans l'empire romain: de César à Dioclétien*, Paris, éditions de Boccard, 2014; S. Lefebvre, *L'administration de l'Empire romain: d'Auguste à Dioclétien*, Paris, A. Colin, 2011.

4   J. C. D'Amigo, *Charles Quint maître du monde, entre mythe et réalité*, Caen, Presses universitaires de Caen, 2004, p. 43; R. Francis, *Le Saint Empire romain germanique : d'Otton le Grand à Charles Quint*, Paris, Seuil, 1926; Grenoble (ed.), *La mort des rois: documents sur les derniers jours de souverains français et espagnols, de Charles-Quint à Louis XV*, textes réunis, traduits et présentés par StanisPerez, Grenoble; Charles V, in Larousse, [online] accessed 28 November 2019.

5   "6 Novembre 1982, Cameroon. Retirement of President Ahmadou Ahidjo replaced by Paul Biya."

6   EncyclopediaUniversalis [online], accessed 28 November 2019.

7   A. Boureau, op. cit., p. 22

8   L. Danto, "La renonciation de Benoît XVI, illustration de la souveraine liberté du pontife romain Réflexions canoniques, in *l'Année Canonique*, 54 (2012): 408.

9   See A. Rey (ed.) *Dictionnaire historique de la langue française*, Paris, Le Robert, 2010, p. 3, 620, 1908; See also, A. Dauzat, *Dictionnaire étymologique de la langue française*, Paris, Larousse, 1938.

10 E. Meyongo, "Controverses autour de l'abdication du pape Célestin V. Un éclairage sur la renonciation historique du pape Benedict XVI," in *Revue de Droit Canonique*, Strasbourg, 64/1 (2014): 69.

11 Zenith, 24 April 2005.

12 A. Boureau (ed.) op. cit., p. 11. According to Alain Boureau, the

abdication is a renunciation of power, it is the pure state of an act of the will in the political or religious sphere. This sovereign authority, which depends on nothing but oneself, decides to abolish itself. He continues that, it is not just relinquishing power, but an act of power.

13 A. Boureau, op. cit., p. 12.

14 The office is understood in an eminently functionalist manner: the function is clearly distinct from the person who holds it.

15 Congregation for Bishops, Directory for the Pastoral Ministry of Bishops, *Apostolorum successores*, n. 226.

The Area of Social Education

1 Joseph Ratzinger, *Faith and Politics*, Ignatius Press, 2018.

2 World Youth Day 2011 in Spain.

Benedict XVI's Concept of Opening a Loophole on What Blocks an African Concept

1 Dr. Anata Mawata Augusta obtained a PhD in social sciences and is of Chadian nationality. She is a lecturer and researcher at the Catholic University of Central Africa. Her work focuses on the family, ageing and life stages, social policies and violence in urban areas. From a methodological point of view, her work is an attempt to go beyond the institutional, essentialist and teleological perspectives of African societies in favoor of a socio-history and an approach based on the everyday culture of these societies.

2 It suffices to analyse the strategies and programmes contained in the countries' emergence projects.

3 Advice that we Africans should make our own.

4 The stone age, age of abundance.

The Impact of Justice and Peace Commissions in the Civic Engagement of Catholic Christians in Cameroon

1 *Africae munus*, n. 1.

2 Ibid., n. 128.

3 *Instrumentum laboris* for the Second Special Assembly for Africa of the Synod of Bishops.

4 Benedict XVI, Message to the Bishops of Mali on his ad limina visit, 18 May 2007.

5   *Instrumentum laboris* for the Second Special Assembly for Africa of the Synod of Bishops, French text published on 19 March. Notes (a) to (e) by DC.

6   John Paul II, Post-Synodal Apostolic Exhortation *Ecclesia in Africa*, 14 September 1995, n. 70: *AAS* 88 (1996): 45.

7   *AM*, n. 18.

8   Lado (2012), p. 172.

9   Essi, *Active citizenship: how to move from information to action?* (2017), p. 67.

10 Yankep, Caroline Claire, *Youth and Active Citizenship in Cameroon*.

11 Kapchie, Sylviane, *Obstacles to citizen engagement in Cameroon* (2017), p. 24.